VICTORIAN BRITAIN
DAY BY DAY

For Mum

VICTORIAN BRITAIN
DAY BY DAY

NICHOLAS TRAVERS

PEN & SWORD
HISTORY

AN IMPRINT OF PEN & SWORD BOOKS LTD.
YORKSHIRE - PHILADELPHIA

First published in Great Britain in 2024 by
PEN AND SWORD HISTORY
An imprint of
Pen & Sword Books Ltd
Yorkshire – Philadelphia

Copyright © Nicholas Travers, 2024

ISBN 978 1 39904 175 1

The right of Nicholas Travers to be identified as Author of this work has been asserted by him in accordance with the Copyright, Designs and Patents Act 1988.

A CIP catalogue record for this book is available from the British Library.

All rights reserved. No part of this book may be reproduced or transmitted in any form or by any means, electronic or mechanical including photocopying, recording or by any information storage and retrieval system, without permission from the Publisher in writing.

Typeset in Times New Roman 10/12 by
SJmagic DESIGN SERVICES, India.
Printed and bound in the UK by CPI Group (UK) Ltd.

Pen & Sword Books Limited incorporates the imprints of Atlas, Archaeology, Aviation, Discovery, Family History, Fiction, History, Maritime, Military, Military Classics, Politics, Select, Transport, True Crime, Air World, Frontline Publishing, Leo Cooper, Remember When, Seaforth Publishing, The Praetorian Press, Wharncliffe Local History, Wharncliffe Transport, Wharncliffe True Crime and White Owl.

For a complete list of Pen & Sword titles please contact
PEN & SWORD BOOKS LIMITED
George House, Units 12 & 13, Beevor Street, Off Pontefract Road,
Barnsley, South Yorkshire, S71 1HN, England
E-mail: enquiries@pen-and-sword.co.uk
Website: www.pen-and-sword.co.uk

or
PEN AND SWORD BOOKS
1950 Lawrence Rd, Havertown, PA 19083, USA
E-mail: uspen-and-sword@casematepublishers.com
Website: www.penandswordbooks.com

Contents

List of Illustrations vi
Acknowledgements ix
Introduction x

January 1
February 20
March 37
April 54
May 68
June 84
July 101
August 118
September 133
October 146
November 160
December 174

Selected Bibliography 190
Index 193

List of Illustrations

1. King William IV. Courtesy of the Wellcome Collection. This work is licensed under a Creative Commons Public Domain Mark 1.0 Licence. King William IV holding a scroll of the Magna Carta in his right hand. Mezzotint by D. Lucas after R. Bowyer, 1830. Public Domain
2. Queen Victoria. Courtesy of the Wellcome Collection. This work is licensed under a Creative Commons Public Domain Mark 1.0 Licence. Queen Victoria. Photograph. Public Domain
3. Prince Albert Courtesy of the Wellcome Collection. This work is licensed under a Creative Commons Public Domain Mark 1.0 Licence. HRH Albert, Prince Consort. Photograph. Public Domain
4. The Prince of Wales. Courtesy of the Wellcome Collection. This work is licensed under a Creative Commons Public Domain Mark 1.0 Licence. Albert Edward, HRH the Prince of Wales. Photograph by G. Jerrard, 1881. Public Domain
5. Isambard Kingdom Brunel. Courtesy of The Metropolitan Museum of Art, New York. Public Domain. Gilman Collection, Purchase, Harriette and Noel Levine Gift, 2005. Public Domain
6. The Great Exhibition. Courtesy of the Wellcome Collection. This work is licensed under a Creative Commons Public Domain Mark 1.0 Licence. The Great Exhibition in the Crystal Palace, Hyde Park, London: the transept looking north. Steel engraving by W. Lacey after J.E. Mayall, 1851. Public Domain
7. The London Slums. Courtesy of the Wellcome Collection. This work is licensed under a Creative Commons Public Domain Mark 1.0 Licence. London Slums. Public Domain
8. Trafalgar Square. Courtesy of The Metropolitan Museum of Art, New York. Public Domain. Anonymous Gift and Purchase, Alfred Stieglitz Society Gifts; 2004 Benefit Fund; W. Bruce and Delaney H. Lundberg Gift; The Horace W. Goldsmith Foundation Fund, through Joyce and Robert Menschel; Susan and Thomas Dunn and Constance and Leonard Goodman Gifts, 2009. Public Domain
9. The Steam Train. Courtesy of Pixabay Licence. Public Domain.
10. The underground railway. Courtesy of the Wellcome Collection. This work is licensed under a Creative Commons Public Domain Mark 1.0 Licence. A trial journey on the first part of the underground railway in London. Wood engraving, 1862. Public Domain
11. The Crimean War. Courtesy of the Wellcome Collection. This work is licensed under a Creative Commons Public Domain Mark 1.0 Licence. Crimean War:

List of Illustrations

Florence Nightingale going around the wards at Scutari Hospital. Wood engraving. Public Domain
12. Queen Victoria visiting the wards. Courtesy of the Wellcome Collection. This work is licensed under a Creative Commons Public Domain Mark 1.0 Licence. Queen Victoria visiting soldiers wounded in the Crimean War. Mezzotint by T.O. Barlow, 1859, after Jerry Barrett. Public Domain
13. Queen Victoria in mourning. Courtesy of the Wellcome Collection. This work is licensed under a Creative Commons Public Domain Mark 1.0 Licence. Queen Victoria in mourning for Albert, her subjects outraged at her neglect of duties. Wood engraving, c. 1861. Public Domain.
14. Prince Albert's funeral. Courtesy of the Wellcome Collection. This work is licensed under a Creative Commons Public Domain Mark 1.0 Licence. The funeral of Albert Prince Consort, in St George's Chapel, Windsor. Wood engraving, 1861. Public Domain
15. Brighton Pier. Courtesy of The Metropolitan Museum of Art, New York. Public Domain. The Elisha Whittelsey Collection, The Elisha Whittelsey Fund, 1972. Public Domain
16. Gladstone. Courtesy of the Wellcome Collection. This work is licensed under a Creative Commons Public Domain Mark 1.0 Licence. Gladstone dancing with Lord Rosebery, who is wearing a kilt, celebrating the Liberal victory in the British General Election of 1880 and a crown. Engraving, 1880. Public Domain
17. The Open Fire. Courtesy of the Wellcome Collection. This work is licensed under a Creative Commons Public Domain Mark 1.0 Licence. Queen Victoria, seated in an armchair by an open fire, day-dreaming about illustrious men of her reign. Colour lithograph by Tom Merry, 1887. Public Domain
18. Charles Dickens. Wikimedia Commons Public Domain Mark. Heritage Auction Gallery. Public Domain.
19. Oliver Twist. Courtesy of the Wellcome Collection. This work is licensed under a Creative Commons Public Domain Mark 1.0 Licence. Oliver Twist, holding a bowl and a spoon, asks for more food, while other children and a woman look surprised. Etching by George Cruikshank. Public Domain
20. British inventors. Courtesy of the Wellcome Collection. This work is licensed under a Creative Commons Public Domain Mark 1.0 Licence. British inventors, politicians and military men, gathered in a room at Buckingham Palace. Engraving by C.G. Lewis, 1863, after T.J. Barker. Public Domain
21. Charles Darwin. Courtesy of the Wellcome Collection. This work is licensed under a Creative Commons Public Domain Mark 1.0 Licence. Charles Robert Darwin. Pen and ink drawing. Public Domain
22. Alfred Tennyson. Courtesy of the Wellcome Collection. This work is licensed under a Creative Commons Public Domain Mark 1.0 Licence. Alfred, Lord Tennyson. Photograph by Elliott & Fry. Public Domain
23. Anthony Trollope. Courtesy of the Wellcome Collection. This work is licensed under a Creative Commons Public Domain Mark 1.0 Licence. Anthony Trollope. Photograph by Elliott & Fry. Public Domain

24. The National History Museum. Courtesy of Pixabay License. Public Domain.
25. Tower Bridge. Courtesy of Pixabay Licence. Public Domain.
26. The Royal Family. Courtesy of the Wellcome Collection. This work is licensed under a Creative Commons Public Domain Mark 1.0 Licence. The Duke of Wellington is presenting a birthday casket to his godson Prince Arthur (later Duke of Connaught) in the presence of Queen Victoria and Prince Albert. Mezzotint by S. Cousins after F.X. Winterhalter, 1 May 1851. Public Domain
27. Wellington's Funeral. Courtesy of the Wellcome Collection. This work is licensed under a Creative Commons Public Domain Mark 1.0 Licence. The funeral car of the Duke of Wellington. Wood engraving, 1852. Public Domain
28. Mr Gladstone. Courtesy of the Wellcome Collection. This work is licensed under a Creative Commons Public Domain Mark 1.0 Licence. W.E. Gladstone represented as Samson destroying the pillars of the British Constitution by abolition of the House of Lords. Colour lithograph by Tom Merry, 24 October 1891. Public Domain
29. Gladstones funeral. Courtesy of the Wellcome Collection. This work is licensed under a Creative Commons Public Domain Mark 1.0 Licence. The coffin of W.E. Gladstone lying in state, attended by five men praying. Drawing by G.B. Scott after A. Kemp Tebby, 1898. Public Domain
30. Elizabeth Garrett Anderson. Courtesy of the Wellcome Collection. This work is licensed under a Creative Commons Public Domain Mark 1.0 Licence. Elizabeth Garrett Anderson. Wood engraving. Public Domain
31. London. Courtesy of The Metropolitan Museum of Art, New York. Public Domain. Gift of Weston J. Naef, in memory of Kathleen W. Naef and Weston J. Naef Sr., 1982
32. The Victoria Memorial. Courtesy of Pixabay Licence. Public Domain.

Front Cover

Queen Victoria. Courtesy of the Wellcome Collection. This work is licensed under a Creative Commons Public Domain Mark 1.0 Licence. Queen Victoria. Photograph. Public Domain.

Courtesy of the Wellcome Collection. This work is licensed under a Creative Commons Public Domain Mark 1.0 Licence. A steam train is travelling across a viaduct at Nanterre with a road, a carriage and horses underneath. Engraving by Lemaitre after C. Rauch. Public Domain

Charles Dickens. Wikimedia Commons Public Domain Mark. Heritage Auction Gallery. Public Domain.

Isambard Kingdom Brunel. Courtesy of The Metropolitan Museum of Art, New York. Public Domain. Gilman Collection, Purchase, Harriette and Noel Levine Gift, 2005. Public Domain

Back Cover

The London Slums. Courtesy of the Wellcome Collection. This work is licensed under a Creative Commons Public Domain Mark 1.0 Licence. London Slums. Public Domain

Acknowledgements

MY SPECIAL THANKS go to Kate Bohdanowicz for her tremendous help in getting this project off the ground, and Charlotte Mitchell for her guidance and advice. Additional thanks also go to Richard Doherty. The author would like to thank the following people and organisations for permission to use copyright material in this book: His Majesty King Charles III and the Royal Archives for granting permission to quote extracts from Queen Victoria's journals; The Houses of Parliament for granting permission to quote from Hansard. Quotes from Hansard contains Parliamentary information licensed under the Open Parliament Licence v3.0. Thanks also go to the Wellcome Collection, the Metropolitan Museum of Art, The Elisha Whittelsey Collection, The Elisha Whittelsey Fund, 1972, Wikimedia Commons and Pixabay for publishing images from their collection. Gratitude also goes to the British Newspaper Archive. Every attempt has been made by the author to ascertain, locate, and contact the copyright holders in this book.

Introduction

THE VICTORIANS CONTINUE to captivate, intrigue and engross contemporary society. In many ways we still live in the shadow of the Victorians. In our institutions, our fashion, our ideas, architecture and infrastructure, modern Britain was forged between the years 1837 and 1901. Superficially, our two generations cannot seem more different. The rigid social conservative values of the nineteenth century appear prudish, out of date, in some cases reactionary, to contemporary liberal times. In other ways, we are more similar than we think. We live in an era of stimulating educational and intellectual questioning, intermingled with seemingly disorientating technological change. The vivid tapestry of the Victorian world interweaves within our own contemporary story.

From Darwin to Dickens, the Great Exhibition and the Industrial Revolution, the Victorian era was an epoch of astonishing political and social transformation. When Victoria was crowned monarch on the warm sticky day of 28 June 1838, few could envisage the unimaginable changes that would unfold in her reign. She arrived into a world dominated by the Georgians; an agricultural country ruled by a cluster of ageing aristocrats who governed parliament undisturbed from democratic influence. When she died, Britain was a country transformed, a nation covered by an interconnected network of railways, industry, factories, commerce and culture. Democracy was rising. Photography, moving film and automobiles were in the ascendant. Powdered wigs, stockings and red military coats were on the decline. For the first time in British history, civil registration came into effect, gaining greater insight into the lives of ordinary Britons. Infrastructural projects had changed the very character of British cities. The foundations of modern Britain were laid.

It's no surprise that some historians regard the century as the most transformative age in modern British history. It was a time of extremes, a time of progress but also pain and poverty. This exploration of Victorian drama sheds new light on many familiar, and unfamiliar, stories of the past, examining the highs and lows of a momentous period. How can we better understand ourselves without understanding the past? This book brings to life key moments in Victorian history that have occurred on every day from 1 January to 31 December. Some discrepancies may exist over some dates, but every effort has been made to verify its contents. This book does not include every single event that ever occurred during the Victorian era. Moreover, each day offers a new, fascinating snapshot into Britain's extraordinary past.

January

1 January

1859 Elizabeth Blackwell becomes the first woman recorded on the Medical Register of the General Medical Council
Few figures have contributed more to the advancement of female medical education than Elizabeth Blackwell. Born in Bristol in 1821, she had originally applied for medical school in Britain but faced unrelenting disappointment and rejection. Undeterred, she relocated to the United States and trained at the Geneva Medical College in New York. Despite the applause, not everyone was impressed by Blackwell's success. Many people, including Queen Victoria, thought it was improper for a woman to serve as a medical practitioner. Her drive and determination paved the way for many new female students who eventually broke down gender barriers in medicine.

1857 Divorce courts were established in England and Wales. Under the Matrimonial Cause Act, secular divorces were made possible for the first time in English history. Women could now legally pursue a civil case to seek a divorce.

1877 On 1 January 1877 Queen Victoria was proclaimed Empress of India in front of a colossal crowd of assembled dignitaries and noblemen. The title had been granted by her beloved Prime Minister, Benjamin Disraeli, who recognised the monarch's love of flattery and imperial pride. Perhaps surprisingly, the responsibility of organising such a ceremony went to Thomas Thornton, a relatively young Anglo-Indian civil servant, who orchestrated an enormous ceremony aimed at cementing a feeling of British invincibility. Victoria did not personally attend the ceremony but was represented by the Viceroy of India.

1883 Augustus Pitt Rivers was appointed the first British Inspector of Ancient Monuments. The imperfect symmetry of Stonehenge in Wiltshire remains one of the great mysteries in British history, and a continued source of cultural, spiritual, and intellectual interest, all thankfully preserved by the Victorians. In 1883, the archaeologist Augustus Pitt Rivers was selected as Britain's first inspector of Ancient Monuments, dedicated to preserving Britain's most treasured, but endangered places. In so doing, he set in motion a legacy of archaeological protection that continues to this day.

1883 Married women obtained the right to acquire their own property. Victorian women faced huge disadvantages in every aspect of society. Before 1883, a wife could not legally own her own home, or land. In the event of divorce, many could find themselves destitute, or even homeless. The changes brought increased provisions to prevent the unfairness prevalent in English property law.

1900 Alfred Austin was appointed Poet Laureate. His selection was initially controversial. To his critics, he was fundamentally unsuited for the role, too lightweight and artistically inexperienced compared to the genius Alfred Lord Tennyson. As a friend of the Prime Minister, some argued that nepotism had reared its ugly Victorian head, a reflection of the government's desire to capitalise on a wave of rising nationalism at the backdrop of the Second Boer War. To his supporters, however, this was an unfair generalisation of his achievements and talents. Austin was the last poet Laureate of the Victorian era. He was also the first Roman Catholic to serve in the role.

2 January

1880 Scandal in the Marlborough set
In the late 1880s the smooth-talking MP Charles Beresford began a short, yet intense affair with Daisy Greville, Countess of Warwick, and fathered her child. By pure coincidence, a love letter written by the countess was discovered by Lady Beresford who quickly submitted the note to her solicitor. The Prince of Wales, a friend of the countess, was deeply horrified by the scandal. He requested the letter be destroyed but Lady Beresford refused. In response, the story became the number one gossip in high society.

1885 A bomb exploded in Gower Street, London. The Fenian threat was an extensive bombing campaign that spread fear and terror across Britain throughout the 1880s. Organised by Irish Republicans against the British Government, the attack was carried out in the tunnel of Gower Street Station on 2 January 1885. No one was seriously injured.

1892 The astronomer Sir George Biddell Air died. The acclaimed astronomer was famous for designing the Airy Transit Circle Telescope, which defined the prime meridian at the Royal Observatory. He was also employed by the British Government to advise on the construction of Big Ben. Many decades later, the astronomer Sir Patrick Moore alleged that the ghost of Airy has occasionally been seen haunting the observatory.

3 January

1901 Lord Roberts is appointed the professional head of the British Army
All morning, a growing crowd of eager bystanders had gathered in watchful anxiety, desperate to get a glimpse of a returning military celebrity, Frederick

January

Roberts. The pageantry could not disguise the many problems inherent in the British Army. Ever since 1899 Britain had been involved in the brutal and bloody Second Boer War. Setbacks had created manic hysteria in the press with renewed fears of a 'fading empire', and British military decline. The Queen's son, Prince Arthur Duke of Connaught, welcomed the new commander with warm affection, and accompanied him through the gilded corridors of Osborne House to meet the elderly Queen Victoria. Roberts spoke candidly and vividly of the problems facing the army. Some American newspapers later remarked, the pessimistic reports by Roberts contributed to Victoria's declining health and, ultimately, her death.

1857 The First Instalment of Wilkie Collins's *The Dead Secret* was serialised in the *Household Words*. Collin tackled several contentious issues in his novels, including illegitimacy, poverty and marriage. His fourth book, *The Dead Secret*, published in 1857, met with mixed reactions.

1883 The Labour politician Clement Attlee was born in Putney. 'Attlee was born and brought up in the Victorian age,' remarked Harold Wilson, 'but there are few men, if any, who have done more in our own generation, to speed the process of change from the country he knew as a young man, to the country in which we are living today.' Much of the misery and hardship of the Victorian world would be reversed under Attlee's government. His administration oversaw the creation of the National Health Service which redefined British society.

1895 Oscar Wilde's *An Ideal Husband* premiered at the Haymarket Theatre

4 January

1884 The Fabian Society, a British socialist organisation, is formed
The nineteenth century was a melting pot of social, cultural, and political questioning, dominated not only by the turmoil of the Industrial Revolution, but the widespread social and political unrest it had unleashed. On 4 January 1884 a small unostentatious house in Osnaburgh Street, London was crammed with a group of eager campaigners, organised by the writer Edith Nesbit to create a new organisation championing the principles of democratic socialism. It was called the Fabian Society.

1891 The Palace Theatre, London was opened. Originally named the Royal English Opera House, its first production was Arthur Sullivan's *Ivanhoe*.

5 January

1855 Anthony Trollope publishes *The Warden*
Trollope is regarded as a Victorian literary titan, although perhaps not as famous with contemporary audiences as the likes of Dickens or Thomas Hardy.

In 1855 he published arguably his first successful book, *The Warden*, set in the fictional county of Barsetshire. Trollope had not originally planned a series when he began the novel, but the immediate popularity soon created demand for a sequel.

1871 The Guild of St George was founded by the philosopher John Ruskin. Its principal aim was the advancement of education, art, craftsmanship and industrial progress, with the wider goal of creating a cohesive, more peaceful society. It was officially recognised by the Board of Trade in 1878.

1886 *The Strange Case of Dr Jekyll and Mr Hyde* was published. Robert Louis Stevenson's legendary novel exposed the duality of human nature, the seemingly unstoppable battle between good and evil. It was initially sold for one shilling and became an enormous commercial success.

6 January

1899 Lord Curzon is appointed Viceroy of India
At just thirty-nine, the talented but aloof Lord George Curzon became the last Viceroy of India of the Victorian era. He remained in the job for six years. Like many politicians of the era, Curzon was an imperialist with a deep conviction in the British Empire, but not always popular with his colleagues or contemporaries. Many found him prickly, pompous and pretentious with a haughty, almost vain disposition which made him increasingly controversial.

1839 The Night of the Big Wind, one of the worst windstorms in British history took place. In Ireland, the storm was so famous it became the stuff of generational legend.

7 January

1896 The actor and writer Arnold Ridley is born in Walcot, Bath
Arnold Ridley is best remembered today as the affable, softly spoken Private Godfrey in the hugely successful BBC comedy *Dad's Army*. Ridley was also a highly accomplished playwright and a decorated war veteran who fought bravely in the Battle of the Somme. He started life in Walcot, a small suburb near Bath, where his father was a gymnastics instructor. After a successful education, he became a soldier during the First World War, and then later a professional performer. He was also the author of the popular play *The Ghost Train*.

1869 The Amateur Swimming Association was established in London with the purpose of encouraging more Britons to exercise.

8 January

1847 A scandalous Royal Wedding takes place
In the small, unassuming church of St John Clerkenwell in London, a stout, bearded gentleman, burdened under a mass of military medals, entered the building to an unnervingly cool silence. His name was Prince George, the first cousin of Queen Victoria, and eldest son of the Duke of Cambridge. George had done something so scandalous for Victorians that it rocked the foundations of aristocratic society, something many friends and colleagues simply couldn't understand. In defiance of traditional custom, and direct convention of the royal family, George had decided to marry Sarah Fairbrother, a poverty-stricken actress, mother of two illegitimate children, and the daughter of a servant, plunging aristocratic Britain into hysterics.

In the context of strict Victorian social hierarchy, his decision was both shocking and intensely controversial. The match was not supported by the palace. No representative of the immediate royal family attended the ceremony, or reception. Nor was Fairbrother granted the title 'HRH'. Her children were similarly barred from the style.

1864 Prince Albert Victor, the eldest son of the Prince of Wales was born. The birth of a new heir is always a momentous occasion, none more so than 1864. Early in the morning of 8 January the heavily pregnant Princess of Wales visited Virginia Waters to watch her strapping young husband play ice hockey on a huge frozen pond. While watching the game, the princess went into labour and was rushed to the nearby Frogmore House. The surprise news of the birth caught everyone off guard. 'We were dumbfounded,' the queen later remarked, 'thank God! She (Alexandra) is safe, but the alarm was great.' Tradition dictated that the Home Secretary attend the birth of a future heir, a protocol that dated back for almost two centuries. In the panic and shock, however, the custom was broken. The labour was also thankfully short and without complications.

9 January

1873 Napoleon III, the deposed emperor of France dies
Napoleon III had resided in England as a guest of Queen Victoria since March 1871 but had found his new life dull and unfulfilling. After losing office following the chaos of the Franco-Prussian War, Napoleon relocated to Chislehurst where he adopted the life of a leisurely country gentleman, hosting dinner parties and glamorous receptions. After two operations in 1872, the Emperor withdrew from public life, and on 8 January 1873 was administered the last rites by a Roman Catholic priest. He died at twenty-five minutes past twelve the following day.

1854 The First Free Lending Library was opened in London. The idea proved popular, especially amongst the middle classes who could not afford the luxury of large personal libraries. The 1850 Libraries Act allowed local authorities to spend money on establishing public libraries but did not provide the funds for purchasing the actual books. Many of the collections were instead donated from private citizens or generous bookstores.

10 January

1863 The First London Underground train goes into operation
The Victorian thirst for technological innovation, invention and discovery was perhaps no better epitomised than the creation of the London Underground. Constructed under the unyielding direction of the Metropolitan District Railway, it was the first underground system in the world, officially opened by William Gladstone. The line ran from Paddington to Farringdon Street, with seven stops at seven stations. As the decade progressed, the underground expanded further across London. Ruthless in their pursuit for domination, the Metropolitan District Railway was prepared to demolish any buildings in its path, even to historic properties. In 1867 they tore down two properties in Leinster Gardens, Bayswater and filled the gap with a fake façade of a house which still exists today. Tragically, several thousand workers were killed throughout the nineteenth century in the construction of railways.

1840 A Standardised Postage Rate was introduced. In the early nineteenth century the national postal system was complex and expensive, inciting huge criticism from the weary public. In 1837 the prominent social reformer, Rowland Hill, advocated that a standardised post rate of one penny should be applied. Any citizen, irrespective of distance, could send a letter for an inexpensive price. His plans led to an enormous upsurge of mail, revolutionising the British postal system forever. In 1839 over seventy-six million letters were posted in Britain. Ten years later that had increased to 347 million.

11 January

1863 The London Underground Opens to the Public
Following its inaugural ceremony, the London Underground was made accessible to the general public on 11 January 1863. Expectations could not be higher. From early morning, hundreds of eager passengers arrived early to get a glimpse of the curious new innovation. By 8.00am Paddington station had become practically paralysed by dense crowds. Thousands squeezed themselves into small carriages causing colossal overcrowding. Much against their wishes, several first-class passengers were forced to travel third class. Tensions seethed and fights soon broke out. It was later estimated that over 30,000 people had attempted to travel the underground, creating unprecedented demands on railway workers and staff. The following day demands on the new line reached even greater heights.

1864 Charing Cross Station was opened. It was constructed by the South Eastern Railway, located near The Strand and Trafalgar Square. A year later, the station also opened a luxurious hotel, built by Edward Middleton Barry, son of Charles Barry who co-designed the Houses of Parliament. The hotel boasted 250 bedrooms with unrivalled views across central London.

12 January

1863 Chaos on the London Underground
On the second official day of the Underground's opening, the demand became completely overwhelming. Steam-powered engines, unsuited for underground travel, were hired to cope with the crowds. Unfortunately, this meant the tunnels were soon filled by thick suffocating smoke, choking the hundreds of passengers on the platform. At Gower Street Station, several staff members became ill and incapacitated. Fortunately, a local business owner called Mr Tilley was on hand to assist intoxicated passengers, taking many to his house and soothing their heads with vinegar.

1887 The formidable figure of the Foreign Secretary, Sir Stafford Northcote, collapsed and died while walking up the staircase of 10 Downing Street. Staff carried his body into the Cabinet Room and laid him down on a coach where a local physician, Doctor Langston, inspected his condition. He was soon pronounced dead, aged sixty-eight.

1895 The social reformer Octavia Hill, together with the Reverend Hardwicke Rawnsley and lawyer Sir Robert Hunter, joined forces to form the National Trust aimed at protecting and promoting places of outstanding historical interest for the nation. Over several years they bought and redeveloped land and property across Britain, saving many buildings from untimely destruction.

13 January

1886 Charles Bradlaugh is permitted to take his seat in Parliament
The corridor to power was characteristically choked with traffic. Endless miles of grey-haired men, dressed in dark frock coats and silk top-hats, colonised the oak-panelled chambers, desperate to get a glimpse of one man: Charles Bradlaugh. Bradlaugh had unleashed an almighty parliamentary storm on a scale never seen before. As a resolute atheist, republican and political activist, his refusal to take the religious oath of allegiance precipitated a vicious period of political drama which eventually led to imprisonment, several by-elections and hefty financial fines. Even then, he refused to change course with his beliefs. Finally, in January 1886, the Speaker of the Commons granted Bradlaugh access to take the oath, speak and vote in the House of Commons. The strange and rather curious episode became known as the 'Bradlaugh affair'.

14 January

1892 The Death of the Prince

14 January 1892. 'A never to be forgotten day!', scribbled the weary Queen Victoria in her diary. A day that would change the course of British monarchy forever, and the face of British history. Prince Albert Victor, the eldest son of the Prince of Wales, grandson of Queen-Empress Victoria, and second in line to the mighty British throne is dead. He was just twenty-eight.

In the early afternoon of 7 January, Albert, known affectionately as Eddy, had returned to Sandringham feeling weak and fatigued. The following day, the prince felt so ill he could barely walk down the stairs and retired to his bedchamber. Doctors diagnosed influenza and inflammation of the lungs. On 13 January Dr Larking, the prince's personal physician, telegrammed Osborne House, informing the queen of an anxious night. The prince was delirious, incoherently muttering and talking to himself. Encouraging early signs had given way to disappointing symptoms of terminal decline. His breathing was laboured and irregular, intermingled with long agonising pauses and an uncomfortable rattle from deep within his chest.

The following morning, the queen's worst nightmare was confirmed. While dressing for breakfast, Victoria's daughter, Helena, burst into the room, clutching the fated telegram from Norfolk. The prince had died shortly after midnight. No part of the country was left untouched by the tragedy. In his younger days, Albert was hailed as the glittering hope and dream of generations. Tall and handsome, he appeared almost as the physical successor of the legendary King Arthur, re-installing a sprinkling of glamour and excitement back to a seemingly austere and economically prudent country.

'Words are too poor to express one's feelings of grief, horror and distress,' remarked Victoria, 'Poor, poor parents, poor May.' The unexpected nature of his death unleashed almost a tsunami wave of sorrow not experienced on British streets for generations. Shops, theatres and pubs were closed and flags lowered to half-mast on every municipal building in the country. Outside the iron gilded gates of Sandringham, a soft drizzle that had sprinkled the area all morning, turned into thick, thundering hail, covering roads with sticky, torturous mud. Dripping with water, mourners gathered silently, cold and wet, shivering and weeping.

Alexandra, though a controlling and dominating character, was enormously fond of her children and rich in mutual affection. Albert's death left an enormous, impenetrable, and ultimately devastating blow from which she never recovered fully. That night, a hymn of grief was sung for the prince at St Paul's Cathedral, and hundreds of services were offered for him across the kingdom. For the Prince of Wales, the tragedy proved almost unbearable.

14 January 1892 ultimately changed the destiny of the British monarchy. Had Albert lived, the future of the United Kingdom, and the royal family, would have been undeniably altered. How would Albert have responded to the tumultuous changes of the twentieth century? The First World War? The rise of egalitarianism and socialism? Who would have sat on the British throne today? We shall never know.

January

The tragic death of the prince also overshadowed other significant events of the day, most notably the passing of Cardinal Henry Manning, Archbishop of Westminster, and prelate of the Roman Catholic Church in England and Wales. By coincidence, his death occurred on the day as those of Cardinal James Gibbons, prelate of the United States, and the influential Papal Secretary, Cardinal Giovani Simeoni. One newspaper appropriately coined it the 'day of death', a never to be forgotten date in Victorian history.

1872 The Scottish Skye Terrier, Greyfriars Bobby, died in Edinburgh. Bobby had gained adulation across the world for quietly guarding his owner's grave for fourteen years in Greyfriars Kirkyard, Edinburgh. The sad revelation of Bobby's passing became international news, with obituaries as far as the United States.

1878 On the cold sunny morning of 14 January 1878, Alexander Graham Bell, the famous British inventor, rang the queen on the telephone. Her Majesty, who was staying at Osborne House at the time, remarked the device was 'quite extraordinary'. It was the first long-distance public telephone call in British history.

1893 History was made in a small Bradford back street. Keir Hardie, a short, unassuming middle-aged Scotsman, together with 130 delegates, hired a large room at the Bradford Labour Institute. With a spring in his step, at around midday, Hardie calmly announced the formation of a new, left-leaning and radical political organisation – the 'Independent Labour Party'.

1895 The Diglake Colliery Disaster. Between 11.30 and 11.40am on the morning a huge pool of water crashed its way into the Audley Colliery Mine, in North Staffordshire, killing seventy-seven men. Over 240 miners, including children, were underground at the time. The aftermath of the tragedy created a lasting legacy, and a painful reminder of the perils of mining for working-class communities. It wasn't until 1979 that a law was finally passed ensuring that mines would have a distance of at least 121 feet between shafts to prevent flooding. On 14 January 2020 a memorial was unveiled, depicting two kneeling miners at Audley Methodist Church.

15 January

1867 The Regent's Park skating disaster
Snow dominated England throughout most of January 1867. In London, a popular boating lake in Regents Park had become a gathering place for ice skaters and onlookers who flocked to the area to enjoy the idyllic winter scene. Tragedy, however, was just around the corner.

On the crisp morning of 14 January, a disaster was narrowly averted when the ice suddenly collapsed, leaving twenty-one people thrown into freezing water. All of the victims survived but the area was mistakenly re-opened the following day.

The next morning, yet more bitter temperatures once again froze the lake, attracting a new influx of crowds. By mid-afternoon, over 2,000 people had gathered, with estimates of as many as 500 people on the ice at the same time.

At 3.30pm, a deep, sinister cracking noise was heard. Within seconds, hundreds were thrown into the water. The scene was chaotic. Rescuers dived into the lake but were paralysed by the freezing temperatures. Others frantically ran to get boats, pulling survivors up with branches from nearby trees. Many others suffered hypothermia and were rushed to the nearby Marylebone Workhouse. The disaster shocked Britain, yet no memorial was ever established. Forty people died in the tragedy.

1859 The National Portrait Gallery was opened in George Street, London. Proposals for a gallery were first raised by Earl Stanhope in 1846 but it took ten years to finally achieve completion. Among the early trustees was Benjamin Disraeli.

1897 Andrew Cunningham enrolled in the Royal Navy. At the age of ten, Cunningham's father asked if his restless son would like to enter the Navy. Ambitious even at a young age, he replied yes, but would like to be an admiral. His wish was granted. On 15 January 1897, he enrolled on board Britannia, an elderly wooden training ship, stationed in Dartmouth. He would go on to become First Sea Lord during the Second World War.

16 January

1840 Chartists John Frost, William Jones and Zephaniah Williams are sentenced to death
The Chartist movement was a major political force throughout the early nineteenth century, driven in the passionate pursuit of parliamentary reform. In November 1839 a large armed protest took place in the Welsh town of Newport, creating shock and terror throughout Westminster. The government feared a revolution, and responded harshly with the three key leaders, John Frost, William Jones and Zephaniah Williams, sentenced to death on charges of treason on 16 January 1840. Fortunately, the sentence was commuted to imprisonment, but they were all shipped off to Tasmania. Jones died penniless in 1873, followed by Williams the following year. Only Frost returned to England and died at the extraordinary age of ninety-three in 1877.

1898 Sir Charles Pelham Villiers, the longest serving MP in the House of Commons died. At ninety-six, Villiers was still an active and sociable Member of Parliament. Originally a radical, he had been elected in 1835, two years before the accession of Victoria, and continued serving his constituency for the next sixty-three years. For the last six years of his life, he also served as 'Father of the House', although never rose to ministerial office. Villiers remains one of the longest serving MPs in British history.

January

17 January

1863 David Lloyd George is born
Although known as 'the Welsh Wizard', Lloyd George actually started life in a small terrace house in Manchester. His father, William George, was a Welsh school teacher who relocated to Pembrokeshire and died of pneumonia. David was raised instead by the firm hand of his tough charismatic uncle, Richard Lloyd, who instilled confidence and encouragement in his nephew, vowing he could achieve anything through hard work and dedication. David Lloyd George is often referred to as the first Welsh prime minister in British history.

1881 Sir William Armstrong's home became one of the first to use electric light. His mansion in Northumberland was constructed to embrace new technologies, including new electric lamps which ran on water through a dynamo-electric generator.

18 January

1881 One of the worst blizzards in British history occurs in southern England
For a few bleak uncertain days in 1881, England came to a halt. Railways, roads and highways were overpowered by thick snow, with many towns cut off from supplies, transport and communication. It was estimated that over 100 people died during the blizzard. When the storm had finally dissipated on 23 January, a mass clear-up began with hundreds of men armed with shovels. Many animals and livestock also perished.

1873 Writer Lord Lytton died. Lytton's quotes are still widely used today. They include the phrases 'the pen is mightier than the sword' and 'in pursuit of the almighty dollar'.

19 January

1901 Queen Victoria reported as seriously ill
By 1901 rheumatism had devastated Victoria's health, leaving the once active and energetic monarch immobile and increasingly dependent on a wheelchair. Her eyesight was poor, clouded by cataracts which worsened at a rapid pace. On 19 January, doctors discovered the queen unresponsive in bed. She had suffered a stroke. Within hours, the grief-stricken Prince of Wales left London for Osborne, arriving frantically that afternoon. Upon entering the bedroom, Victoria expressed a remarkable end to her forty-year hostility against her son and spoke with enormous and unusual tenderness. The prince, who had for so long suffered an unsteady, painful relationship with his mother, was overcome with emotion. A bulletin was later published announcing that the queen's health had declined and was causing much anxiety. At 6.00pm a second bulletin was released published a slight improvement. The world held its breath.

1848 The writer Isaac D'Israeli died. Unfortunately, he never lived to see his son, Benjamin, rise to the dizzy heights of prime minister. Born to Italian-Jewish parents, Isaac had prospered during the early nineteenth century as a writer and bibliophile but was largely regarded as an outsider in the snobbish, hierarchical world of high society.

20 January

1843 Terror comes to London
20 January 1843. A young civil servant left Charing Cross Station for his usual daily walk to Downing Street. His name was Edward Drummond. Having started his career as a clerk in HM Treasury, Drummond had risen to become the private secretary of four British prime ministers, including the incumbent, Sir Robert Peel. Unknown to him, Drummond was being followed.

As he walked towards the entrance of the iconic number ten, a young and dangerous character suddenly approached him from behind. With a sudden jerk, the man pulled out a pistol, took aim, and at point-blank range, fired a bullet straight into Drummond's back. He collapsed immediately.

The incident shocked London. The assassin was later identified as Daniel McNaghten, a twenty-nine-year-old woodturner from Scotland who had intended to shoot the prime minister but had mistaken Drummond for Peel. Remarkably, Drummond was not immediately killed. With the aid of policemen, he managed to stand and eventually even walk back to his private residence. The bullet was also successfully removed but infection soon set in. He died on 25 January. Curiously, Drummond's death had also raised questions of medical mistreatment. One doctor later published a letter arguing the poor man died not because of the actual bullet, but from medical mistakes in the aftermath of his injuries.

1853 The Royal Photographic Society of Great Britain was founded. It would be several years until photography was commercially available for ordinary citizens, but the society set in motion increasing professional respect for the art of photography.

1896 Death of Prince Henry of Battenberg. 'An awful day,' wrote Queen Victoria, 'it is almost impossible to describe it.' While dressing for breakfast, Victoria received a sudden, unexpected knock at her bedroom door. It was her son, Prince Arthur Duke of Connaught. 'I felt sure there was something wrong.' she recalled, 'still more so, when he said he wished to speak to me alone.' The maids were ordered out of the room and the corridor cleared of eavesdroppers. With deep emotion, Arthur informed her that Prince Henry of Battenberg had died. He was only thirty-seven years old. Henry's wife, Princess Beatrice, had already begun breakfast when Arthur informed her of the news. The Queen, grief-stricken with sadness, clasped Beatrice in her arms and sobbed. 'I felt as if my heart must break,' she remarked, 'God in his mercy help us.'

January

1900 John Ruskin, arguably the most significant art critic of the nineteenth century, died. Ruskin's philosophy was bold and unapologetic. He regarded art as a vivid expression of personal morality. His belief that art could transform lives was equally mirrored in his huge appreciation for architectural conservation and he was highly critical of the perceived greediness of the modern industrial age.

21 January

1855 Anti-Crimean War riots erupt in London
The vicar of St Martin's in the Field gazed timidly from his presbytery window with alarm and apprehension. All morning, a growing crowd of angry protesters had gathered in London's Trafalgar Square, furious at the conduct of the Crimean War. Wagons skidded and skated across the ice, as mobs furiously began pelting stones, snowballs and rocks at passing traffic, quickly descending into violence. By midday, police had arrived armed with truncheons but were hastily pelted with snow. Reinforcements were called from the nearby barracks, by which point over 1,500 people had crowded into the vicinity. Fierce fighting ensued. Eventually, after several hours of violence, calm was restored and the ringleaders arrested. The disturbance became known appropriately as the 'Snowball riots'.

1840 The first woman doctor in Scotland, Sophia Jex-Blake, was born in London. She was a leading pioneer for female education.

22 January

1901 Queen Victoria dies
The Queen was dead. Long live the King. Victoria's passing brought to a close, the then, longest reign in British history. She had died surrounded by her children and grandchildren at Osborne House. The shockwave of grief and astonishment was felt in almost every region of the globe. In the United States Senate, news of the death was passed around by doorkeepers. Both houses of Congress were adjoined, and the American flag lowered to half-mast by most government buildings. The court ball in Vienna was cancelled under direct instruction of Emperor Francis Joseph. In Berlin, Germany declared a state of official mourning.

In London, the sad mood was matched by equally grey drizzly weather. Shops, theatres, public houses and markets were closed. The huge cumbersome blinds of Mansion House were slowly lowered as the bells of St Paul's Cathedral tolled a mournful lament for the late sovereign. The Dean of St Paul's later sent six candelabras, which had been used at the funeral of the Duke of Wellington, to Osborne. Many tourists arrived at London theatres only to be turned away and find the doors shut with huge black-bordered signs announcing mass cancellations. As news spread further across the country, enormous crowds flocked to Buckingham Palace and St James Palace where a solemn notice had been placed on the outside gates.

Victoria gave her name to an age. Her sixty-three-year reign had cemented almost unprecedented continuity. Without her, the future seemed bleak, unfamiliar and unsettling. Victoria was born into a world that no longer existed. A pre-industrial Georgian age, where the throne was shaky, periodically damaged by her peppery Hanoverian uncles. Although intensely political and frequently unpredictable, Victoria established the precedent for modern British constitutional monarchy, a system which exists above the contentious, divisive world of politics. By 1901 she reigned over the largest Empire the world had ever seen. Now she was gone.

1846 Robert Peel delivered a landmark speech regarding the Corn Laws. The debate was one of the most divisive political topics of the nineteenth century and ultimately split the Conservative Party in two. For decades, the laws had protected the price of British wheat from international rivals, something supporters argued gave considerable encouragement to arable farmers. For critics, however, the laws represented the worst example of aristocratic self-interest, a policy designed to mechanise parliamentary influence to safeguard itself against cheaper foreign corn that would benefit poorer communities. For Peel, the issue was particularly complicated. A large number of Tory MPs benefitted from the laws, making abolition unpopular in the party. For the country, however, he felt abolition was necessary. On 22 January 1846, Peel delivered one of his most famous addresses in the Commons, pushing for the end of the laws. Unfortunately for Peel, many Tory MPs never forgave him and he resigned as prime minister just six months later.

1889 Carlo Pellegrini died. The flamboyant, funny and exuberant Italian artist Carlo Pellegrini monopolised Victorian aristocratic society with his wit and charisma, becoming good friends with the Prince of Wales and other members of British public life throughout the 1880s. He had first arrived in England penniless and heartbroken after a series of personal tragedies and, allegedly, lived under Waterloo Bridge as a homeless man. Within a few years, however, he had established himself as a gifted and noteworthy caricaturist, working under the alias 'Ape' for the popular magazine *Vanity Fair*. With his big beard and larger than life persona, he became a foremost Victorian celebrity. Ever a good talker, Pellegrini claimed he always kept a cigar perched in his mouth at all times, even while sleeping. Unfortunately, he died young of lung disease in 1889 aged just forty-nine.

23 January

1874 Prince Alfred marries Tsar Alexander II's daughter, Maria Alexandrovna
It was called the wedding of the decade. On the morning of 24 January 1874, St Petersburg reached a crescendo of excitement as the glamorous figure of Maria Alexandrovna, daughter of Tsar Alexander II, married the dazzling son of Queen Victoria, Prince Alfred, in a mesmerising Orthodox ceremony hosted at the Winter Palace.

The beauty of the ceremony could not disguise the many months of controversy that had raged behind the scenes. The Queen was opposed to the marriage. She distrusted

January

the Russians, and hated the Tsar who, she feared, would manipulate the marriage to gain influence in British society. In Russia the feeling was similarly hostile. No British royal had ever married a Romanov. The Tsar also worried that Maria would fail to adjust to Britain and dislike her new infamously temperamental mother-in-law.

Just a few weeks after the engagement Victoria requested Maria visit Scotland where they could meet for the first time, but the Tsar refused. Later, the Queen demanded an Anglican ceremony be performed after the Orthodox Mass, ruffling the feathers of the Russian court. As relations between Russia and Britain declined again in the 1870s, Maria became horrified at Victoria's rampant anti-Russian feeling. Oblivious to the dramas, the public celebrated the wedding like any other royal event. In Edinburgh, the day was marked with a tremendous bonfire lit on the summit of Arthur's Seat followed by a spectacular firework display.

1899 The influential British judge Lord Alfred Denning was born in Hampshire. His remarkable life would span the entirety of the twentieth century and yet he almost died shortly after his birth. He was born prematurely and was so small he was nicknamed 'Tom Thumb'. Although physically petite, Denning would nevertheless have a large and long influence over the legal affairs of the United Kingdom.

24 January

1895 Lord Randolph Churchill dies
Winston Churchill awoke with terror. Winter had colonised London, turning the usually bustling city into a haven of white sleeping snow. While staying at a friend's house on 24 January, Winston was alerted that his father, Randolph, was gravely ill and appeared to be on the brink of death. Quickly getting dressed, Churchill sprinted across the icy Grosvenor Square, to reach his father's bedside just in time. Randolph died shortly afterwards. He was just forty-five years old.

His long illness meant that many obituaries had been already drafted weeks in advance and were published almost immediately the following morning. Beyond the echoing of praise and condolences came a real sense of unfulfilled, unconquered political potential. He had wrecked his parliamentary career in 1886 in a self-defeating resignation letter to the prime minister, Lord Salisbury. Instead of promotion, the remaining years were clouded by disappointment, boredom and devastating illness. No consensus has ever been properly established over the precise cause of Randolph's death. While widespread theories suggested syphilis, others argued he may have suffered from a brain tumour. Winston Churchill died seventy years to the day on 24 January 1965.

1896 The celebrated artist Frederic Leighton was awarded a peerage. Leighton was a Victorian artistic colossal. As the President of the Royal Academy of Arts since 1878, his artwork was respected from prince to pauper, making him the first British artist to be awarded a peerage, bestowed through the personal intervention of William Gladstone. Unfortunately, it was also the shortest peerage in history. The following day, Leighton suffered a heart attack and died at 3.05am.

25 January

1858 The wedding of Queen Victoria's eldest daughter, Victoria, to Crown Prince Frederick of Germany takes place in Windsor
The royal couple were married at Windsor with the majestic music of Mendelssohn's *Wedding March* thundering out across the chapel for the first time in British history. Preparations for the big day had begun, literally, years in advance. Throughout the 1840s, Albert had watched with growing unease as much of continental Europe seemed gradually moving towards republicanism, casting aside their old traditional reverence for monarchy. His dream was for a grand European alliance, whereby his children would marry various members of other ruling families, cementing peace and, most importantly, preventing the likelihood of future war and disharmony. The engagement of Victoria and the Crown Prince of Germany was a vivid and seemingly perfect fruition of this dream. The proposal had occurred in Balmoral, everything choreographed by Albert himself to ensure the perfect romantic setting. Amid the heraldic trumpets, the full-dress uniforms, the ceremonial splendour, the marriage most importantly cemented Anglo-Germanic relations. Victoria became the new Crown Princess of Germany and relocated to Berlin where she died over forty years later in 1900.

1851 The first segment of Charles Dickens' *A Child's History of England* was published. It became such an immensely popular and influential book that it was later incorporated into the educational curriculum until the early twentieth century. Dickens had originally written the book for his own children.

26 January

1885 General Charles Gordon is killed in Khartoum
Gordon, the national hero, was dead. Several months earlier, the charismatic commander had been dispatched to Khartoum to administer an evacuation of civilians and soldiers during the Mahdist War. Against their wishes, Gordon remained in the city and organised a large-scale defence, garnishing praise from the British press and but vehement hostility from Westminster. As the campaign drew on, William Gladstone reluctantly ordered a relief force to help Gordon's troops, but they arrived too late. Gordon was killed by the Mahdist forces on 26 January, plunging the country into despair.

On the morning of 2 February, the Prime Minister awoke to the cacophony of angry chants pounding down Whitehall. Soon, a large and extremely hostile crowd gathered outside Downing Street. Stones were pelted through the windows, rocks fired at the entrance. Angry mobs also appeared at parliament. Fights broke out in the streets. Gladstone was labelled a murderer, a traitor, and a coward. The queen, who had long hated the Liberal leader, exploded in a fit of rage. In a harshly worded telegram, which was later leaked to the press, she passionately condemned the government. Few prime ministers could have survived such an onslaught of public and political attacks. The crisis even put a strain on Gladstone's health: he began suffering 'overaction of the bowels' and other physical disturbances. The Liberal government collapsed in June.

27 January

1859 Queen Victoria's first grandchild, Prince Wilhelm of Germany, is born in Berlin

It was not an easy pregnancy. On the morning of 26 January, the quiet solemnity of Crown Prince Palace in Berlin was ablaze with panic. The recently married Princess Victoria had gone into labour but was suffering from severe life-threatening complications. Administered by the British doctor, Sir James Clark, and the German physicians Eduard Martin and August Wegner, the crown princess was given heavy doses of chloroform and other drugs to ease her agonising pain, making her unconscious.

Observing the baby's arm elevated behind his head, Martin forcibly pulled his left arm down sharply, tearing the brachial plexus, and damaged the network of nerves that conducts signals from the spinal cord to the arm, hand and shoulder. The child was delivered in the early hours of 27 January, unconscious, and was violently slapped by the midwife until he awoke screaming and crying. By this point the bedroom had become hot and sweaty. Tension filled the corridors like smoke, corroding any feelings of optimism for a healthy baby. Back in London, the queen was growing even more restless. Hourly updates revealed little, and soon false rumours emerged that both the infant and mother were dead.

Despite the trauma of the event, both survived. Much to his personal embarrassment, Wilhelm suffered a deformed hand for the rest of his life and was subjected to various painful medical examinations throughout his childhood. In the harsh militaristic environment of nineteenth-century Germany, his disability became a source of shame and arguably contributed towards his complex personality in adulthood.

1855 Mary Seacole embarked for Constantinople. The life of Seacole continues to inspire and fascinate people as an example of selflessness and devotion. Born in Jamaica in 1805, Seacole moved to England in the 1820s but also travelled extensively across South America, the Bahamas and Cuba, working as a nurse for the sick and vulnerable. In 1855 she embarked for Constantinople with the aim of opening a hotel for injured British officers in the Crimean War. Having previously applied and been denied funding for the trip by the Crimean Fund, Seacole financed the trip independently but suffered huge racial prejudice. Her work is fondly remembered today. In 1872 a bust of Seacole was unveiled at the Royal Academy of Arts, carved by the sculptor Prince Victor, nephew of Queen Victoria.

28 January

1886 The Conservative government falls

A week is a long time in politics. Despite gaining office in 1885, by January 1886 the Conservative cabinet, led by Lord Salisbury had collapsed. On the evening of the 26th, the Liberal MP Jesse Collings tabled a vote of no confidence in the government. The Conservatives were defeated, and Salisbury resigned as prime minister two days later. The queen was devastated by the news. Just twelve months earlier, Gladstone had been lambasted as a traitor after the disaster of Khartoum. On 1 February, he returned to Number 10 to form his third administration.

1896 On 28 January 1896, a young, speed-loving motorist named Walter Arnold became the first man to be fined for speeding in the United Kingdom. He was driving at 8mph. Arnold was a fun-loving fellow and one of Britain's first car dealers who championed the modern motor as an alternative to horse-driven transport. Alarmed at the speed of his vehicle, however, a policeman followed Arnold on his bicycle and, after an exhausting five-mile chase, finally arrested him on the spot. The fine was levied at one shilling.

29 January

1856 The Victoria Cross is instituted
Since the Crimean War, calls for a new and prestigious military decoration had thundered out across the country. Unlike many other European nations, Britain did not have a formal system to reward gallantry within the armed forces for soldiers irrespective of rank or class. Many acts of courage would go unnoticed, or unappreciated. Finally in 1856, the Victoria Cross was established by royal warrant to recognise acts of extraordinary bravery in the face of the enemy. Legend has it, the first medals were actually cast from the bronze of Russian guns captured in Crimea. The inscription was originally planned to read 'For Bravery' but was later changed on the recommendation of Queen Victoria to 'For Valour''. Recipients were also entitled to a £10 per annum annuity, the equivalent of around £750 today, and the post-nominal letters VC after their name.

1839 On the cold Tuesday morning of 29 January, a nervous Charles Darwin stepped into St Peter's Anglican Church in Maer to marry his first cousin Emma Wedgewood, granddaughter of the famous Josiah Wedgewood. The Darwin's would go on to have ten children and remained married for forty-four years.

30 January

1891 The MP Charles Bradlaugh dies in London
The contentious and colourful life of Charles Bradlaugh came to an abrupt and premature end on 31 January 1891. He was just fifty-seven. The remaining years of his life had been clouded in darkness and tragedy. In December 1890 his beloved daughter, Alice succumbed to typhoid fever and meningitis, after which his own health declined rapidly. The end came for Bradlaugh in the early hours of the morning. His funeral, held four days later at Brookwood cemetery, was attended

by thousands of grief-stricken mourners, among them David Lloyd George and the young Mohandas Gandhi. His robust defence of his convictions left a long and potent legacy. In 2016 a bust of Bradlaugh was added to the Parliamentary Art Collection.

1869 Benjamin Disraeli became the first prime minister to be caricatured by *Vanity Fair*.

31 January

1855 Ministerial crisis
Foul weather rocked and raged the gardens of Buckingham Palace as the portly figure of Lord Derby, the Conservative leader, prodded up the gilded stairs for a hugely consequential meeting. Lord Aberdeen had resigned as prime minister the previous day, leaving the country without a leader. Superficially at least, Derby seemed the most likely candidate. Born into an aristocratic family, he had served briefly as prime minister in 1852 and possessed a wealth of political experience. To everyone's amazement, however, he declined the offer and Britain was thrown into ministerial chaos. The queen, with a sting of irritation, accused Derby of renouncing his responsibility. Benjamin Disraeli was particularly furious. In the next few days, Whitehall descended into crisis.

1858 The *Great Eastern* steamship was launched. It was the largest and greatest ship in the world, a shining example of Victorian innovation but also a blistering disappointment. Designed by Isambard Kingdom Brunel and John Scott Russell, the five-funnelled steamship was created to reflect Britain's booming engineering power. In reality, it proved so big that no harbour was large enough to cope. With much sadness, it was eventually sold in 1864 and taken to pieces some years later.

Undated

1872 William Jerrold's book *London: A Pilgrimage* published
In January 1872 Jerrold published a landmark book, co-written with the French author Gustave Doré, exploring the cruel realities of Victorian urban life. The book was met with considerable controversy, especially over its candid, brutal descriptions of unrelenting poverty. The immense squalor and deprivation were depicted with forensic and meticulous detail. Some reviewers found it too graphic, criticising the work for 'inventing' or exaggerating the extent of poverty.

February

1 February

1901 Queen Victoria's body returns to London
The late monarch had written meticulous instructions to be followed after her death, including a number of preparations to take place before the funeral. Firstly, Victoria wanted several items placed inside her coffin. This included a lock of hair from John Brown, a sprig of Balmoral heather, photographs of family members, jewellery, a cast of Prince Albert's hands and Albert's dressing gown. Lastly, a bunch of fresh flowers was to be placed softly into her hands, strategically placed by undertakers to hide a photograph of John Brown which was positioned in her left hand.

In the immediate hours after her death, Victoria's plain oak coffin lay in state at Osborne House which had been decorated with heavy black drapes and enormous wreaths. The biggest wreath came from the King of Portugal, garnished with a large crown of lilies resting on a cushion of violets. After a short service held at the private chapel, her body was carried into the main deck of the Royal Yacht *Alberta* and arrived in Kent the same day.

1867 The Blue Plaque Scheme was established. One of the great joys of London is the numerous blue plaques dotted in and around the capital, providing a visual story of the city's illustrious and interesting inhabitants. The scheme was initiated in 1867, orchestrated by William Gladstone to provide a physical reminder of London's rich history. The first plaque was dedicated to the poet, Lord Byron.

1873 The Royal Naval College was opened in Greenwich. Notable graduates of the college included the 9th Marquess of Queensberry, famous for his role in the downfall of playwright Oscar Wilde.

2 February

1901 The state funeral of Queen Victoria
Many of the rich and fascinating traditions of British state funerals derived from Queen Victoria's, although much of this was accidental. As the daughter, wife, mother and grandmother of a soldier, Victoria wanted a military funeral with her coffin carried by gun carriage. Amidst the tolling of haunting church bells,

the funeral procession passed a regiment of mournful bystanders in Windsor for a formal service held at St George's Chapel. As her coffin was solemnly placed onto the gun carriage, however, the horses became spooked. They refused to budge and stubbornly stood silently. Despite numerous attempts to rectify the problem, sailors from the Royal Navy were called in to perform the ritual, thus starting a precedent which continues to this day. Sadly, it was also reported that 1,305 people were injured during the funeral in a stampede. Several were treated by St John Ambulance Association, and twenty-four people were taken to St Mary's Hospital

1843 Rose Leclercq, the first actress to play Lady Bracknell, was born. Leclercq started life in Liverpool, the daughter of struggling actor Charles Clark and Margaret Clark, a ballet mistress. She enjoyed a successful career on stage but died young of influenza in 1899. She was just fifty-six.

3 February

1852 The House of Commons chamber is opened
The House of Commons is a testament to Victorian architectural creativity and ingenuity. The designers, Charles Barry and A.G. Pugin, both yearned to create a grand, imposing atmosphere to fit the legislative gravitas of a bustling country, but with a degree of intimacy, maybe even aggression, that makes debates in the commons so legendarily robust.

Upon completion in 1852, the writer George Bradshaw described it as the greatest building in the world. For many politicians, however, the chamber seemed remarkably small, so small it only seated two thirds of all members. In early debates, several MPs were forced to stand in the doorway or inside the lobby. In the summer, the chamber would also become extremely hot and uncomfortable. Barry didn't seem to care much for the taller members, the likes of whom were cramped by the significant lack of legroom. The lofty Lord Salisbury, who stood at six foot four found himself particularly disappointed with the design, preferring to stand in the entrance of the chamber, rather than squeeze himself through hours of languid debates.

Another significant feature of the commons was the green leathered benches, a marked difference from the red benches of the Lords, a purposeful illustration of the hierarchy between the two chambers. The commons was markedly less opulent, less ornamented and less grand than the upper chamber. Ironically, the importance of the lower chamber would significantly increase throughout the Victorian era, something which was arguably not reflected in the final designs.

1896 Lord Leighton's funeral was held at St Paul's Cathedral. Leighton was granted the unprecedented honour of lying in state in the grand Octagon Room of the Royal Academy of Arts for two days before the funeral. Among the hundreds of wreaths included personal messages from the Prince of Wales, Kaiser Frederick of Germany and former Prime Minister Lord Rosebery, who also sent private condolences to the family. On Monday the 3rd, his coffin was carried into the courtyard of Burlington House and placed onto a horse-drawn hearse. Over thirty carriages carrying Britain's great and good followed behind, as well as the American, Austro-Hungarian, French, Chinese, Italian and Spanish Ambassadors. Prime Minister Lord Salisbury who was expected to attend was forced to cancel at the last-minute owing to a cold.

4 February

1845 A Memorable State Opening of Parliament
Victoria only attended the State Opening of Parliament four times in her reign, and after 1845 who could blame her? While proceeding to the House of Lords chamber, the Duke of Argyll, who was carrying the crown, suddenly jerked. In front of hundreds of spectators, the priceless crown fell from its gilded cushion and crashed onto the floor. When the Victoria and Albert had retired into the Robing Room, the mortified Duke brought in the crown. The Queen later remarked that it looked like a squashed pudding. The peers looked on in utter horror.

1868 Constance Georgine Markievicz was born. Markievicz takes her name in history as the first woman elected to the House of Commons, although she never personally took her seat. She was born in Buckingham Gate, London, the eldest daughter of the famous Arctic explorer Henry Gore-Booth, who owned large amounts of land in Sligo. In 1900, she married the Polish playwright, Casimir Dunin Markievicz, who styled himself 'Count Markievicz' and eventually settled in Dublin. Constance was an active member of the Irish Citizen Army and ardently supported the Irish Republican Brotherhood. She was sentenced to death for her involvement in the 1916 easter rising but her charge was commuted. Two years later, she ran as the MP for the Dublin St Patrick's constituency, emerging victorious with 66% of the vote. She never sat in the Commons.

5 February

1838 The Oxford and Cambridge Club opens to members
Designed by Sir Robert Smirke, the club was an impressive example of Greek revival architecture, dominated by a rich neo-classical interior. Soon after its completion, a particularly infamous story circulated of some snobbish visitors from the Guards Club who had dropped by during the August recess. 'These middle-class fellows certainly know how to enjoy themselves,' they mocked. The Duke of Wellington, who was sitting opposite, slowly lowered his newspaper with a steely gaze. The formidable face of the Iron Duke today hangs in the dining room. Nor was the club immune from Victorian controversy. William Gladstone famously resigned his membership after hearing members of staff were not permitted to attend church on Sundays.

February

1852 On 5 February 1852 an almighty tragedy hit the sleepy town of Holmfirth in Yorkshire. In the mid-afternoon, the embankment of the Bilberry reservoir collapsed completely, pouring out approximately eighty-six million gallons of water. Eighty-one people were killed and many homes totally destroyed. Several shops, barns and warehouses were also damaged.

6 February

1838 Actor Henry Irving is born in Somerset
The transformation of British theatre from a discredited occupation into an admirable profession owes much to the work of Henry Irving. He started life in Somerset, born into a working-class family with no theatrical background. After his professional debut in 1856 his career survived enormous ups and downs, yet he became one of Britain's most respected personalities of the age. In 1895 he bridged the class divide by becoming the first British actor to be knighted.

1855 Lord Palmerston became prime minister for the first time. Palmerston was never a popular figure in the royal court. It was no secret that the queen disliked him intensely, both politically and personally. His colourful private life raised eyebrows in socially conservative society and his popular appeal to the press created hostility with many traditional colleagues who regarded him as a political ruffian.

1899 Prince Alfred, the grandson of Queen Victoria and eldest son of the Duke of Edinburgh died in mysterious circumstances on the evening of 6 February. He was just twenty-four years old. Rumours surrounding Alfred's health had murmured ever since his absence at his parents wedding anniversary in January. Less than a month later, the prince was discovered dead in his bedchamber. Speculation varied, with some suggesting Alfred had suffered a nervous breakdown and killed himself with a revolver in his bedroom. Others, however, proposed he was actually suffering from syphilis, consumption or even a tumour.

7 February

1845 Crisis at the British Museum
On the evening of 7 February, a drunken man fell into a priceless Portland Vase. Museum security in the nineteenth century was not as sophisticated as today and, unfortunately, the vase took several months to repair. When it was finally returned a few months later, it was situated safely behind a secure glass cabinet.

1865 The first edition of the popular magazine *The Pall Mall Gazette* was published. It included two items by Anthony Trollope.

1885 Douglas Haig was commissioned as a cornet in the 7th Hussars. Haig enjoyed rich aristocratic connections throughout his career, most notably with the royal family. He would later command the British Expeditionary Force during the First World War, but his legacy remains controversial.

1895 The brutal winter of 1895 was one of the coldest of the Victorian era, killing hundreds across the country. Many of the victims were centred in poorer communities where coal was unaffordable for struggling families.

8 February

1886 The infamous West End riots breaks out in London
An elderly Conservative peer was quietly settling himself down in a comfy leather armchair, enjoying the peace and sobriety of London's Carlton Club. Nestled within oak-panelled walls, fine carpets and magnificent portraits, the elderly peer began to snooze, unaware that his palatial peace was soon about to be shattered. Quite literally. At ten o'clock, a brick, thrown with formidable force, smashed through the window, landing plump in the centre of the floor. Within minutes a second stone was thrown, and then a third, and then a fourth. The club was under attack.

Earlier that morning, a meeting organised by the Fair Trade League (FTL) had come into conflict with a counter-demonstration led by the Social Democratic Federation. While the protest had started peacefully, things quickly got out of hand. The crowd swelled at over 10,000, many armed with rocks, bricks and weapons which they soon used to attack various buildings across London. The police were taken by surprise. Later the march turned towards Regent Street and, then, Oxford Street where worried shopkeepers rushed to board up their windows. Numerous properties were damaged. The inadequacy of the police response created fury throughout Britain who felt that law and order was breaking down before their eyes.

1840 Prince Albert was promoted to Field Marshal in the British Army. A few months later, he was also appointed as Colonel in Chief of the 11th Hussars. Albert took his new rank seriously and developed an intense interest in British military affairs.

1855 The Mysterious 'Devil's Footprints' appeared in Devon. After a night of heavy snowfall across south-west England, local residents in the Exe estuary awoke to find large and terrifying footprints stamped across the fields and lanes of more than thirty different locations in Devon. The footprints had no logical explanation. They appeared on several fields, walls, rivers and even houses, with further sightings in Dorset and Lincolnshire. Samples of the footprints were published in the *Illustrated London Times*, depicting a trail of hoof-like marks, immediately leading to speculation that the culprit was the devil. In subsequent weeks, several theories circulated over its origins, including hopping wood mice, badgers or even donkeys. More outlandish guesswork suggested that kangaroos may have been responsible, although these were widely dismissed. Some even doubt the validity of the event entirely, suggesting the phenomenon was either made up, or exaggerated by word of mouth.

1900 Snow disrupts Big Ben. The first winter of the new century was viciously cold for Londoners. In February, snow had fallen so heavily that the famous bell of Big Ben in St Stephen's tower stopped chiming for over eight hours.

9 February

1841 Queen Victoria saves Prince Albert's life in an ice-skating accident
Albert's death in 1861 is widely regarded as an untimely tragedy, although his demise could have easily been a lot earlier. On 9 February 1841 the royal couple had decided to ice skate on the frozen lake in Buckingham Palace gardens. They were accompanied by one lady in waiting but no security. Suddenly, the ice collapsed, and Albert was thrown into freezing cold water. Victoria screamed and tried desperately to pull him out. After two minutes he escaped and was rushed back to the palace for a hot bath. It was a very narrow escape.

1872 Speaker John Denison retired as Speaker of the House of Commons. Denison was the second-longest-serving Speaker of the Victorian era, and the first occupant of the grand Speaker's House in the Palace of Westminster. Unfortunately, Denison was not overtly impressed by the new building and complained of the draughty rooms on the ground floor. He subsequently ordered the construction of a grand porch to be built in order to keep out the 'rush of cold air'. His coat of arms, which still survives, was placed over the entrance. Denison also established the constitutional convention 'Denison's Rule'. He died less than a year after leaving office.

10 February

1840 Wedding of Queen Victoria and Prince Albert
The marriage of Queen Victoria and Prince Albert was a critical moment in British history. Arguably the greatest royal love story in modern times, the wedding had profound consequences on the nation, and the world and left a potent legacy for generations.

The queen awoke at 8.45am. The weather, predictably, was cold and wet, but not bad enough to dampen the public spirits. Assisted by the charismatic Duchess of Sutherland, Victoria was the first British royal to popularise the modern white wedding dress, something which was becoming increasingly fashionable throughout the century. At noon precisely, Prince Albert, his father and his brother left their accommodation for the Chapel at St James's Palace, creating a wild roar of excitement. At St James's Park, spectators were so ecstatic some even climbed trees to get a better view of the magnificent procession.

Meticulous planning for a royal wedding had begun many years in advance. Since childhood, Victoria knew she was destined for an arranged marriage. Details had been organised when Victoria was only a young child, although her very first encounter with Albert proved rather disappointing. The princess found her future husband dull, quiet and rather plump. Albert was also very shy, reserved and more naturally inclined for study than socialising. To make matters worse, the German delegation had come down with a nasty bout of a gastric virus. Victoria, meanwhile, was more infatuated by a parrot which had been given to her as a gift. Thankfully, subsequent meetings proved more successful and the two later fell madly in love.

In reality, the marriage was far less tranquil than the modern image suggests. It was tumultuous, dominated by Victoria's fierce temper and Albert's rigid social conservative values. Nevertheless, upon his death, the queen would be forever tormented with grief. She would refer to 10 February as the happiest day of her life. In the long winter of widowhood, it became a source of comfort, reflection, nostalgia and loss.

1871 A dreadful storm, known as the Great Gale struck the north coast of England. Nine volunteers courageously sailed out into a lifeboat to rescue the poor sailors caught in the raging water. Seventy people drowned in total and thirty ships were destroyed.

11 February

1884 Queen Victoria publishes her book *More Leaves from The Journal of A Life In The Highlands*
No British sovereign had previously published a book. Within days of the release, the work became an instant best seller, with over 100,000 copies sold. Unsurprisingly, Victoria's children were not happy, especially as John Brown featured more prominently than her own family. Even more worryingly, Victoria announced the commencement of a second book, a full-scale biography of Brown which would be released to the public. The household exploded with mortified shock. After furious rows, it eventually fell to the jittery Dean of Windsor to persuade her to terminate the project. Victoria was enraged. She erupted into a fierce temper and accused the dean of class prejudice. Nevertheless, despite her anger, she took his advice. Whether or not the manuscript survives is a matter of debate, although it is likely the drafts were deliberately destroyed after her death by Princess Beatrice.

1845 In February 1845 gossip emerged that Prince Albert was about to be proclaimed king. The rumour became so widespread that it was later discussed in parliament. 'It was not a good practice,' replied the exasperated Robert Peel, 'for honourable Members to ask Ministers to give explanations with respect to newspaper rumours.' Contrary to inaccurate reports, Albert retained the title Prince Consort until his death.

February

1895 The lowest-ever UK temperature was recorded. If you were unlucky enough to be in Braemar, Aberdeenshire on 11 February 1895, you would have encountered −27.2°C temperatures, (measured as −17°F).

12 February

1881 The philanthropist Baroness Burdett Coutts ignites scandal by marrying her secretary
As one of the wealthiest women in Britain, Coutts was commonly regarded as the most 'eligible bride' in Victorian England. Like many aristocrats, however, she was not immune from society gossip or scandal. In 1839 she became infatuated with the venerable Duke of Wellington, who was fifty years her senior. Defying popular convention, she proposed marriage to the duke in February 1847. Wellington politely declined, but the news created ridicule throughout the gossip-ridden avenues of high society. In 1881 the esteemed baroness suddenly announced her engagement to her young American-born secretary, William Bartlett. The scandal was perceived as worse because Coutts was over thirty-five years older than Bartlett, who quickly gained a reputation as a gold-digger. Rumours even circulated that the marriage was manipulated by Bartlett to steal her fortune. More significantly, a clause in Coutts's stepmother's last will and testament forbade her from marrying a foreign national. In defying her wishes, she was forced to give up three-fifths of her income.

13 February

1849 Lord Randolph Churchill is born in London
The third son of the 7th Duke of Marlborough, the young Randolph was a boisterous, robust and unpredictable child, qualities that arguably manifested themselves into a tumultuous adulthood. His mother, Lady Frances Churchill, was the goddaughter of the Duke of Wellington, and a strong dominant presence in the family. After Eton, Randolph was enrolled at Oxford University where he was disciplined for drunkenness and smashing the windows of a hotel. Despite his short life and long illness, he would dominate Victorian politics with colour and controversy, carving a name for himself as a charismatic, if contentious, political giant.

14 February

1852 Great Ormond Street Hospital is opened
The hospital was established after years of campaigning by the paediatrician Charles West who had advocated for a hospital solely dedicated for children. Only ten beds were initially available when the hospital opened in 1852 but it was expanded quickly. West's association with the hospital ended in 1877 after a series of disagreements with the hospital management. West later claimed his conversion

to Catholicism was a major factor in his declining popularity. Great Ormond Street would go on to become one of the world's leading children's hospitals.

1895 Oscar Wilde's *The Importance of Being Earnest* was performed for the first time. The two central characters, Algernon and Jack, were played by George Alexander and Allan Aynesworth. Since 1895 the play remains as popular as ever. Numerous stage, radio and film adaptations have followed in several languages, yet it remains at heart a tale of Victorian aristocratic absurdity.

15 February

1848 The Caledonian Railway is opened
Whereas previous generations had criticised the Scottish countryside as a ragged, untamed and 'savage' landscape, the Victorian railways introduced many to the vivid realities of a truly beautiful country. For the first time in history, English tourists were able to visit the Highlands with relative ease, without months of exhausting travel, and explore new areas which were previously unreachable. In 1848 the famous Caledonian Railway opened. The views of unspoiled, unravaged hills and mountains became an immense attraction for the area and led to a great demand for hotels and hospitality for the local economy.

1894 On 15 February the usually calm serenity of the Royal Observatory in Greenwich was rocked with tragedy. Martin Bourdin, a twenty-six-year-old French anarchist residing in FitzRoy Street, accidently blew himself up with explosives. Miraculously, Bourdin was initially still alive, but with devastating injuries. Although able to speak, he withheld the names, motives or targets of his anarchist campaign. Police carried his body to the Seamen's Hospital in Greenwich where he died just thirty minutes later.

16 February

1887 The 10th general meeting of the British Beekeepers Association (BBA) is held
Baroness Burdett-Coutts, president of the association, marked the tenth anniversary of the BBA with a special meeting hosted at 105 Jermyn Street, Piccadilly. Coutts had gained a reputation as the 'queen of the poor' due to her charitable donations which extended from social housing to wildlife and prisons. She was also the first woman in British history to be ennobled in recognition of her charitable achievements, especially in helping deprived children in East London. Under her leadership, the BBA championed the preservation of natural habitat from creeping urbanisation and industrialisation which was slowly destroying much of England's green areas. Burdett Coutts is also credited for financing the commemorative statue of the popular dog 'Greyfriars Bobby' in Edinburgh.

February

1841 Lord Cardigan was tried in the House of Lords after being accused of injuring an officer during a duel. He was initially released, but later retried. After a short legal case, he was acquitted.

17 February

1867 Princess Alexandra's illness
During her pregnancy with her third child, Princess Alexandra was diagnosed with rheumatic fever and became dangerously ill. The after-effects of the disease left her extremely weak for several months. She also became permanently deaf in one ear. A photograph was released in September 1868 to show Alexandra standing and physically recovered. The evidence brought huge relief to the worried public, but the consequences of the illness left life-changing problems, including a pronounced limp.

1854 The popular painter John Martin died on the Isle of Man. In his lifetime, Martin was a divisive figure in the art world, condemned heavily by critics such as John Ruskin for presenting grand theatrical works which were considered outdated by the 1840s. The public meanwhile adored him and his paintings now fetch considerable prices at auctions.

18 February

1895 The Albemarle Club scandal
The tobacco-scented tranquillity of London's Albemarle Club had been temporarily halted by the appearance of a middle-aged peer, the Marquess of Queensberry, marching through the lobby with vehement rigour. He demanded to see a member, Oscar Wilde, playwright and author. The porter refused. Infuriated, the Marquess left a small card in the lobby entrance: 'For Oscar Wilde, posing as somdomite'. Queensberry, whose son Lord Alfred Douglas, had been accused of having sexual relations with Wilde, was determined to pursue revenge. After much deliberation, Wilde pursued charges for defamation of character. As for the Albemarle, the reputation of the club was devastated by the trial and eventually moved to a new location to distance itself from controversy. It finally closed in 1941.

1888 England's football team wins its greatest ever victory against Ireland. The final score was a 13-0 victory. It remains England's greatest-ever football result in history.

19 February

1838 The notorious Spring Heeled Jack strikes for the first time
On 19 February 1838 a teenage girl named Jane Alsop was relaxing at her father's house when a sudden, loud, thunderous knock thudded on the front door. It was a

policeman. Calmly and without panic, he informed her that the local constabulary had captured a terrifying monster called 'Spring Heeled Jack', a horrid beast with clawed hands and eyes of red-hot fire. Clutching a candle, Alsop travelled with the policeman to see the creature for herself where she discovered a hideous apparition in a black cloak vomiting white and blue fire. Suddenly, the beast turned in her direction. Gripping her by his claws, he tore off her arms and ripped her neck. Screaming, she ran back to the house and was rescued just in the nick of time.

The real identity of Spring Heeled Jack was never found, with many suspecting the story to be either false or exaggerated for popular attention. News of the incident spread quickly. Rumours circulated in the town that his appearance was extra-terrestrial or perhaps even paranormal. In the decades following, 'Spring Heeled Jack' became one of the most famous folk stories in Victorian history. Tales of the beast would strike terror (or laughter) across the country. His legend became so infamous by the late nineteenth century that he became a well-known 'bogeyman' for children, who were told he would re-appear to badly-behaved youngsters unless they worked hard at school.

1849 On 19 February 1849 sixty-five young people were tragically killed in the Theatre Royal, Glasgow. A man in the upper gallery had inadvertently dropped a lighted paper near the stage which created a small fire. Panic swept the hall, creating a mass stampede. It was Glasgow's worst theatrical tragedy. Almost all of the casualties were under the age of twenty.

20 February

1874 Benjamin Disraeli forms his second government
The queen could barely control her excitement. Victoria was the first sovereign in British history to exercise constitutional restraint on her power, yet she remained a highly political individual with strong opinions and passionate, sometimes contentious beliefs. Disraeli injected a new level of energy and charm into her weekly meetings which Victoria found electrifying. With Disraeli, she felt the same level of intimacy, friendship and companionship that she did with Lord Melbourne some thirty-five years earlier. Disraeli was a tremendous talker, a raconteur and a gossiper, balancing constitutional formality with real genuine amity. As for his cabinet, despite vowing never to serve under Disraeli, the talented Lord Salisbury was eventually couched back into government. The former prime minister's son, the 15th Earl Derby, was also appointed as Foreign Secretary, while Sir Stafford Northcote became the Chancellor of the Exchequer. The government would last six years.

1855 Queen Victoria greeted wounded servicemen at Buckingham Palace. The encounter created a deeply emotional impression on the queen. A painting of the event by George Housman Thomas was later commissioned.

February

1867 Princess Louise, the daughter of the Prince of Wales was born. Louise matured into a shy and conservative character who disliked the intensity of media interest. By the time of her death in 1935, her public profile had faded so significantly that one newspaper inadvertently published a photograph of her late aunt, also called Louise. The error was indicative of her unfussy and low-key approach to royal life.

21 February

1848 The *Communist Manifesto* is published in London
One of the most profound moments in political history took place in a small backstreet publishing house in London on 21 February 1848. Karl Marx, a thirty-year-old philosopher from Prussia, had set out his plans for radical political re-organisation and change. The document predicted revolution in Europe and the eventual overthrow of capitalist dominance over society. Less than twenty-four hours later, revolution swept across France, seemingly threatening the stability of other European neighbours in the process. The *Communist Manifesto* would become one of the most influential pamphlets ever published.

1852 The government of Lord John Russell resigned. 'Ministerial Crisis" was the headline of many newspapers that morning. The Prime Minister, Lord John Russell, had frequently clashed with his foreign secretary, Lord Palmerston, whose strong opinions on foreign policy aggravated and even embarrassed the weary prime minister. On 26 December 1851, Russell forced Palmerston to resign, but the decision backfired overwhelmingly. Seething with anger, Palmerston turned his wrath against the government and, in 1852, turned a debate on a militia bill into a full-throttle vote of no confidence. 'I feel so anxious,' wrote the queen, 'lest this trial should disturb the present peaceful & prosperous condition of the country … Palmerston's claptrap speech was in very bad taste.' Russell resigned as Prime Minister. Not for the first time in Victorian politics, Britain was plunged into uncertainty and disarray.

1896 The first public screening of a film in Britain took place in London. The Polytechnic Institute established a display of the Lumière brothers' adventurous, moving picture contraption called the Cinématographe.

22 February

1859 George Lansbury is born in Suffolk
Lansbury began his career in the heat and turmoil of the 1870s, working as a railway contractor and later as a poor law guardian. His interest in politics began early, regularly attending debates in parliament with Gladstone and Disraeli. Having fought two unsuccessful elections himself in the nineteenth century, Lansbury was finally elected to parliament in 1910 and emerged as leader of the Labour party in 1932. Lansbury was also the grandfather of the actress, Angela Lansbury.

1886 The head of the Metropolitan Police, Edmund Henderson was forced to resign owing to widespread dissatisfaction with the police's response to a riot in the West End of London.

1888 Anna Kingsford died in London. She was the first medical student in Britain to graduate with a medical degree without having experimented on a single animal. A staunch animal rights' campaigner, Kingsford also established a successful food society which advocated vegetarianism. Sadly, she died young, aged just forty-one, from pneumonia.

23 February

1870 The Mordaunt scandal
No royal scandal had rocked the House of Saxe-Coburg as vehemently as the Mordaunt Affair. For a long time, the queen had regarded the Prince of Wales as a reckless, wayward and fundamentally irresponsible youth, grossly unfit for the demands of modern monarchy. As she jealously guarded her power, the prince indulged himself in luxury away from the stuffiness and prudence of the royal court. He became a party prince, a hard-drinking, hard-smoking, charismatic entertainer, frequently hosting glamorous social gatherings and conducting several affairs with high-profile women. In 1870, his lifestyle would create serious controversy for the family.

Among the many friendships the prince enjoyed was with Sir Charles and Lady Harriet Mordaunt, a respectable aristocratic couple from Warwickshire, who had deep political connections with the Conservative party. When Sir Charles was frequently away in parliament, the prince began a short passionate affair with Lady Mordaunt who later confessed the scandal. Sir Charles returned home to discover his wife and the prince in the house together. Furious, he dragged his screaming wife into the gardens, marched her to the stables and made her watch as he killed two of her favourite ponies in front of her eyes. In 1869, Sir Charles began divorce proceedings.

The incident had become deadly serious. To reverse public scrutiny, Mordaunt's family argued that Harriet had gone 'insane'. On 23 February 1870 the prince was called to give evidence in court, the first time ever that a Prince of Wales had been cross-examined by barristers, and a source of immense embarrassment to the queen. Luckily for him, the barrister was unduly lenient. No awkward or embarrassing questions were asked, and the prince denied any impropriety. As for Lady Mordant, she was later admitted to an asylum where she died in 1906.

1852 Earl Derby formed a minority Conservative government. 'I had hoped that Lord Derby would not succeed,' wrote the queen, 'yet I am wrong.' In 1852, the fifty-two-year-old stout country squire, Lord Derby, formed his first government following the downfall of Lord John Russell. Unfortunately for Derby, the

February

Conservatives did not hold a parliamentary majority. The government was shaky. In the House of Lords, the ever sarcastic Duke of Wellington mocked the new cabinet as 'the Who? Who? Ministry', owing to the lack of prominent names. In December 1852, after just eleven months, the government collapsed.

24 February

1855 Florence Nightingale depicted as 'The Lady with the Lamp' was published in the *Illustrated London News*.
Each year a small ceremony is performed at Westminster Abbey where a lamp is carried to the high altar. It commemorates the life and work of a remarkable Victorian heroine, Florence Nightingale, also known as the 'lady with the lamp'. Born into a privileged family, Nightingale experienced a deep religious calling as a young woman, guiding her to a life of public service. She became a nurse, travelled to Constantinople during the Crimean War and organised care for wounded and disease-stricken soldiers. Contrary to misconceptions, Nightingale did not actually carry a roman oil lamp, but a Turkish lantern which she purchased at a market. Nevertheless, the image catapulted her to unprecedented fame. It transformed her into a national heroine, a symbol of Victorian motherly virtue and Christian compassion, yet also overlooked her significant intellectual and pioneering abilities.

25 February

1899 Adrian Carton de Wiart enrols in the Army under a false name
Carton de Wiart was often referred to as the 'unkillable soldier'. With his black eyepatch, clipped moustache and one arm, he became the stuff of legends. Ironically, Carton de Wiart was originally advised against the army. Despite the disapproval of his father, he enlisted in 1899 under a pseudonym. In the Second Boer War, he was severely wounded, both in the groin and the stomach. In the First World War, he was wounded again eight times, and was awarded the Victoria Cross. He received further recognition in the Second World War serving as Winston Churchill's representative in China. His notoriety was such, in later life, he became something of a military celebrity.

1879 The infamous Victorian murderer Charles Frederick Peace was executed. Peace was among the most feared criminal of the century but was eventually overshadowed by the terrifying reputation of Jack the Ripper.

1885 Princess Alice of Battenberg was born in Windsor Castle. She was the eldest child of the queen's granddaughter, Princess Victoria of Hesse and by Rhine. Alice is perhaps remembered today as the mother of the late Prince Philip, Duke of Edinburgh.

1890 The British pianist Dame Myra Hess was born in London. Hess came to national attention during the Second World War, organising concerts at the National Gallery for Londoners to escape the stress of wartime bombing. The concerts became extremely popular and she was awarded a Damehood in 1941.

26 February

1884 Covent Garden explosion
Late on the afternoon of 26 February, two police constables were quietly exiting the Bow Street police station, when they observed a sudden flash of lights in the direction of the Covent Garden Theatre, followed shortly by two enormous explosions. The two men hastily sprinted to the theatre where they discovered a severely injured man called Harry Cardwell who was bleeding heavily in the road. His beard was burnt and a thumb partially missing. Much of his hair was also singed. The incident had occurred hours after a bomb explosion at London's Victoria Station, spreading fears of a terrifying nationwide terror attack. Investigations concluded Cardwell was actually a fireworks artist who had experimented with chemicals, causing an accidental explosion. Earlier the same day, a bomb had been discovered in the cloakroom of London's Victoria Station, injuring seven members of staff. It was suspected that the terrorist Fenian Brotherhood was behind the attack. Bombs were also found in the cloakrooms of Charing Cross, Ludgate Hill and Paddington station.

27 February

1847 A historic Cambridge chancellery election
Prince Albert was considered the most obvious choice for the vacancy, especially in light of his famous intellectual credentials. Unfortunately for him, the contest did not run smoothly. Shortly after the nominations opened, the tough-talking Earl of Powis launched a highly politicised campaign, bolstered by a strong group of aggressive supporters from St John's College. Albert emerged victorious, but with just 117 votes. To celebrate his success, a grand fireworks display and banquet was held in the university grounds. On 25 March, he was formally appointed Chancellor in Buckingham Palace.

1848 The Composer Hubert Parry was born in Bournemouth. He was the youngest son of Thomas Parry and his wife Isabella Fynes-Clinton. Thomas did not approve of his son's fascination with music, advocating instead a more stable profession. After the untimely death of Isabella, Parry suffered a solitary childhood. After attending Oxford University, he worked briefly as an underwriter at Lloyd's of London until finally pursuing his musical passion professionally in the 1870s.

1868 Benjamin Disraeli became premier for the first time, coining the famous phrase, 'I have climbed the greasy pole.' Until the twentieth century, British

February

general elections were sprawled out over long and agonising weeks. Governments could be formed or broken before the final results were even announced, as was the case in 1874. The election was the first to be held by secret ballot and, much to Disraeli's delight, resulted in a comfortable Conservative victory. His charm and affability were magnified by his ability to work with difficult political colleagues, many of whom regarded him with immense distrust, or even disdain. Disraeli's first government was defeated at the December 1868 election.

1900 The British Labour Party was formed by Keir Hardie at the Congregational Memorial Hall. Other important founders included Ramsay MacDonald, who later became Labour's first ever prime minister, and future foreign secretary, Arthur Henderson.

28 February

1874 The Tichborne trial concludes
In 1873, a middle-aged Australian butcher called Tom Castro emerged, claiming to be the heir to the wealthy Tichborne estate in Hampshire. Twenty years earlier, Sir Roger Tichborne had died in a shipwreck but his body was never found. The legal case that followed captivated Victorian society and became one of the most controversial trials of the era.

Castro was heavily supported by many working-class commentators, but the establishment opposed him massively, revealing a tangible split in public opinion. Ironically, although most journalists doubted Castro's credibility, Lady Tichborne passionately acknowledged him as her son and even supplied money to him. The case went on for many months and Castro was later alleged to be an imposter whose real name was Arthur Orton from London.

Orton was sentenced to fourteen years' hard labour but the drama was not over. His lawyer, Edward Kenealy, was accused of unprofessional and disrespectful conduct throughout the case and was professionally disbarred from practising law. After the motion, Kenealy then launched his own public movement called the Magna Carta Association, which called for Orton's validity. In 1875, he was elected as an MP for Stoke-Upon-Trent, and later called for a Royal Commission into the Tichborne case. Ultimately, his actions failed. Orton died penniless in 1898. Interestingly, although most supported the ultimate verdict, in later years some doubts emerged about whether Orton may actually have been telling the truth. The case remains a source of controversy.

29 February

1872 The Queen survives an assassination attempt
Leap Day 1872. Victoria, accompanied by her children Arthur and Leopold, escaped the stuffiness and intensity of court to take a short drive in the open landau

to enjoy some much-needed fresh air. The crowds, as always, cheered and waved as the royal party left the security of Buckingham Palace and circled around the neighbouring parks, basking in the comfortable winter's sunshine. As the queen returned, however, a crisis was about to occur.

A young man, dressed in shabby clothes and holding a pistol, scaled the fence at Buckingham Palace. Upon entering the grounds, he ran across the courtyard without detection. Just as the queen's carriage clattered back through the garden entrance, the man sprinted up to her and raised his gun. Almost without hesitation, the queen's servant, John Brown, violently wrestled the man to the ground. Prince Leopold nearly fainted from fright. 'I was trembling very much and a sort of shiver ran through me,' the queen wrote, 'with all my heart I thank God for his great mercy and for preserving me once again.'

The event terrified Britain. In reality, the gun wasn't loaded but the incident clearly showed a failing in royal security. The man was later identified as an eighteen-year-old called Arthur O'Connor, a Irish republican, who claimed he only used a pistol to frighten the queen. His motives were the release of Irish political prisoners held in British prisons. Rather predictably, he instead was also sent to prison, and was eventually transported to Australia. As for John Brown, the heroic action met with widespread congratulations, and he later received a special honour for bravery.

March

1 March

1869 The Prince of Wales establishes the Marlborough Club
By the late 1860s, all was not well in Clubland. Whites, the oldest and most venerable club in London, had declared civil war against its members by officially banning smoking inside its hallowed walls. The Prince of Wales was furious. He resigned his membership and, in 1868, formed his own club to provide an agreeable, and appropriately smokey, place to enjoy free and unrestricted access to tobacco. A small property was purchased in Pall Mall for £18,000, conveniently close to his London residence, Marlborough House. It was thereafter named the Marlborough Club. The prince loved the place so much that his favourite chair was permanently left vacant in case of his appearance.

1851 Marble Arch was relocated to Hyde Park. The beautiful arch was designed by John Nash as a grand entrance to Buckingham Palace. Regrettably, by the late 1840s, the once majestic white exterior had become discoloured by years of thick Victorian smog. Plans for an enlargement of the palace also meant that the arch was deemed impracticable, and so was moved to the more appropriate location of Hyde Park. Contrary to misconception, the arch did not prove too small for the royal carriages, something which was proved at Queen Elizabeth II's coronation in 1953.

1855 Footballer George Burrell Ramsay was born in Glasgow. Ramsay is often described as the world's first professional football manager. He began his career in 1876, making his professional debut for Aston Villa, and emerged as a moderately successful footballer in his own right. In the 1880s he branched into management, leading the team to its greatest professional results. He remained in the post for forty-two years.

2 March

1882 Another assassination attempt on Queen Victoria
On the morning of 2 March 1882, the cobbled courtyard of Eton College was swarming with Etonians, dressed in their silk top hats, tails and umbrellas, flocking to the station to see a most important royal visitor. As Victoria exited the platform, a loud gunshot was heard across the crowd. Suddenly, a man was jostled to the ground.

The scene was chaotic. Eton boys struck him on the head with their umbrellas, while policemen stormed into the scene amidst a sea of screaming onlookers. The man was identified as Roderick Maclean, a twenty-eight-year-old Scotsman. He was tried for high treason but declared insane. He was later transferred to Broadmoor Hospital, where he died over thirty years later of natural causes.

1854 Courtier and officer Sir John Conroy dies. The queen despised Conroy to the bitter end, blaming him, not only for a miserable childhood, but the estranged, sometimes toxic, relationship with her mother, the Duchess of Kent. Despite a generous pension, Conroy died in colossal debt. In the years following, some commentators argued that Conroy may have been Victoria's real biological father, owing perhaps to an affair with the duchess. Others, however, refute the claims as idle gossip.

3 March

1884 The Third Reform Act debated in parliament
By the mid-1880s calls for political reform had grown louder, especially among the working classes who were still denied proper political representation. In Gladstone's own words, why was it fair that 'the lower stratum of the middle class is admitted to the exercise of the franchise, while the upper stratum of the working class is excluded'. The bill was debated in parliament in 1884, creating fierce and tough arguments. After being misquoted by an angry opposition member, Gladstone doggedly barked back, 'pardon me, that was not my argument. I said no such thing. If my right honourable friend chooses to quote me, he might quote me correctly.'

1869 The composer, Henry Wood was born in Oxford Street, London. Wood is commemorated every year at the Last Night of the Proms with a special bronze bust placed in front of the organ, decorated with an elaborate floral chaplet. After the proms' season concludes, the bust is returned to the Royal College of Music and an annual memorial ceremony is conducted at St Sepulchre's Church.

1894 William Gladstone retired from politics. After sixty years in the House of Commons, and a combined total of twelve years as prime minister, the elderly, stooping figure of William Gladstone stood down at the grand age of eighty-four. For many Liberals, his disappearance was a watershed moment in British politics. The queen, whose blatant hostility had not dimmed in recent years, refused to offer him a knighthood or a peerage.

4 March

1884 A Royal Commission on housing established
By 1881, the population of the UK had skyrocketed to almost 30 million, leading to screaming levels of urban deprivation and overcrowding. In 1884, a royal

commission was established, with Lord Salisbury working closely alongside Cardinal Henry Manning, Sir Charles Dilke, the Prince of Wales and several other public figures. The findings concluded that widespread action was needed, although nothing radical was ever put in place.

1890 The magnificent Forth Bridge was opened by the Prince of Wales. Constructed by John Fowler and Benjamin Baker, the bridge took eight years to build and was made entirely from steel. Measuring 2.5 kilometres in length, over 4,000 workmen were employed on the project, of whom fifty-seven died. Upon completion, it was the longest bridge in Britain.

1878 The Scottish Catholic Church was re-established by Pope Leo XIII.

5 March

1894 Lord Rosebery was appointed Prime Minister
Queen Victoria had taken the decision without consultation, or even advice from the British government, and had inadvertently stirred a hornets' nest from within the Liberal party. At just forty-seven, Rosebery was the youngest prime minister since Robert Peel, and the first born during her reign. Compared to more experienced colleagues, he was regarded as an upstart, creating tense feelings of jealousy and suspicion from within the government. These problems would be exacerbated greatly as the months rolled on.

1894 The Local Government Act was given Royal Assent. The act required all parishes with a population over 300 to elect parish councils. Crucially, women could vote in the parish elections but were still excluded from wider national elections.

6 March

1867 Cortolvin wins the Grand National
Horse racing had traditionally been the bastion of the upper classes, yet the arrival of the Victorian railways once again redefined the nature and dynamics of British society. A new generation of racing fans emerged, many of them hailing from the middle class, who would travel in great numbers to the various sporting venues. In 1867 the beautiful stallion Cortolvin won the Grand National. The jockey was Johnny Page, the son of a humble farmer from Warwickshire.

1893 The Liverpool Overhead Railway was opened. Technically, the railway had been officially opened a month earlier by Lord Salisbury, but did not begin its first public service until March. It was the first British railway to install automatic signalling, passenger escalators and electric multiple units. Although popular with local townsfolk, several accidents occurred in the first few weeks of its opening.

7 March

1874 The Duke and Duchess of Edinburgh arrive in England
The newly-married Prince Alfred and Princess Maria Alexandrovna of Russia arrived in England to a rapturous applause. It was Maria's first encounter with England and she was genuinely touched by the multitude of loyal crowds, many of them armed with British and Russian flags. The Queen, despite her private misgivings, was equally impressed by Maria's charm, good looks and excellent English. The goodwill, unfortunately, would not last long.

The new princess did not prove popular. Maria disliked Britain. She found Buckingham Palace dull, Windsor Castle dingy and Queen Victoria obstinate and difficult. She disliked British food, manners and customs. She complained that the weather was dreary and the conversation poor. As the months rolled on, her relationship with Princess Alexandra became dangerously bad. To complicate matters even further, Maria was the Grand Duchess of Russia and the Duchess of Edinburgh, creating confusion about which title should come first. Tensions finally came to blows one day at Balmoral, where the Princess refused to leave the bath unless a fire was lit. After Maria had left, the Queen immediately entered and ordered all the windows to be opened and water thrown on the fire.

1842 A daguerreotype of Prince Albert, taken on 7 March 1842, is believed to be the first known photographic image of a member of the British royal family. Albert visited a small independent studio run by William Constable to see for himself the new and exciting medium of photography. The daguerreotype was delivered to Buckingham Palace a few days later, gaining the approval of Queen Victoria. Little over a century later, the royal family would arguably become the most photographed family in the entire world.

8 March

1867 Lord Cranborne resigns from government
Debates over electoral reform raged throughout much of the 1860s. In 1867 the Tory government led by Lord Derby introduced a Reform Act designed to change the electoral representation in the country. Although introduced by the Conservative government, the bill aggravated many Tory members who were unhappy at its alleged 'radical nature'. The most vocal critic was Lord Cranborne who publicly denounced Disraeli in vehement terms, labelling him an adventurer, an opportunist and a cad. He resigned from the government, vowing never to serve in the government again.

9 March

1870 Queen Victoria receives Charles Dickens at Buckingham Palace
Despite sharing a mutual admiration for each other, the two icons had never previously met. Dickens had declined four invitations from the palace owing to

his busy schedule, although in his youth, had professed a great crush on the young monarch. The queen similarly was an enormous admirer of Dickens and particularly appreciated his dedication to the poor. As a young princess, reclusive and socially isolated, she escaped the monotony and dullness of Kensington Palace enraptured in the tales of Oliver Twist and his heartbreaking life of adversity. Finally, in 1870, Dickens and the monarch met in Buckingham Palace and enjoyed a convivial evening. After the reception, the queen favourably remarked in her journals of his pleasant voice and friendly manner. Three months later Dickens succumbed to a stroke and died.

1881 The Labour politician Ernest Bevin was born in the rural village of Winsford, Somerset. The illegitimate son of Diana Bevin and an unknown father, he shares this location with another foreign secretary, Boris Johnson, who lived in the area some eighty years later. Bevin grew up with the sting of Victorian illegitimacy and received little formal education. After a brief stint as a lorry driver, he was first introduced to politics through the Bristol Socialist Society, and later joined the Labour Party.

1892 The famous writer and garden designer Vita Sackville-West was born amidst the grandeur and beauty of Knole House, Kent, the former residence of England's archbishops of Canterbury. She would become a novelist, poet and later garden designer, remembered chiefly for creating the much loved garden at Sissinghurst Castle.

10 March

1863 The wedding of the Prince of Wales and Princess Alexandra of Denmark takes place in Windsor
'I felt as I should faint,' scribbled the weary Queen Victoria, 'only by violent effort could I succeed in masking my emotion.' The sound of the angelic choir heralded memories of potent painfulness for the recently widowed monarch, whose mind was immediately drawn to the colour and optimism of 1840, her own wedding, held in the same chapel twenty-three years earlier. 'Oh! What I suffered in the chapel,' she recalled mournfully, 'it was indescribable.'
    The wedding of the Prince of Wales to Princess Alexandra of Denmark brought mixed feelings for the queen. Just two years had passed since the demise of her beloved husband, whose absence was intensely poignant. The Prince of Wales similarly suffered a complicated and fractious relationship with his fiery mother. Ever since his seventeenth birthday, the queen had been in search of a steady-headed bride who would mould her supposedly 'wayward' son into a sensible future sovereign. In 1858 a list of potential brides was drafted with Alexandra, the eldest daughter of the future Danish King, placed at number five. After years of deliberation, Alexandra was shortlisted to the top, an excellent choice for strengthening Anglo-Danish relations. In September 1862 the royal couple were engaged, and Alexandra arrived in England fresh from Copenhagen in March the following year.

The wedding itself was not without controversy. Firstly, the venue was unpopular as many visitors could not travel as easily to Windsor as London. The chapel itself was smaller than Westminster Abbey, meaning fewer seats were available, hence fewer invitations, creating disappointment among some aristocrats of a 'royal snub'. During the ceremony, the young Prince Wilhelm of Germany (later Kaiser Wilhelm II) also became agitated and bit his uncle on the leg. Nevertheless, as the ceremony ended, the guns on the Long Walk in Windsor Park thundered out to wild screams of exhilaration. The magnificent reception was held at St George's Hall, followed by official photographs. The wedding cake, placed in the centre of the royal table, weighed around eighty pounds. A sign perhaps of the queen's mournful nature, in official photographs, the monarch was depicted gazing at a bust of her late husband positioned in the left side of the picture. In death, as in life, his presence weighed heavily over the family.

1850 Spencer Gore, the legendary tennis player, was born in Wimbledon, London. Gore takes his place as the first gentlemen's singles' Wimbledon champion in history. After a short professional career playing for Surrey Cricket club, he transferred to tennis in the 1870s and defeated William Marshal in straight sets to become the 1877 Wimbledon champion. The success would not last as he was defeated the following year and retired.

1864 Precisely a year after the prince's wedding, the nation celebrated another milestone with the christening of Prince Albert Victor, the eldest son of the Prince of Wales. Having endured a brutally harsh childhood of his own, the Prince of Wales was determined to shun the rigorous educational practices of the time, favouring instead a relaxed, progressive upbringing which distanced itself from conventional Victorian beliefs. His children were allowed to flourish as individuals and pursue individual pursuits beyond the rigid conformity of academic rigour. Victoria, less than sympathetic with the modern methods, complained bitterly that his children were 'ill-bred', fragile, intellectually inferior and ignorant. She was equally unimpressed with the parents' decision to keep Albert Victor in London, a poisonous city of pollution. To complicate matters unfortunately, Albert Victor was a sickly child, something which Victoria was quick to blame on Alexandra.

1866 The opera singer and actress Amanda Aldridge was born in south London. Aldrige's father, Ira Aldridge, was a pioneering African American actor renowned for his electrifying performances of Shakespeare. Despite suffering terrible racism, Amanda followed her father's steps into the theatrical profession, but also trained as an opera singer and later a teacher who educated hundreds of students in the arts.

11 March

1864 The Great Sheffield Flood disaster
Heavy rainfall caused huge flooding throughout the winter of 1864. On 11 March, the Dale Dyke Dam collapsed, killing over 200 people, and destroying hundreds of

homes. Over 600 properties were damaged, and 700 animals drowned. The tragedy also shone a light on faulty engineering practices, leading to tighter regulations for large-scale structures in Britain.

1884 Alfred Tennyson was appointed a baronet. Having previously twice declined a baronetcy, Tennyson accepted the honour in 1884, taking his place in the House of Lords on 11 March. He was given the title 'Baron Tennyson, of Aldworth in the County of Sussex and of Freshwater in the Isle of Wight'.

12 March

1868 Attempted assassination of Prince Alfred
Victoria was not the only British royal to suffer an assassination attempt. In 1868, Prince Alfred came dangerously close to death on a planned excursion to Clontarf in New South Wales, Australia. While attending a small sailors' picnic overlooking the harbourside, Henry O'Farrell, a thirty-five-year-old Irishman approached the prince slowly and, without warning, fired a bullet directly into his back, hitting his spine. In a tumult of panic and confusion, O'Farrell was thrown to the ground by a local coachmaker, William Vial, and then attacked by a large crowd of onlookers who assumed, wrongly, the prince was dead. Luckily, the wound was not fatal. With constant supervision by six nurses, the prince was quickly nursed back to health. O'Farrell was hanged for treason.

1881 History was made on the cloudy morning of 12 March 1881 when the twenty-five-year-old Andrew Watson made his professional and outstanding debut as the first black international football player in British history. As a player for numerous clubs, including Queen's Park, he was picked to play for Scotland against England. Until recently, however, Watson's career had been sadly overlooked by most historians. Thanks to research conducted by the National Records of Scotland, more information about his fascinating life and legacy has now been revealed.

1890 Joseph Sutherland, the last British survivor of the Battle of Trafalgar, died. His passing closed a long and prominent chapter in British history. For many, he represented an old Georgian world which was fast disappearing under the heat and smog of Victorian modernity and technological change. News of his death was reported in several national newspapers.

13 March

1879 The Duke of Connaught's wedding to the Prussian Princess Louise
The wedding took place in a stupendous ceremony in Windsor, described by some as the grandest royal wedding of the decade. State dignitaries, ambassadors, foreign

and cabinet ministers arrived on a special train from London, including William Gladstone who glittered like a ceremonial Christmas tree in his ornate state robes. Many more extra trains were scheduled to bring thousands of spectators into Windsor, regulated by an even bigger body of policemen drafted from neighbouring counties to control the huge crowds.

14 March

1883 Karl Marx dies in London
Marx is commonly cited as one of the most influential political thinkers of human history. He died a 'stateless person' at his home at Haverstock Hill following a battle with bronchitis, but the news was not released until two days later. Inaccurate reports noted he had died in Paris which was later corrected by his friends. In accordance with his wishes, Marx was buried in a non-religious ceremony at Highgate cemetery, attended by Friedrich Engels.

1885 Gilbert and Sullivan's opera *The Mikado* premiered in London.

1898 Winston Churchill published his first book, *The Story of the Malakand Field Force*, commenting on his personal experience on the North West Frontier. Churchill was determined to carve a name for himself as a writer, and wrote a second book, *The River War*, just a year later.

15 March

1862- The foundation stone is laid by Queen Victoria at the Royal Mausoleum
The costs of the new building was financed privately by the Queen and the Prince of Wales, eventually coming to an estimated £200,000, the equivalent of over £19 million today. When finally completed, the Mausoleum was a beautiful shrine to Romanesque architectural opulence. The exterior was designed in the form of a Greek cross, built from granite and Portland stone, accompanied by Australian copper on the roof. The interior was a lavish feast of colour and grandeur. Victoria would be buried at the Mausoleum thirty-nine years later, laid together with her beloved husband.

1856 James Buchanan resigned as the US Ambassador to the UK. He later became the President of the United States in 1857.

1891 The engineer Sir Joseph Bazalgette dies in London. Bazalgette was distinguished for the creation of a central sewerage system in London which helped ease periodic cholera epidemics in the city.

March

16 March

1861 Queen Victoria's mother, the Duchess of Kent, dies at Frogmore House, Windsor
The relationship between the Duchess and her daughter had been strained for several years, especially since Victoria's accession. During the royal wedding in 1840 the queen purposefully made a point of kissing the Dowager Queen Adelaide on the cheek, but merely shaking her mother's hand. It was a visual expression of the monarch's hostility, something which never healed. In the remaining years the duchess was side-lined from court and isolated from exclusive royal events. Fortunately, in the last years of her life, their relationship slowly improved and Victoria was left genuinely devastated by her death.

Shortly after her passing, Victoria discovered her mother's papers in Kensington Palace which exposed real, heartfelt words of affection for her daughter. The Queen's sadness turned to guilt. She blamed Conroy for exploiting the tensions between them and sowing wickedness. Devastation became almost overwhelming. In the following years, Victoria had many of her mother's letters placed in a gilded book for posterity and erected a window in her memory at the Royal Chapel of All Saints in Windsor. The Duchess was later buried in Frogmore Gardens which was also renamed, The Duchess of Kent's Mausoleum, designed by Prince Albert's favourite architect, A.J. Humbert.

1867 Joseph Lister published a landmark paper on antiseptics in *The Lancet*. The document proposed that carbolic acid could be used by doctors to destroy germs and prevent infection and disease.

17 March

1883 Queen Victoria badly injured in a fall
While walking down a steep flight of stairs at Windsor Castle, the sixty-three-year-old queen fell suddenly. Her loyal servant, John Brown, heard the crash and immediately rushed to her aid. Her leg was severely swollen and very painful for several weeks. At a meeting with the Home Secretary the following day, she was forced to lie on the sofa. She remained in a wheelchair until early July and suffered terrible, sometimes unrelenting, pain. She never fully recovered and suffered rheumatism for the rest of her life.

1873 The first woman cabinet minister, Margaret Bondfield, was born in Chard, Somerset. The Bonfields were a highly politically brood with a strong awareness of social justice and socialist political causes. Her father, William Bondfield, was a smart, self-educated lace-worker who is credited as an early inventor of a flying machine. In his younger years he was heavily involved in the Chartist cause for greater political inclusion. Just a few months after her birth, however, William was dismissed from his factory work and thrown into poverty. Anxiety hovered over the family for months, later inspiring Margaret to take up active political involvement and eventually emerge as the first woman cabinet minister in British history.

18 March

1848 Queen Victoria's fifth daughter, Louise, is born at Buckingham Palace
Louise was an unconventional, independent and rebellious princess and a staunch supporter of the arts and sciences. An intelligent and highly talented woman, she frequently found the narrow, limiting constraints of royal life restrictive and dull. She suffered an unhappy marriage with the Duke of Argyll and was dogged by rumours of extra-marital affairs. When the sculptor Joseph Edgar Boehem died in Louise's presence, gossip erupted that the two were lovers. She was herself a gifted sculptor but was never able to properly fulfil her artistic potential. She died in 1939.

1854 The Alhambra Theatre was opened in Leicester Square. It was famed for popular music hall performances and hilarious comedy. Sadly, the theatre was demolished in 1936 and replaced by the Odeon Luxe Cinema.

1869 The future prime minister Neville Chamberlain was born in Birmingham. The second son of Joseph Chamberlain and Florence Kenrick, Neville was ironically not considered suited for a career in politics and was sent to the Bahamas instead in an ill-fated business venture.

1883 John Brown was hired by Queen Victoria to investigate an alleged assassination attempt on the writer Lady Florence Dixie in Windsor Great Park.

19 March

1874 The City of London congratulates the Duke of Edinburgh
The ceremony was organised by the City of London to congratulate the newly married Prince Alfred and Maria on their recent marriage since most of the organisers were unable to attend the wedding in Russia. The Lord Mayor, accompanied by a large deputation of senior figures, arrived at the Guildhall at around midday and then proceeded in a grand horse-drawn procession to Buckingham Palace. Along the route church bells rang in jubilation as large crowds gathered to watch the spectacle.

1896 The River Thames Meeting took place in London. Flooding of the River Thames had often worried the Victorians. In the 1890s heavy rain had caused major problems for Londoners, especially in the vicinity of Chiswick and other districts close to the river. In 1896, the queen wrote a letter to the President of the

Board of Trade, Charles Ritchie, urging the government to act on preventing the recurrence of such regular devastating floods which had wrecked the lives of so many inhabitants. The meeting, chaired by Ritchie, argued that measures needed to be designed to limit the extent of damage. Despite this, little was meaningfully achieved.

1896 The charismatic firebrand Admiral Charles Beresford launched a damning attack on the Royal Navy on 19 March at a large Conservative meeting in Birmingham. Beresford argued the 'panic' of failing naval defences in Britain was not the fault of Lord Salisbury, or the government, but the 'rotten system' in which they worked.

20 March

1878 The 'Marriage of the Year' occurs in London
The wedding of the handsome millionaire Lord Rosebery to the fabulously wealthy Hannah de Rothschild was the social event of the year, but also the scene of considerable controversy and, in some cases, prejudice. The romance met with the disapproval of aristocratic London, where Hannah, as a Jewish woman, was deemed unsuitable and undesirable as the wife of a leading politician. Rosebery's mother refused to attend the ceremony. Hannah's parents, who were also disapproving of the romance, refused to send any male relatives. Despite the immediate problems, the couple refused to renounce their love. Hannah was instead given away in the ceremony by the dazzling presence of Benjamin Disraeli. They remained married until her death in 1890.

1842 George FitzClarence killed himself in London. FitzClarence was the illegitimate son of King William IV and had suffered a turbulent, melancholy life of stress and disappointment. His relationship with his father was often stormy, dominated by fierce volcanic arguments and disagreements. After the king's death, he served as aide-de-camp to Queen Victoria, but suffered increasingly from gambling and drink addictions. Some suspected he also suffered from porphyria like his grandfather, King George III. Sadly, in 1842, FitzClarence shot himself, first on his hand, and then in his mouth.

21 March

1871 Queen Victoria's daughter Louise marries John Campbell in Windsor
The wedding marked the first royal marriage between a daughter of a sovereign and a British subject since 1515. The romance had also created tension. Campbell's father, the Duke of Argyll, was a prominent Liberal and friend of William Gladstone, creating fears that the palace would be dragged through the murky waters of controversial British politics. Campbell himself had also served as an MP for

the Scottish constituency of Argyllshire, although made little lasting impression. Despite murmurings, the queen remained doggedly supportive of the marriage. As the first royal wedding in five years, the ceremony also attracted huge numbers of spectators, comparable to previous state occasions.

1889 London County Council was established. It became the largest municipal body of the era, founded by Lord Salisbury for the purpose of easing the many problems faced by the capital. It was credited for systematic housing reforms and remained in existence until the 1960s. Ever the pessimist however, Salisbury later worried the council would create a breeding ground for 'socialistic experiments' and 'a new revolutionary spirit'.

1861 The comedian Albert Chevalier was born in London. Chevalier specialised in cheeky cockney humour of old London, making his professional debut at the age of eight, starring in Shakespeare's *Julius Caesar*. Later he specialised in comedy, becoming a household name in the 1890s for his hilarious interpretation of cockney life. Although comedic, his acts also shone a spotlight on the hard, often painful, realities for working-class communities in Victorian London.

22 March

1888 The English Football League was formed
On 22 March 1888, representatives from twelve English football clubs met together in a small unpretentious hotel in Fleet Street to form their own sports association. It would become known as the English Football League. Indeed, the growing popularity of football throughout the nineteenth century owed somewhat to the advancement of the interconnected Victorian railways. For the first time in history, fans could travel across the country, supporting their teams in away games and other functions. Arguably, the league would never have been formed without the railways.

1855 The neo-classical artist Dorothy Tennant was born. Tennant enjoyed her first exhibition at the Royal Academy in 1886, aged just thirty-one. She went on to enjoy considerable artistic success. Tennant was also the wife of explorer Henry Morton Stanley.

23 March

1887 Queen Victoria visits Birmingham
Birmingham snoozed in warm sunshine, the perfect weather for a most important visit from Queen Victoria. By the 1880s, the once grim town had blossomed into one of Britain's greatest cities, a testament to the ingenuity and innovation of Mayor Joseph Chamberlain and other key figures. The transformation was made

more remarkable by the sheer speed of its urban redevelopment. Slums were cleared and depilated houses demolished. Roads were widened and public libraries were established, including a renowned university. Driving in an open landau, the queen was deeply impressed with the newly built municipal buildings. Later, she laid the foundation stone for the Victoria Law Court, named, appropriately, in her honour. Although admiring the city, she unfortunately found the locals 'rough' and quite poor.

1891 Allan Noel Minns, a distinguished doctor and war hero, was born in Norfolk. Minns was the eldest son of Allan Glaisyer Minns, the first black mayor in British history. In the First World War, Minns was twice Mentioned in Despatches, and was awarded the Military Cross for bravery, followed by the Distinguished Service Order. Sadly, his life was cut short in a tragic motorcycle accident in 1921, aged just thirty.

24 March

1877 The infamous Boat Race
The annual Oxford and Cambridge boat race of 1877 caused quite a splash, but not necessarily for the right reasons. For the first time, no winner was declared, with both teams coming side by side in a dead heat. Both claimed victory but the result remained inconclusive. The many hundreds of spectators who had lined the Thames were deeply disappointed.

1895 Oscar Wilde was advised to drop his charge of criminal libel against the Marquess of Queensbury. His decision to launch legal action was risky and heavily tilted against him. On 24 March, close friends advised him to drop all charges in order to avoid public stress or, worse, condemnation. Wilde ignored the pleas. He pressed on with his libel charge, lost and was sentenced to prison. He died in poverty five years later.

25 March

1868 The Foreign Office is opened
The Foreign Office remains a vivid illustration of the restrained imperial architecture that defined the mid-nineteenth century. Lord Palmerston had previously rejected plans to design the building in an exuberant neo-gothic style, favouring instead an understated Italianate palace, partly to reflect British continuity with ancient Rome, but also to keep costs down. Inside was a salubrious feast of imperial grandeur, decorated wall to wall with ornate paintings of the British military past, dominated by large imposing portraits of colonial governors. In the words of one civil servant, it was purposefully designed to 'impress foreigners'. The offices were so grand that the future prime minister Lord Salisbury even decided to work there fulltime.

On 25 March 1868, a large reception was hosted in the new premises to celebrate its completion. Like many other Victorian buildings, however, by the 1960s the Foreign Office was threatened with demolition. The outcry was loud enough to deter planners, but its future remained uncertain until 1970 when it achieved Grade I listed status. Palmerston did not live long enough to see the building completed. He died in 1865 but is remembered with a bust located near the exit.

1843 The Thames Tunnel was opened. The Tunnel was the first of its kind to be constructed under a body of water. Masterminded by Marc Isambard Kingdom Brunel, father of Isambard Kingdom Brunel, construction work was initially beset with problems, costing several thousands of pounds. In 1828 a collapse in the tunnel killed two miners and almost killed Brunel. To make matters worse, a few months later, Marc suffered a paralysing stroke. He insisted on attending the opening ceremony but died a few months later. The Thames Tunnel was later used by the London underground.

26 March

1867- Disraeli's Reform Act speech
The 1867 Reform Act was yet another example of the titanic dramas that dominated Victorian politics, and one which arguably still influences public life today. Following the death of the doggedly traditionalist Lord Palmerston in 1865, the notion of political change once again resurfaced. Although the 1832 Reform Act had widened the political franchise, it did not extend to the growing numbers of middle-class men who were growing restless for representation. Championed by the Chancellor, Benjamin Disraeli, in 1867 the government proposed a series of changes which, Disraeli argued, would strengthen British democracy. His dazzling address to the Commons was described by one commentator as the speech of the session. When he retired to his country house for the Easter recess a month later, he was widely regarded as the driving force of the government; the prime minister in everything but name.

27 March

1883 John Brown, loyal servant and friend of Queen Victoria, dies
With the exception of her husband, John Brown was perhaps the most significant man in Queen Victoria's life. Their friendship was close and genuine, supplemented by a similar sense of humour and companionship which was deep, meaningful and unpretentious. Unsurprisingly, the relationship had also caused quite a stir in high society. In many eyes, the very concept of a monarch becoming friends with a servant was not merely improper, but deeply unacceptable. Gossip emerged that the two were lovers, with Victoria unkindly mocked as 'Mrs Brown'. Despite Brown's robust health and a healthy appetite for life, in 1883 he contracted pneumonia. Both

of his parents had lived into their eighties, but Brown unfortunately succumbed to the illness aged just fifty-six. The queen was devastated with his loss, and soon ordered the erection of a statue in his honour in the grounds of Balmoral.

1893 Tsar Nicholas II visited the United Kingdom. During his travels, Nicholas took the unusual step of visiting the House of Commons, where he watched a debate from the public gallery. His presence was not particularly welcome. One fearful Liberal grandee worried that the disorderly scenes in parliament would discourage the Tsar from democracy altogether. Fortunately, he needn't have worried as Nicholas was said to have been deeply impressed.

28 March

1884 The Queen's youngest son, Prince Leopold, dies in France
Leopold had been diagnosed with haemophilia as a child and died tragically young aged just thirty in 1884. Having suffered from joint pain the previous winter, the prince had been advised by doctors to holiday amidst the sun and sanctuary of Cannes, where the warmer weather was deemed conducive for rest and relaxation. On 27 March, Leopold suffered a fall in his villa, badly hitting his head and his knee. The following morning, he was discovered dead, casting the royal family into deepest despair. The queen collapsed when courtiers informed her of the news. 'I am a poor desolate old woman,' she wrote, 'my cup of sorrow overflows.'

1854 The Crimean War began after Britain and France declared war on Russia, creating a wave of anti-Russian sentiment in England. The British government, led by Lord Aberdeen, feared Russian military expansion in the Balkans.

29 March

1871 The Royal Albert Hall is opened
No other hall in London evokes Victorian Italianate architecture better than the Royal Albert Hall, named in memory of the queen's lamented husband. The opening ceremony was a landmark event, not least because it marked one of the earliest occasions since Albert's death when Victoria appeared in public. With tears in her eyes, the queen was so impressed with the building that she remarked the hall reminded her of the British constitution. Doors to the venue were opened early to allow a huge throng of expected visitors, and by 11.00am, almost half of the 8,000 seats were taken. One verse of *God Save the Queen* was sung, followed by a short speech by the Prince of Wales who praised its architectural innovation. After his address, the queen read a short speech which was then followed by prayers from the Bishop of London. Finally, the Hall was declared open and the second verse of the national anthem thundered out across the building, followed by guns in Hyde Park. It has remained an icon of London ever since.

1859 The 3rd Marquess of Waterford died in a tragic accident. The famous marquess was a colourful, handsome but hard-drinking fellow who enjoyed a notorious reputation. He first made headlines in 1837 when he and a group of friends purchased large quantities of red paint and vandalised the town of Melton Mowbray in Leicestershire. The evening became so legendary: the term 'paint the town red' became synonymous with drunkenness. Each man was fined £100, but a few weeks later he was involved in another scandal. The marquess sadly died on 29 March 1859 in tragic circumstances after a horse-riding accident.

1899 Queen Victoria was treated to a performance of the Italian composer Leoncavall at Buckingham Palace. He played the opera *La Boheme* and three pieces from *Pagliacci*.

30 March

1851 The 1851 Census takes place in Britain
The 1851 Census was the first British census to register citizens' marital status, relationship to the head of the household and details of disability. The total population was recorded as over twenty-one million. For genealogists, the Victorian period was indeed a landmark era for ancestral research. The registration of births, marriages and deaths was formally introduced in England and Wales in 1837. Scotland followed in 1855 providing the most thorough and detailed of genealogical resources in the UK. Ireland began registration on 1 April 1845 but it was not formally adopted for the whole country until 1864.

1856 The Crimean War officially came to an end. Relief back in England was widespread, yet it couldn't reverse the years of terror, heartbreak and suffering the war had caused. Nevertheless, the immediate news created an initial period of joy, leading many people to celebrate in the streets until the early hours.

31 March

1870 General Charles Grey, the Principal Private Secretary to the Sovereign, dies
'Poor dear General,' remarked Queen Victoria, 'I could not bear to think I should never look again on his face in this world!' Charles Grey, the second son of the former prime minister, Earl Grey, had served as the queen's reliable, dependable, and loyal private secretary since Albert's death in 1861, steering her through the worst torments of grief and solitude. Following a short illness, Grey died at 10.20pm on Thursday 31 March, plunging Victoria into yet another wave of grief. His rich experience and wisdom were deeply valued by the monarch who relied on him increasingly for support, guidance and advice. Grey was succeeded by Sir Henry Ponsonby.

March

1855 The novelist Charlotte Bronte died during pregnancy with her unborn child after suffering from severe morning sickness. The official cause of death was listed as 'phthisis', although many suspected other causes such as hyperemesis gravidarum.

1880 The 1880 general election was called. Disraeli had initially called a meeting to discuss the possibility of an early general election. The Conservative government had grown deeply unpopular, especially since a devastatingly poor harvest which left many farmers in poverty. Fearful of defeat, the cabinet decided against an election. Just moments before the meeting concluded, a messenger burst into the room with shocking news that the Tories had taken Southwark, a long-held Liberal safe seat in a by-election. Disraeli was so shocked by the news he threw caution to the wind and called a general election. The decision backfired spectacularly. He was defeated by a large majority.

April

1 April

1841 The Royal Botanic Gardens at Kew are opened
Kew Gardens were opened largely thanks to the work of William Cavendish, President of the Royal Horticultural Society, who pushed for increased funding for horticulture and scientific research. Administered under the directorship of William Hooker, and later his son Joseph, the park significantly increased in size by almost 75 acres and achieved huge national and scientific status. In 1848 the Palm House was constructed by the architect Decimus Burton and is today regarded as Britain's most renowned Victorian glass-and-iron structure. Later, in 1863, the even larger Temperate House opened, housing some of the biggest plants in the park. Unfortunately, Kew's success was not universally well received. In the 1870s the Liberal politician Acton Smee Ayrton, together with the famous scientist Sir Richard Owen, argued that Kew should not receive government funding or be allowed to expand as an independent scientific institution. Owen was concerned that Kew would surpass the National History Museum. He also held a personal grudge against Hooker whom he disliked intensely.

1892 The first London-Paris telephone system was opened.

1900 The Irish Guards were formed by order of Queen Victoria who was deeply moved by stories of heroic Irish soldiers during the Second Boer War.

2 April

1891 The Scottish entertainer Jack Buchannan is born in Scotland
Born Walter John Buchannan to working-class parents in Dunbartonshire, he started his career under the alias 'Chump Buchanan', working mainly in Glasgow to limited success. After the First World War, he reinvented himself again as 'Jack Buchannan', finding huge acclaim playing the quintessential upper-class English gentleman. He even took part in the first transatlantic television broadcast, organised by John Logie Baird.

1873 British trains were fitted with toilets. The idea of having lavatories on trains was initially dismissed as impractical although, by 1873, it had finally become a reality.

April

3 April

1895 The Oscar Wilde trial begins
The first day of Wilde's trial was reported extensively by the national press. Outside the court, scenes almost of hysteria unfolded with colossal crowds flocking into the area like birds. Queensberry's lawyers were led by the powerful Edward Carson who later became an influential Irish unionist politician. Queensberry had also hired a team of private detectives to dig up information on Wilde and his private life. The famous playwright was questioned vigorously by Carson who repeatedly inquired into his association with several younger, less wealthy men. The day ended with growing alarm among Wilde's supporters. It was not a promising start.

1862 The polar explorer Sir James Clark Ross died. Ross was an early trailblazing navigator of Antarctica, but his work was largely overshadowed in later decades by the dazzling status of Captain Robert Falcon Scott. In 1848 Ross discovered the famous Transantarctic Mountains, along with an enormous ice shelf that was later named in his honour. Ross was also immortalised by the Ross Sea and Ross Island, both in tribute to his lifelong work in polar exploration.

4 April

1900 The Prince of Wales survives an assassination attempt
The sooty platform at Nord Station in Brussels was packed with anxious sightseers, craving a glimpse of the Prince and Princess of Wales on their way to Denmark to celebrate Alexandra's father's eighty-second birthday. At 5.30pm, the train was about to move when a young man rushed onto the platform and approached the carriage. Within a few metres from the royal couple, he levelled his gun and fired two sporadic shots at short range. Remarkably, none of the royal party was injured. Back in London, Sir Francis Knollys, the prince's private secretary, received the news via cable, and quickly telegrammed the palace and the prime minister. The news created horror across Britain. The queen, who was staying at the Viceregal Lodge in Dublin, was informed immediately by Princess Helena at around 7.15pm. The would-be assassin, Jean-Baptiste Victor Sipido, was a sixteen-year-old boy employed as a local apprentice. He was quickly tackled to the ground by police and arrested without resistance. Services of thanksgiving were later offered for the royals in several cathedrals across England. Sipido was later acquitted.

5 April

1847 World's first municipal park opens in Birkenhead, Merseyside
Birkenhead was the first purpose-built park in the world, designed exclusively for the enjoyment and recreation of local Liverpool citizens. Joseph Paxton, the brainchild behind the Crystal Palace, was given the responsibility of creating

a welcoming and open space in the heart of an urban city. The popularity of Birkenhead meant that many similar parks were subsequently created.

1862 Anthony Trollope was elected as a member of the Garrick Club. Clubland was very important for wealthy Victorians, none more so than the Garrick Club, a bastion for influential artists and writers. Trollope's nomination was seconded by fellow writer William Thackeray. Two years later, he was also elected as a member of the famous Athenaeum Club in Waterloo Place.

1899 The funeral of MP Richard Chamberlain took place in Key Hill, Birmingham. Chamberlain was largely overshadowed by his brother Joseph and later, his nephew Neville Chamberlain who became prime minister.

6 April

1843 William Wordsworth was appointed Poet Laureate of the United Kingdom
Apart from Tennyson, Wordsworth was perhaps the most famous poet laureate of the Victorian era and yet he wrote relatively little in the role. The renowned writer was initially reluctant to accept the position, partly due to his age. After the death of Robert Southey in March 1843, the vacancy was offered to Wordsworth, who at seventy-three, felt he was too elderly for the prestigious and demanding role. Only after personal intervention from Robert Peel did he finally agree, but with direct assurances that there would be little writing requirements. Wordsworth remained in the role until his own death in 1850 but did not compose any new works publicly during that time.

1895 While relaxing in London's fashionable Cadogan Hotel the playwright Oscar Wilde was approached by his friend Robbie Ross, who had news of upcoming trouble. He urged him to leave the country and flee to France, but Wilde refused. Later the same night, policemen arrived on the premises and arrested Wilde on charges of gross indecency.

7 April

1853 Queen Victoria's youngest son, Leopold, is born at Buckingham Palace
Victoria was the first British sovereign to receive chloroform during childbirth, a somewhat controversial and risky decision at the time. The news of Leopold's healthy arrival came with great relief throughout the country. To mark his birthday, in 1859 the queen hosted a large children's fancy dress party held in the Ball Supper Room at Buckingham Palace. Children from six to fourteen were invited, with both Leopold and his older brother Arthur attending as the medieval princes of King Henry IV. A watercolour painting of the event was later commissioned.

April

1871 Tragically, Leopold's eighteenth birthday also coincided with a terrible family tragedy. Prince Alexander, the newborn child of the Prince and Princess of Wales, succumbed to an infection shortly after midnight on 7 April. He was under a day old.

8 April

1848 Revolutionary fears threaten the Queen
Damp and dreary weather greeted the royals as their weary carriages exited Buckingham Palace under an atmosphere of panic and emergency. Political unrest in Britain had reached a thunderous climax, illustrated vividly by the 1839 Newport rising, where approximately 4,000 Chartist sympathisers took part in an armed protest. In February 1848 revolution spread through France, toppling the monarchy of Louis Philippe and spreading through other regions of Europe. For Robert Peel, the risk for Victoria was too high. The royals were carted away from London to the sanctuary of Osborne House on the Isle of Wight. The move was unnecessary. No serious anti-monarchist threat emerged in her reign and Victoria remained an immensely popular figure for most of her life.

1838 The SS *Great Western* made its maiden voyage. The vessel was Isambard Kingdom Brunel's first major project and, at sixty-five metres long, the longest steamship in the world. The voyage began in Bristol for New York but was unexpectedly delayed by early problems. Just before reaching the port of Avonmouth, the ship was badly damaged by a fire, during which Brunel was injured in a fall. Passengers were so spooked by the incident; over fifty people cancelled their bookings. Only seven passengers were eventually present for the maiden voyage on 8 April. It arrived in America fifteen days after leaving England, making it the second steamship to cross the Atlantic, a record missed by just one day. Luckily for Brunel, the *Great Western* proved a success and remained in operation until 1856.

1886 William Gladstone introduced the First Irish Home Rule Bill to the Commons. Rumours had whirled around for months that Gladstone was about to announce his support for Irish Home Rule. The prospect was controversial. While supporters argued it was only fair that Ireland exercise more autonomy over it decisions, critics warned it would mean the break-up of the empire. Even the Liberals were split by the question. Some members formed a separate party called the Liberal Unionists, led by Lord Hartington and Joseph Chamberlain

9 April

1838 The National Gallery opens in London
The original gallery opened in 1827 but was heavily mocked as a national embarrassment, a poor reflection on British architectural talent. In 1838 a new

building was constructed in Trafalgar Square, designed as a splendid example of new Victorian confidence. Twenty-nine years later, Edward Middleton Barry proposed an even bolder redesign of the existing structure with an enormous dome located in the centre. The plans did not meet with the gallery's approval, with many critics accusing Barry of 'plagiarising' the dome of St Paul's Cathedral. The gallery remains in the same location today.

1894 At a lavish ceremony hosted in Marlborough House, the Prince of Wales, on behalf of the council of the Society of Arts, awarded Joseph Lister the prestigious Albert Medal. The award was granted for Lister's outstanding achievements, especially for discovering the antiseptic methods for treating wounds.

10 April

1848 The Kennington Chartist Rally
On the chilly morning of 10 April 1848, two cumbersome hackney carriages arrived outside the Houses of Parliament. Inside, they held two halves of a chartist petition, with the signatures of almost two million angry, disgruntled and discontented citizens demanding radical political change. Not too far away, the calm lawns of Kennington Common had become overpowered by over 100,000 protesters, desperate to express their rage at the slowness of political change.

Chartism was not a new movement. Disapproval at the unfair political nature of British democracy had raged for decades, yet this was undeniably the largest political rally of the era and deeply alarmed the government. Police were deployed throughout the city, with armed guards placed outside key landmarks, including the bank of England. Cannon were even installed on the Tower of London. Faced with the prospect of potential bloodshed and violence, the chartist leader, Feargus O'Connor, urged his followers to conduct themselves peacefully with no incitement to aggression. A daguerreotype of the event was taken and is currently held by the Royal Collection Trust. The rally ultimately was unsuccessful. Chartist demands for more democratic representation remained unfulfilled for many years.

1877 The first human cannonball act took place at London's Royal Aquarium on 10 April, delivered by the courageous teenager Rossa Richter. Like a lot of Victorian actors, Ritcher started her career as a child star working in pantomimes and music halls. Her mother was a dancer and her father was a talent agent, who trained his daughter in circus acts and dancing. She was only seventeen when she began her legendary cannonball act which shocked and amazed Londoners. In 1879 she performed it again in Portsmouth but was badly injured. In 1891 Richter was involved in a more serious accident while performing and retired. She died in 1937.

1869 The Royal Philatelic Society London was founded. The organisation was established for stamp collectors with early members including the future King George V. The society remains the oldest of its kind in the world.

April

11 April

1844- The London Ragged School Union is established
In the dark, rather damp quarters of 17 Ampton Street, near Gray's Inn Road, a group of grey-haired elderly gents gathered in a small, sparse room to discuss the future of British education. Together, after long discussions, the men formed a radical organisation: the Ragged School, a charitable institution aimed at providing free education to the underprivileged and destitute children of London. The idea was not entirely a new one. The concept of a free school had first been discussed by an eighteenth-century tailor, Thomas Cranfield, who established nineteen free schools for deprived children. The ragged schools, however, were more ambitious in size and scale, led by the Union's first President, Lord Shaftesbury. Additionally, Shaftesbury used his position in the House of Lords to further the cause of free education. Another famous supporter was Charles Dickens.

1864 An extraordinary scene took place in London, with the arrival of the Italian general, Giuseppe Garibaldi, who was visiting Britain for a twelve-day tour. As many as half a million Londoners scrambled into Trafalgar Square with some folk even climbing lampposts and Nelson's iconic plinth to get a glance of his passing carriage. Crowds eventually became so dense that Garibaldi's procession was halted by the thick mass of supporters; it took five hours to reach his intended destination.

1890 Joseph Merrick, known as the 'Elephant Man' died. As a child, Merrick suffered severe physical deformities and was nicknamed the 'Elephant Man'. After a traumatic childhood, he found employment in a cruel 'freak show' until being taken into care by Dr Frederick Treves. He received good treatment and became a popular local figure, renowned for a kind and sensitive nature. Sadly, Merrick died at only twenty-seven.

12 April

1891- The oldest active serviceman in the Royal Navy, Provo Wallis, celebrates his 100th birthday
By 1891 the venerable figure of Admiral Provo Wallis was still doggedly refusing to retire even after his 100th birthday. Born in 1791, Wallis had joined the Royal Navy as a young man and never saw a need to change. Congratulatory telegrams came from far and wide, including Queen Victoria, the Prince of Wales and several military leaders. He remains the oldest Admiral of the Fleet in British history.

1864 Charles Dickens hosted a charity dinner for the University College Hospital. The dinner raised over £1,500 for the hospital, the equivalent of over £130,000 today.

1864 Louie Henri was born in Paddington, London. She was one of the first actresses to portray Queen Victoria on film, starring in the popular silent movie *Sixty Years a Queen*, released in 1913.

1868 On the morning of Easter Saturday 1868, the senior politician, the 2nd Marquess of Salisbury died. Being a public holiday, there was no telegraph service to inform his son, Lord Salisbury, who later became prime minister. He instead discovered the news purely by chance the next morning at Guildford railway station.

13 April

1886 The 8th Earl of Shaftesbury kills himself in a London cab
Shaftesbury was the oldest son of the much-celebrated philanthropist, the 7th Earl, but had suffered an unhappy life with huge financial debts and personal stress. While seated in a London cab near Oxford Street, he shot himself in the head. A group of onlookers soon gathered around the vehicle and miraculously the Earl was still alive. He died later that day from his injuries.

1869 A destructive fire broke out at the Junior Carlton Club in Pall Mall, threatening to spread to the neighbouring buildings. Fortunately, no one was killed.

1892 Royal Air Force commander Arthur Harris was born in Cheltenham. Harris became a controversial figure during the Second World War, nicknamed 'Bomber Harris' for his advocacy of bombing campaigns against German cities.

14 April

1857 Queen Victoria's youngest daughter Beatrice is born at Buckingham Palace
It was not an easy pregnancy. The thirty-eight-year-old Victoria suffered such intense pain during the labour that her physician, John Snow, took the controversial decision of administering chloroform, a seemingly risky choice at the time. The Church of England and the medical profession were deeply unhappy with Snow's decision, but the queen was said to be delighted. She forever described it as the 'blessed' chloroform.

1864 Allan Aynesworth, the first actor to play Algernon in *The Importance of Being Earnest*, was born in Sandhurst.

1868 The National Society for Women's Suffrage held its first meeting, hosted at the Manchester Free Trade Hall. The society was founded by Lydia Becker, an amateur scientist, who was credited for forming the modern suffragette movement that emerged in the twentieth century.

April

1876 The barrister Cecil Chubb was born in Wiltshire. He was the last private owner of Stonehenge which he donated to the nation in October 1918.

15 April

1874 Lord Randolph Churchill married Jennie Jerome at the British embassy in Paris
Lord Randolph was first introduced to Jerome by the Prince of Wales at a glitzy social party. As a glamorous American socialite, Jerome was not widely popular in stuffy aristocratic British circles. She found it difficult to acclimatise to the social scene, especially with Lord Randolph's mother who deeply disapproved of the relationship. The wedding was hosted in the small chapel of the British embassy in Paris.

16 April

1889 Charlie Chaplin is born into poverty in South London
Chaplin's childhood was bleak, bitter, deprived and traumatic. There is no official certificate of Chaplin's birth, although it is believed he was probably born in East Street Market, where a blue plaque today marks his life. Both his parents were failed actors and suffered an unhappy, complicated marriage. In 1896 Chaplin was committed to the Lambeth Workhouse, followed by the Central London District School for poor children. In 1898 his mother's health deteriorated and she was committed to a mental asylum. Chaplin was sent to live with his alcoholic father who died prematurely in 1901.

1894 On 16 April 1895 the bull-necked, starch-collared Chancellor, William Harcourt, presented his budget to a packed House of Commons. The plans were intensely controversial. Firstly, he intended to raise income tax, aggravating wealthy landowners. Secondly, he also established death duties. Prime Minister Lord Rosebery was deeply unimpressed. Weeks earlier he quarrelled bitterly in cabinet, arguing the policies would hurt the party's richest supporters, maybe even risking an exodus to the Tory party. Harcourt dismissed the concerns as 'rubbish'. The incident exposed deep levels of infighting within the British government and would ultimately contribute to its collapse.

1896 The National Trust purchased its first property, Alfriston Clergy House in Sussex. The total cost for the building was just £10; repairs came to over £300.

17 April

1888 Winston Churchill enrolled at Harrow School.
In his own words, Churchill was ill suited to the inflexibility and rigour of Victorian academic life, something his parents deeply resented. After narrowly passing the

entrance exam in 1888, Churchill did not excel or enjoy his studies. Outside the stuffy, oak-panelled classrooms of Harrow, the restless youth found solace in physical exercise and cadets. He enjoyed fencing tournaments, running and sports. Despite his loathing of school, Churchill grew to develop a huge admiration for his teacher, Robert Somervell, who saw potential in his youthful spirit. The two remained in contact for several years until Somervell's death in 1933.

18 April

1893 Austen Chamberlain delivers his maiden speech
On 18 April 1893 Chamberlain delivered an enormously successful maiden address, recalled by some colleagues as the greatest parliamentary performance of his career. 'It was a characteristic speech,' recalled David Lloyd George, 'faultless in matter and in style.' Another observer, Winston Churchill, still not a MP himself, was crouched on the floor of the public gallery listening to events from above. Even Gladstone, not known for emotion, was apparently impressed.

1881 The National History Museum was opened in London, showcasing a huge collection of specimens, skeletons and fossils existing in natural history. The museum also included several books and manuscripts relating to natural science. The magnificent building was designed by Alfred Waterhouse and opened to stupendous acclaim.

1892 Alfred Roberts, mayor of Grantham and father of Margaret Thatcher, was born in Ringstead, Northamptonshire.

19 April

1881 Benjamin Disraeli dies
Following Disraeli's defeat at the 1880 election, most expected a triumphant political comeback. In a private letter to a senior Tory grandee, the ageing leader vowed to act with the same youthful and energetic manner as before. In reality, the former premier would not even live a year. By March 1881 his health took a serious turn for the worse. He was suffering from bronchitis, but also heart failure and other ailments. He spoke again briefly at a party meeting on 26 March and was hailed as a champion, yet behind the scenes real worry began to grow that Disraeli was seriously ill. He spent the last few weeks of his life bedridden, drifting in and out of consciousness at his home in Buckinghamshire. At 4.30am on 19 April Disraeli died peacefully aged seventy-six.

1882 The following year, the acclaimed scientist Charles Darwin died following a battle with angina. His death received substantial international coverage.

April

1882 The Battle of the Braes took place in Scotland. Throughout the nineteenth century, thousands of Scottish crofters were cruelly evicted from their homes by landlords hoping to save money, casting many families into poverty. In 1882 a group of highlanders resisted eviction in Braes on the Isle of Skye. The local laird, Lord MacDonald, instructed police to issue eviction notices, which were subsequently burned by furious crofters. Fifty policemen arrived at the scene to be greeted with stones and sticks. Violence ensued and several people were injured. What became known as the 'Battle of the Braes' would create widespread sympathy for the crofters, yet evictions continued for many years to come.

20 April

1861 William Morris establishes his own arts company
By the 1860s the perceived harshness of the modern industrial revolution had created a renewed interest in the quieter, supposedly simpler age of pre-industrial Britain, a country absent of tall menacing chimneys and modern factories, or regiments of overcrowded and unsanitary houses. The Arts and Crafts movement drew its inspiration from the past, a return to an idealised version of Medieval England. In 1861, the artist William Morris founded his own arts company which created furniture, wallpaper and stained glass in the medieval gothic design. The movement would expand greatly throughout the nineteenth century, eventually becoming one of the most influential groups in British art.

1899 Lady Margaret Rosebery married Liberal MP Robert Crewe. The wedding at Westminster Abbey was the biggest society event of the year, attracting such big crowds that it almost rivalled the queen's diamond Jubilee. The wedding cake was enormous, standing six-feet tall and decorated with both families' coats of arms within the corded silk ribbon.

21 April

1843 Queen Victoria's favourite uncle, the Duke of Sussex, dies
In the years of the queen's youth, the duke was commonly seen as Victoria's favourite uncle, although his status in Buckingham Palace had faded greatly in the years preceding his death. He was the ninth child of George III and renowned for his liberal political views and championing of the arts. The duke had been unwell for some time with Erysipelas, but his death was unexpected. After lunch, the queen visited him at Kensington Palace where she encountered a large throng of spectators outside the gates eager for fresh updates. Servants stood in tears. He died later the same day with his brother, Prince Adolphus, by his side.

22 April

1848 The Treason Felony Act of 1848 is passed in response to the French Revolution
It would be no exaggeration to say the 1848 revolution that had swept France ruffled many feathers in England. Westminster feared a copycat revolution occurring in Britain, a not so improbable threat, considering the recent fears over a chartist uprising that had caused sleepless nights for some aristocrats. In 1848 the Commons drafted a Treason Felony Act which made it illegal to advocate, plot or devise the abolition of the monarchy.

1884 A large and unusually powerful earthquake ripped through the sleepy Essex town of Colchester, causing considerable damage and widespread shock across the community. The earthquake hit originally at around 9.00am. At 4.6 on the Richter scale, it was the most destructive English earthquake since 1580. Over 1,000 buildings were damaged, including a Norman church, which was later demolished.

23 April

1888 Queen Victoria met Emperor Franz Joseph I of Austria in Innsbruck.
The meeting was significant, not least because of the geo-political implications. Austria-Hungary was increasingly regarded as a major European power and many British policymakers saw a potential future for an Anglo-Austrian friendship. Many years later, Britain and Austria-Hungary would be at war, and the close relations would appear almost a distant memory.

1880 William Gladstone formed his second government on 23 April, although not everyone was pleased. Victoria vowed she would rather abdicate than have 'that man' in Number 10. Even her anger, however, could not reverse the democratic process. Gladstone's meeting with the Queen was not a pleasant one. Furious with his attacks on Disraeli during the election, she reminded him of the many 'falsehoods' in his statements.

24 April

1857 The Whigs win the General Election
Many regarded the 1857 election as little more than a popularity contest for the publicity-seeking Lord Palmerston who yearned for another term as prime minister. As the most famous, colourful and contentious politician of the decade, the Whig campaign focused heavily on his credentials, especially emphasising his merits and charisma as leader, while at the same time depicting the Tories as weak and ineffective. Palmerston returned to Downing Street with an increased majority of 377 seats, the greatest election result for several years.

April

1862 Writer Arthur Christopher Benson was born. He is perhaps most recognised for writing the lyrics of the patriotic tune *Land of Hope and Glory* in 1902.

1880 The Amateur Athletic Association of England was formed by three men from Oxford University.

1882 Military commander Hugh Dowding was born in Scotland. Dowding served as chief of RAF Fighter Command during the Battle of Britain and is credited for providing strong, assured leadership during the early stages of the Second World War.

25 April

1843 Queen Victoria's second daughter, Princess Alice, is born at Buckingham Palace
Alice was born at 4.05am at Buckingham Palace. Many hoped the child would be a boy, and even some Privy Councillors offered 'condolences' to Prince Albert upon confirmation of the news. Alice would mature into a highly intelligent, gifted, artistically talented young woman who showed an enormous skill for literature, languages and music. She became a foremost and highly popular member of the royal family.

1897 Over fifty years to the day, Princess Mary of Teck gave birth to a daughter, also called Mary, at York Cottage, Sandringham. In most royal biographies, Mary is regulated to either to a few lines or a minor footnote. Never a fan of the limelight, the unassuming princess was a formidable, if overlooked, figure in national life and became the first female chancellor of a British university.

26 April

1881 Benjamin Disraeli buried in Buckinghamshire
Despite the offer of a state funeral, Disraeli was buried at his request in the unassuming parish church of St Michael and All Angels'. Royal protocol meant the queen did not attend the ceremony but sent a posy of primroses for the coffin and later visited his graveside personally. The monarch was represented by the Prince of Wales and Prince Leopold. Almost the entire Conservative cabinet attended, including former enemy the 15th Earl Derby who had quarrelled bitterly with Disraeli in the years before his death.

1897 A bomb planted by a Russian anarchist group injured sixty innocent commuters at Aldersgate Street station. A thirty-five-year-old father of two named Harry Pitts later died of his injuries. He is tragically considered the first man killed in a terrorist attack on the London Underground.

27 April

1880 The Conservative Party is defeated at the General Election
Disraeli was devastated by the defeat. At a meeting at Bridgewater House a few weeks later, he rallied the party faithful like never before. As he finished a thunderous speech, a group of impassioned Tory MPs sang Gilbert and Sullivans rousing song *He is an Englishman*. No faction was powerful enough to rival his authority although, behind the scenes, things were quite different. Disraeli's health was ailing. Queen Victoria was equally disappointed at the prospect of another Gladstone government.

1883 The Royal Red Cross was established to award exceptional services in military nursing. The first recipient was Florence Nightingale.

28 April

1862 Columbia Square opened
In the 1860s, Baroness Burdett-Coutts purchased land in London to form the Columbia Market Buildings, built by the extremely talented architect Henry Darbishire. In 1862 the model block of flats was completed at Columbia Square with each apartment constructed with a functioning water system and a high standard of physical cleanliness. Poor hygiene, overcrowding and bad sanitation was a hallmark of urban Victorian areas, something which Burdett Coutts was determined to eradicate. A large laundry room was placed on the top floor to give easy access to cleaning facilities, and a reading room for residents to relax and unwind.

1877 Stamford Bridge stadium was opened as a new host for the London Athletic Club, the oldest independent track and field club in the world. The stadium, which has since been rebuilt, is now home to Chelsea FC.

29 April

1879 The English conductor Sir Thomas Beecham is born in Lancashire
Beecham emerged as a foremost musical giant in the twentieth century, leaving an indelible mark through his innovative and exceptional interpretations of classical music. He started life in Lancashire, born in a modest house near his grandfather's laxative factory known as Beecham Pills. His family were extremely wealthy, but tumultuous, dominated by his parents' explosive relationship. After an expensive education at Rossall School and Oxford University, Beecham studied musical composition in Liverpool and became a self-taught conductor. In 1899, however, he faced personal crisis when his father, Joseph, committed his wife to a mental asylum, which Beecham desperately attempted to reverse. In securing her release,

he was subsequently disinherited by his father. Fortunately, their relationship was slowly repaired. In the twentieth century, Joseph financed many of Beecham's most notable musical projects.

30 April

1851 The Sutton Tunnel railway accident
Train crashes were distressingly common in Victorian Britain. Barely a month went by without some story of railway accidents or errors appearing in the newspapers, sometimes resulting in large casualties. On the fateful afternoon of 30 April 1851, a particularly tragic incident occurred in the crowded area of Sutton. The community was heavily crowded with visitors attending the Chester Cup horse-racing show. After the races had finished, a train crash occurred in the Sutton Tunnel, killing nine people and injuring numerous bystanders.

1857 Princess Mary, the last surviving child of King George III, died. The Royal Scots Fusiliers formed a guard of honour as her body was carried from Cambridge House to Paddington Station for a formal burial at Windsor. Prince Albert and the Prince of Wales attended the funeral.

1865 Admiral Robert FitzRoy died. He was the founder of the Met Office, a national weather service to form meteorological predictions. He initially established the organisation to advise fishermen for their safety at sea.

May

1 May

1851 The Great Exhibition opens in London
'A day to live forever,' wrote the jubilant Queen Victoria, 'one of the greatest and most glorious days of our lives.' The Great Exhibition was an event like no other, a world fair that showcased Britain's best and brightest technological and industrial advancements like never before. It was the most successful show of its kind, unquestionably the most remarkable and undeniably the most celebrated festival of the century.

The royal couple arrived early to see the exhibits for themselves. Victoria wore a bright pink dress to stand out in the crowd of over 40,000 visitors. The highlight was undoubtedly the magnificent Crystal Palace in Hyde Park, the first-ever glass building attempted on such an enormous scale in Britain. Other less famous technologies included George Jennings' curious invention called the 'halting stations', also known as street toilets. Over the course of five months, over 800,000 visitors used the facilities, with each compartment containing a hair comb, a towel and a shoe-shine. Customers were required to pay one penny, hence the expression 'to spend a penny' as a euphemism for using a lavatory. Later the same day, the royal family appeared for the first time on the balcony of Buckingham Palace, the start of a long tradition of balcony appearances which continues to this day. 'One felt so grateful to the great God,' recalled Victoria, 'whose blessing seemed to pervade the whole great undertaking.'

1840 The World's first postage stamp, the Penny Black, was released in Britain. It completely transformed the nature of the British postal system.

1863 The first instalment of Charles Dickens's last completed novel *Our Mutual Friend* was released. The book dealt with a tangled web of complicated love, a theme that weaved through much of his personal life throughout the 1860s.

1873 David Livingstone, the British Christian missionary was dead. He succumbed to internal bleeding caused by dysentery, plus a secondary cause of malaria. His body was later transported back to England, where it lay in No 1. Saville Row until a funeral at Westminster Abbey. His eldest son, Robert, had died previously in the American Civil War.

1875 Alexandra Palace nicknamed 'The People's Palace' was re-opened. The magnificent building was designed as a place of recreation, artistic discovery, education and entertainment, erected on a 190-acre site in London. Named after Princess Alexandra, the palace was destroyed by a fire just sixteen days after opening, killing three members of staff. Nevertheless, thanks to its initial popularity, the complex was rebuilt and re-opened in 1875.

1877 The Grosvenor Gallery opened its first exhibition. The gallery was created to provide an alternative to the traditional art displayed at the Royal Academy, founded by Sir Coutts Lindsay, who wished for greater diversity in art. Many of the pieces exhibited were considered unconventional for the time, including the work of Edward Burne-Jones.

2 May

1845 Yarmouth suspension bridge disaster
In 1845, the usually sleepy, tranquil town of Great Yarmouth became the place of immense national tragedy. Yarmouth suspension bridge was constructed in 1829 and stretched across the River Bure, becoming a popular and notable landmark. On 2 May a circus performance was staged under the bridge with hundreds of spectators gathering to watch, including several children. At 5 20pm, however, disaster struck. The seemingly impregnable bridge collapsed, killing almost eighty people below.

1869 *The Malay Archipelago* by Alfred Russel Wallace was published. The book was a popular travelogue, providing an interesting account of Alfred Russell Wallace's eight years travel across the Malay world. Wallace was a prominent British naturalist with a reputation for zoological and biological research and worked closely with Charles Darwin.

1870 Disraeli published his successful novel *Lothair*. Disraeli's dual role as a politician and author cemented suspicion in the Commons, especially among older colleagues who regarded him as an opportunistic fame-seeker with no aristocratic background or even a university education. His first novel *Vivian Grey* was an almighty failure and led to ridicule. Undeterred, Disraeli published several subsequent books to moderate success, including the popular novel *Lothair* which was released to wide acclaim.

3 May

1891 John Fisher is appointed Admiral Superintendent of the dockyard at Portsmouth
John Fisher entered the navy, in his own words, 'penniless' and poor. By 1891, however, he was hob-nobbing with the rich and famous, eating lunch with Queen Victoria and dazzling dinner guests with the Prince of Wales at glamorous parties.

Fisher's appointment as Admiral Superintendent of the dockyard at Portsmouth cemented his reputation as a naval highflyer. In his position, however, he increasingly clashed with another up-and-coming admiral, Charles Beresford, whose boisterous, energetic personality jarred with Fisher's own unpredictable character. The feud became extremely public and damaging. Beresford, known in the press as 'Charlie B', was a dashing, silver-haired, silver-tongued aristocrat with a similarly enthusiastic and egotistical personality. It would become one of the most tumultuous war of words in the nation, in which both men would split the Victorian Navy in two.

4 May

1896 Hotel Cecil is opened
Before the Victorian era, hotels were often considered disreputable places of ill-repute. Rich country gentlemen were more inclined to stay at their clubs or return home after a long hard day's business in London. The nineteenth century modified this image. Towards the 1880s and 90s, new, ultra-luxurious and fashionable institutions emerged, none more so than the Hotel Cecil which boasted the most exquisite cuisine in London. Its opening night on 4 May promised to be a landmark event for hospitality in Britain. All the great and the good attended, including representatives from foreign embassies, top-hatted and white-tailed journalists, pompous politicians and glamorous peers. Coincidentally, the property was also built on the site of Salisbury House, a colossal aristocratic mansion owned by Prime Minister Lord Salisbury, which he sold for a huge sum of money. The conservative government, dominated by Salisbury's chums and relatives, was later nicknamed 'Hotel Cecil' to highlight its alleged nepotistic nature.

1896 The first edition of the *Daily Mail* was published. While most newspapers of the time were around one penny, the *Daily Mail* was just a halfpenny. Its content was concise and coherent, and proved immensely popular with the public. Three years later, new printing facilities were purchased and, by the dawn of the twentieth century, circulation reached over a million.

5 May

1857 The Art Treasures of Great Britain opened in Manchester.
It was one of the largest, grandest, most spectacular, most stupendous exhibitions of fine art in British history, attracting over one million eager and impressed visitors. Everyone who was anyone attended – Queen Victoria, Tennyson, Disraeli, Dickens, dukes and duchesses. The millionaire manufacturer Titus Salt was so impressed that he hired three trains to take over 2,000 workers to visit. A temporary hotel was even constructed to accommodate the enormous number of travellers. The exhibition ended prematurely after news of the Indian Rebellion. The buildings

were brought down the following year. Despite the initial success, the event did not generate huge profits, with the biggest beneficiaries being the railways who saw a considerable boost in their revenues.

1883 General Archibald Wavell was born in Colchester, Essex. He would find fame as a leading military commander in the Second World War.

1896 The film *Oxford and Cambridge boat race* became the first moving picture to be premiered outside London. It was also displayed in Cardiff Town Hall.

6 May

1882 The Phoenix Park murders occur in Dublin
On 6 May 1882, the Chief Secretary of Ireland, Lord Frederick Cavendish, and the senior civil servant, Thomas Burke, were brutally murdered in Phoenix Park, Dublin. The culprits were members of the Irish Republican Brotherhood who wounded both men in their backs with surgical knives. The following morning the prime minister announced their deaths to a stunned and emotional House of Commons.

1838 The Guards' Chapel was opened in Wellington Barracks. It was later redesigned in a majestic Lombardo Byzantine style with a vivid marble interior. Unfortunately, much of the Victorian structure was damaged by a V.1 flying bomb on Sunday 18 June 1944, killing 121 and injuring another 141.

1896 The Prince of Wales became the first recipient of the Royal Victorian Order (RVO). While most honours were bestowed on advice of ministers, the RVO was established at the personal request of the queen for services to the monarch.

7 May

1839 The bedchamber crisis
Victoria was a stubborn, steely and, occasionally, reckless character, illustrated clearly during the infamous 1839 bedchamber crisis. Following the fall of the Whig government in 1839, and the removal of her beloved Lord Melbourne as prime minister, the queen faced the prospect of a new leader. Robert Peel was a tough-talking Tory who lacked the charm and conversational mastery of Melbourne. Suspecting that the palace was anti-Tory, Peel requested that the queen dismiss her ladies of the bedchamber who were married to Whig peers. Victoria refused. She declined to comply with the government's wishes, and Peel resigned as prime minister. The reaction in the press was fury. It was the last occasion where a British monarch had so publicly disobeyed her elected prime minister. Critics argued that the incident revealed the queen's inexperience but also, more significantly, her naivety about the dangers of modern politics.

1885 The 1st Earl of Dudley died in London. Dudley was a popular character in high society, known for his long, knotted hair, earning him the nickname 'Fixie Wig'. His ancestral home, Dudley House, is one of the oldest surviving aristocratic properties in London.

8 May

1838 The People's Charter was published
The Victorian era throbbed and pulsated with political agitation, a reflection of the harsh realities of the Industrial Revolution and the radical changes it created in British society. In 1838 the political activist William Lovett and the London Working Men's Association, published the famous 'People's Charter'. It was hailed by many as the 'magna carta of the nineteenth century', a concise list of six demands which would form the ideological foundation of the Chartist movement. The document's points included universal suffrage and a secret ballot, both of which were eventually achieved but after many decades of fierce and often painful battles

1855 Queen Victoria hosted her first ball in the new Grand Ballroom at Buckingham Palace. The ballroom measured thirty-four metres in length and fourteen metres in height, making it the most palatial room in the palace. The organ had originally belonged to the Royal Pavilion in Brighton and was extended and redecorated by Gray & Davison. Unusually for the time, the ballroom was also illuminated with gas, the power equivalent to around 1,000 wax candles.

1889 The Composer Edward Elgar married Caroline Alice Roberts in Brompton Oratory, one of London's largest Roman Catholic churches. Caroline Roberts, who was eight years his senior, descended from a wealthy Anglican family who were extremely disapproving of her decision to marry a poor, penniless Catholic composer. She was subsequently disinherited.

9 May

1874 Chelsea Embankment opened
The project was masterminded by the engineering genius of Sir Joseph Bazalgette, a respected civil engineer who is also credited for constructing London's modern sewage system that significantly reduced cholera deaths in the capital. Bazalgette had been given the task of easing London's infamous flooding from the river Thames, something which had afflicted Chelsea for several years. The embankment was officially opened by the Duke of Edinburgh.

1881 Lord Salisbury became leader of the Conservative Party in the Lords. The elevation was not initially welcomed by the naturally shy and introverted Salisbury who disliked the gruelling social events, shaking hands with seemingly endless lines of grey-haired dignitaries, and muttering ritualised small talk and social pleasantries.

1887 Buffalo Bill's Wild West Show opened in London. After stupendous success in the United States, on 9 May Bill moved his show to London, opening with massive crowds and sold-out audiences. The tour was so successful that the Prince of Wales later asked for a private performance, followed by a royal command performance for the Golden Jubilee. The queen was said to be deeply impressed.

1860 The writer J.M. Barrie was born in Kirriemuir. He is acclaimed as the author of *Peter Pan*. Ironically, Barrie almost never became a writer. His anxious family strongly urged him to pursue a more stable career.

10 May

1849 The British actor William Charles Macready nearly killed in a riot
The famous actor William Charles Macready visited the United States in April 1849, but vowed never to return. In previous months, Macready had quarrelled bitterly with the American actor Edwin Forrest, who had publicly criticised his performance of Hamlet some years earlier. The rivalry between both actors became increasingly bitter. On 7 May Forrest's fans purchased a mass of tickets for Macready's *Macbeth* at the Astor Opera House, and chucked eggs, vegetables and even shoes at the actor. On the 10th, an even bigger disturbance occurred. As the play began, an estimated 10,000 anti-Macready protesters gathered outside the theatre and began fighting with police. Some attempted to set fire to the building and pelted the windows with stones. Later a riot broke out. Several people were killed and numerous injured. Macready returned to England sad and deeply shaken by the events.

11 May

1892 Margaret Rutherford, Oscar-winning British actress, is born in Balham
Margaret Rutherford's childhood was overshadowed by tragedy and unremitting personal sadness. Her father, William Benn, suffered from severe mental illness and, in 1883, killed his own father with a chamber-pot. He was discharged from Broadmoor in 1890 but was subsequently re-admitted in 1903. Following Margaret's birth, the family emigrated to India for a short while but returned to London in 1895, where her mother, Florence, committed suicide. Those traumatic experiences left Margaret with painful bouts of anxiety throughout her life. She would go on to become one of Britain's most popular and best-loved actresses. She was also the cousin of Labour politician, Tony Benn.

1890 Olympic runner William Applegarth was born. He is best known for his tremendous performance during the 1912 Olympic Games, winning Gold for the 4 x 100 metres relay. Applegarth was professionally guided by Sam Mussabini who also coached fellow Briton, Harold Abrahams.

12 May

1842 The first Bal Costumé is held at Buckingham Palace
It was the queen's first fancy-dress ball held at the palace and, understandably, the number one social event of the year. Over 2,000 guests were invited, including many aristocrats who spared no expense on designing the most extravagant costumes. The royal couple came dressed in elaborate mediaeval uniforms, a nod perhaps to the Arthurian legend which was becoming increasingly popular in Victorian literature. The party was such a titanic success that Edwin Landseer was hired to paint the occasion. A second Bal Costumé was held in 1845.

1842 The Royal Children Employment Commission published its first report. It concluded that children as young as five were working long devastating shifts in the British coal industry. Nothing substantial was done to rectify the problems.

1862 The Ulster Hall, one of the grandest concert halls in Ireland, was opened. Many Victorian figures performed in the hall, including Charles Dickens who gave a recital of his works. Randolph Churchill made a passionate speech there.

13 May

1893 The Imperial Institute Kensington is opened
Like most Victorian cities, by the 1880s London was dominated by thick satanic pollution, leaving public buildings disfigured, ruined, or unrecognisable from their original colour. Plans for an expensive hall in Kensington were unsurprisingly controversial. With so many other buildings damaged by smog, it was feared that the Imperial Institute would become yet another wasteful project. Fortunately, its designer, T.E. Colcutt, was determined to create a superb example of architectural elegance to rival the best cities in the world. The foundation stone was laid by Queen Victoria, followed in 1886 by a grand inaugural ceremony performed by Prince Christian. Despite surviving two world wars, the institute was marked for demolition in the 1950s, creating mass public uproar. It seemed ironic for a building that had provoked so much controversy in construction, mirrored similar levels of anger in its destruction.

1842 Composer Arthur Sullivan was born in Lambeth. Arguably one of Britain's best loved composers, Sullivan's collaboration with W.S. Gilbert earned him legions of dedicated Victorian fans and admirers throughout the world Born into a musical household, Sullivan would boast of playing almost every instrument in a military band. His father, Thomas Sullivan, was an Irish bandmaster who taught him the basics of musical composition, but strongly encouraged a more stable profession. As an adult, his enduring success and lasting fame made him a national celebrity and a highly respected figure in musical theatre.

1874 Anglo-Russian relations in the mid-1870s had taken a turn for the better, resulting in a visit by Alexander II to London. The Tsar suffered a turbulent and somewhat strained relationship with Queen Victoria, but his visit was marked with warmth, respect and friendship.

14 May

1900 The Olympic Games open in Paris
The 1900 Olympics opened with spectacular fanfare. It was the second time that British athletes had competed in the modern Olympic games and they enjoyed far greater success than 1896. Britain came third in the medal league table with fifteen gold medals and eight silvers. It was also the first Olympics where British athletes were known as Team Great Britain rather than the United Kingdom. Among the most notable successes was Laurence Doherty who won in both the singles and the doubles tennis tournaments.

1881 Mary Seacole died in London. Seacole is warmly remembered for her tireless work and sacrifice during the Crimean War and overcoming racial prejudice and social criticism. In later years, Seacole served as the personal masseuse to the Princess of Wales but was not financially wealthy. She died of a stroke on 14 May 1881 at seventy-five.

1889 The National Society for the Prevention of Cruelty to Children was launched. It was founded by a Congregationalist minister, Benjamin Waugh, who was increasingly appalled by the poverty and misery of working-class life.

1894 Blackpool Tower was opened. Designed by Frank Matcham, it stood at 518-feet tall. The Tower has since become a symbol of Blackpool.

15 May

1899 John Fisher selected to lead the British delegation at the Hague conference
The conference, which opened on 18 May, was attended by a multitude of world leaders and representatives to address world peace. The talks established the Geneva Convention, and formal statements on the laws of warfare and war crimes which would have a lasting significance into the twentieth century. To represent the British government, Lord Salisbury sent the dogmatic but dazzling Admiral John Fisher. Like many negotiators, Fisher's tactic was to remain quiet during the formal meetings

and lobby hard during the lunches, when leaders were at their most relaxed. The same year, after nearly forty-five years in the service, Fisher was appointed as Commander-in-Chief of the Mediterranean Fleet, one of the most prestigious positions in the navy, defending a crucial sea link between Britain and its Empire.

16 May

1865 Henry Manning appointed Archbishop of Westminster
Henry Manning was a fascinating but largely overlooked ecclesiastical leader of the nineteenth century. Just fourteen years after his conversion from Anglicanism to Roman Catholicism, Manning was appointed as Archbishop of Westminster by Pope Pius IX. During his tenure, he greatly expanded the number of Catholic schools in England and oversaw the purchase of the land to construct Westminster Cathedral.

1890 The Queen hosted a huge glittering reception with the French, Turkish and Spanish ambassadors, accompanied by various royal and political figureheads. Music was provided by the band of the Coldstream Guards.

1898 Having returned from a holiday in Cannes in early 1898, William Gladstone was diagnosed with cancer. The sad news was eventually made public and in May he was reported to be seriously ill.

17 May

1873 Vincent Van Gogh arrives in London
The artist arrived in England with a considerable salary of £90 per year, working for the Goupil Gallery which sold paintings of high quality. As a keen walker, Van Gogh would often spend his weekends strolling around the sights and sounds of London, especially the National Gallery and the British Museum. He submerged himself in English literature, especially the works of Dickens, his favourite author. He was also deeply impressed by Britain's advocacy of new technology such as electricity and streetlights. Interestingly, Van Gogh created some of his lesser-known works in England, including a sketch of Streatham Common. He left London in 1874 and relocated to Paris.

1887 Charles Parry's *Blest Pair of Sirens* was performed for the first time in St James's Hall, London. The composition was an outstanding success and remains popular. It is acknowledged as one of the greatest pieces of Victorian English choral works.

1899 Queen Victoria laid the foundation stone of the Victoria and Albert Museum in London.

May

18 May

1853 Britain's first public aquarium was opened in London Zoo.
The famous Fish House was the first of its kind in England and a considerable fascination for Victorian zoo visitors. It exhibited over 300 marine species in glass tanks, followed later by Britain's first insect house, which opened in 1881. The Zoo also housed a number of interesting animals, including a quagga and Tasmanian tigers, both of which are now extinct. Queen Victoria never visited the zoo, although a post-box bearing her cypher remains intact within the premises.

1855 The Queen presented Crimean War medals in a special ceremony on Horse Guards Parade. She was deeply moved by the event, especially by three men who were severely wounded.

1870 Actor Leedham Bantock was born. Bantock was the first actor to portray Santa Claus in a moving picture. He was born into a prosperous middle-class family in London and entered the acting profession in his early twenties. He died in poverty in 1928, aged fifty-eight.

19 May

1898 William Gladstone dies
Gladstone had been a constant, if controversial force in national life, a key protagonist in some of the greatest political dramas of the nineteenth century. His life spanned a total of eighty-eight years, over forty years longer than the average life expectancy of the time. In the House of Lords, Prime Minister Lord Salisbury described his former adversary as 'the most distinguished political name in this century'. William Harcourt paid tribute to him as 'not only a great Statesman, but a great Gentleman', while Lord Rosebery focused on his personal kindness. More critical remarks came from other commentators who highlighted his many controversies and contentious policies.

1900 The last Crystal Palace Saturday concert took place. Commencing in 1855, the Crystal Palace hosted a series of Saturday musical concerts throughout the era which grew in national prominence. To cope with its booming popularity, the concerts were expanded across several months, organised and led by the charismatic musical director August Manns. By 1900, however, demand had decreased, and its last performance was held on 19 May.

20 May

1867 John Stuart Mills argues for the extension of the electoral franchise to women
The pursuit of female political enfranchisement was a long and contentious political question which grew with prominence steadily throughout the nineteenth

century. In 1867 the Liberal parliamentarian and philosopher John Stuart Mills proposed an amendment to the 1867 Reform Bill which would admit women into the electoral franchise. 'The exclusion of women,' he argued, 'merely as women is also repugnant to the particular principles of the British Constitution. It violates one of the oldest of our constitutional maxims.' The date also coincided with his sixty-first birthday which he celebrated after the speech. His amendment was unsuccessful and women remained excluded until the twentieth century.

1840 York Minister's nave roof was accidentally destroyed by a fire. A workman had left a candle burning in the south-western tower. The nave roof was soon alight and almost totally destroyed. Fortunately, most of the building remained intact.

1880 The foundation stone of Truro cathedral was laid in Cornwall. The cathedral was designed in the style of Victorian Gothic revival, constructed on the site of the sixteenth-century church of St Mary the Virgin which was demolished in October 1880.

1884 Lady Cynthia Crewe Milnes was born. She was a prominent courtier who devoted much of her life to improving social conditions in East London. The twin daughter of the 1st Marquess of Crewe, in later years she became the 'Woman of the Bedchamber' to Queen Mary. She broke the tragic news of King George VI's death to Mary in 1952.

1899 The Brighton Palace Pier, commonly known as Brighton Pier, was opened. It was the second, and most ambitious, pier designed for the Brighton seafront, built to replace the famous Chain Pier which collapsed in 1896. A new, grander structure was created to survive the excesses of the turbulent English weather and provide a source of entertainment for visitors.

21 May

1873 A fatal accident occurs at the Junior Carlton Club
In 1873 three young men who had been dining at the Junior Carlton Club suffered a terrible misfortune. They had just left the smoking-room at around 11.00pm and were proceeding down the upper staircase, when they suffered a fall. It was alleged that one gentleman, Frank Graham, challenged his friend to jump from the top. Before the other man had accepted, Graham lost his balance, whirled over the banister and fell from a height of sixty feet. He was severely injured with devastating internal injuries. A physician, Dr Prothereo Smith, who was in the club at the time, administered to the victim and moved his body to an apartment for rest. He was given chloroform to ease the pain but died the following morning.

1839 Queen Victoria was formally proclaimed Queen of New Zealand.

22 May

1859 Arthur Conan Doyle born in Edinburgh
Best known for his creation of the popular detective Sherlock Holmes, Arthur Conan Doyle started life in 11 Picardy Place, Edinburgh to Anglo-Irish parents. His mother, Mary Foley, was born in Ireland but his father, Charles Doyle, was English with Irish ancestry. Charles was an alcoholic and the family suffered unremitting periods of instability. When Arthur was just five, he was sent to live with the Scottish educational reformer Mary Burton, who helped disadvantaged and vulnerable children. In 1867 he moved back with his parents but was soon moved on again to a Jesuit independent school in England, financed by his wealthy uncle. Later the following decade Doyle was enrolled in a secondary school in Austria. He finally returned to Britain in 1876 to study medicine at the University of Edinburgh Medical School.

23 May

1851 The MP, Richard Lalor Sheil dies
Sheil was a long-standing Irish MP with a notorious reputation for eccentricity and excitability. Sheil's oratory was unique, colourful and often controversial. His voice was loud, high-pitched and sometimes inaudible due to his false teeth. To the shock of British society, he died suddenly in Italy two months before his sixtieth birthday. The cause of death was listed as gout in the stomach, although many commentators also suspected his highly excitable character was a contributing factor. His funeral, attended by members of the diplomatic court, was held at the magnificent church of San Michele Visdomini in Florence. His body was later returned home to Ireland and buried.

1857 The photographer Signor Caldesi was summoned by Queen Victoria to make a series of photographs of the royal children.

24 May

1899 Queen Victoria's 80th birthday
Victoria was the first queen in British history to celebrate an eightieth birthday. To commemorate the occasion, Walter Parratt, the Master of the Queen's Music, proposed a collection of choral songs, created by thirteen British composers. These included Edward Elgar and Hubert Parry. After breakfast, Victoria was entertained by the Windsor and Eton Amateur Madrigal and Choral Societies, followed by a march-past of 2nd Battalion Scots Guards. A thanksgiving service was later held at St Paul's Cathedral. In the evening, over 200 representatives assembled in the Hotel Cecil for a celebratory dinner. The country would not celebrate a monarch's eightieth birthday again until her great-great granddaughter, Queen Elizabeth II.

1847 On 24 May a fatal railway accident occurred when a carriage carrying passengers to Ruabon in Wales, fell through the Dee bridge into the river. Five people were killed. The incident provoked criticism of the bridge designer, Robert Stephenson.

1877 Lillie Langtry met the Prince of Wales for the first time. The infamous affair between Langtry and the prince was one of high society's best-kept, if most scandalous, royal secrets. The two first met at a dinner party hosted by the explorer Sir Allen Young where the prince took a shine to the twenty-three-year-old beauty. Langtry, who had been married since 1873, also became the mistress of the Earl of Shrewsbury and Prince Louis of Battenberg, creating a tangled web of confusion and scandal. When she became a professional actress in 1881, the prince used his position to promote and advance her career and remained on good terms until his death.

25 May

1850 The first hippopotamus moves to London Zoo
Obaysch was the first hippopotamus in Britain since prehistoric times. Born in 1849, he had been captured near the White Nile River in Africa and donated by the Viceroy of Egypt in return for deerhounds. Obaysch arrived in London on 25 May to wild excitement. His popularity was such that over 10,000 visitors flocked to London Zoo just to see him, with visiting figures doubling in the year 1850 alone. Obaysch became a national celebrity but sadly died in March 1878.

1871 The first Bank Holiday was established in England and Wales. The original concept was proposed by the Liberal MP John Lubbock. The Bank holiday Act meant that all banks would close on certain days of the year, ensuring a brief public holiday for the hardworking folk of Britain.

1878 Gilbert and Sullivan's *HMS Pinafore* was performed for the first time in The Opera Comique, Westminster. The show was such a success that it was revived nine years later to colossal acclaim. It had a profound impact on the development of musical theatre with the song *He is an Englishman* becoming a particular hit with the patriotic Victorian public.

26 May

1867 Princess Mary of Teck born
Mary started life in Kensington Palace. Her mother, Princess Mary Adelaide, was born in Hanover, the youngest daughter of the queen's uncle, Prince Adolphus. Her father, Francis, was four years younger and was not considered wealthy or

distinguished in royal circles. The Tecks were fond of spending money and quickly found themselves burdened by deep dangerous debt. Financial necessity meant the family was eventually uprooted abroad, relocating to the sunnier climes of Florence in 1883 where they lived in hotels and villas. The young Princess Mary gained a significant understanding of Italian history, language, culture and art. When she returned to England in 1885 she was regarded as a highly cultured and well-educated young lady.

1857 The royal family were photographed together at Osborne House. Little did they know that a century later, photography would become a regular, if unwelcome, reality of modern royal life, and a daily normality for working royals. The queen's decision to have the family photographed was historic. It gave a fascinating glimpse into her young family before the bleakness and misery of Prince Albert's death, and also revealed her growing interest in new technology. The public adored the snaps. It led to a considerable upsurge in photographic interest.

1868 The last public execution took place in London on 26 May. Public hanging was formally abolished in Britain a few days later.

1897 Bram Stoker published his highly acclaimed novel, *Dracula*. It depicted a vampire who is eventually hunted down and killed.

27 May

1898 William Gladstone's body lies in state at Westminster Hall
Following Gladstone's death, the government agreed that only a state funeral would be fitting for a statesman of such historic stature. At around 2:50pm on Thursday 26 May, his coffin was carried into Westminster Hall to lie in state. The following morning, hundreds of spectators arrived outside. Ministers, civil servants, peers and paupers intermingled to pay their last respects. By 8.00pm, Gladstone's sons, Herbert and Henry, together with his physician, Dr Bliss, and Mr O'Tier, entered the hall to stand vigil beside the body throughout the night. The imposing government offices which Gladstone had dominated were closed and their curtains drawn. Flags were flown at half-mast across the entire capital.

28 May

1898 William Gladstone's state funeral
The funeral was one of the few occasions that captured much of the Victorian high society together on grainy, black-and-white moving film. To the queen's dismay, the Prince of Wales not only attended the service, but also served as a pallbearer. Furious, she wrote demanding to know the 'precedent' for his decision. Later in the abbey a large statue was installed, suitably positioned next to his arch-rival

Benjamin Disraeli. The two are facing opposite ways, an indication that in death, as in life, the figures remain bitter rivals.

1859 All Saints', Margaret Street was consecrated. It was designed by William Butterfield, a leading Gothic Revival architect, who was closely associated with the Oxford Movement in the Church of England. The church is richly decorated with colourful, dazzling imagery, ornate mosaics and a spectacular painted ceiling.

29 May

1842 Queen Victoria survives an assassination attempt
Victoria and Albert were quietly cruising along the Mall on the morning of 29 May when a young man, armed with a pistol, took a shot at the monarch at terrifyingly close range. Fortunately, the trigger failed and the man vanished into Green Park. The next day, however, he re-appeared. Refusing to be intimidated by the would-be assassin, the royal couple decided once again to travel in an open carriage and show their faces to the cheering spectators. Security guards mingled with the crowd and quickly apprehended the man. His identity was revealed as John Francis, who was later charged with treason, punishable by death. Luckily for him, Victoria commuted his sentence to life imprisonment.

1873 Prince Friedrich, Princess Alice's fifth son, tragically died after suffering from haemophilia. His death at just two years old was a devastating blow to the royal family, and he was greatly mourned in Britain and Germany.

30 May

1884 A co-ordinated terrorist attack hits London in several locations
A co-ordinated attack, orchestrated by the Fenian Brotherhood, brought horror to the streets of London. The first bomb exploded in the evening outside Scotland Yard, headquarters of the Metropolitan Police. A second bomb exploded in the Junior Carlton Club in St James's. A third bomb exploded outside the home of the elderly, illness-stricken Conservative MP, Sir Watkin Williams-Wynn. The windows of the house were completely smashed, leaving thousands of pieces of glass in the street, and damaging nearby buildings. The Junior Army and Navy Club was also badly damaged. A final bomb was located at Trafalgar Square but, thankfully, never exploded. Within minutes, large numbers of police descended into London looking for the culprits.

1891 The Trooping the Colour was postponed due to bad weather. The ceremony took place a few days later but was considerably toned down. For the first time ever, no salute was taken, with neither the queen nor the Prince of Wales attending.

May

31 May

1838 The Battle of Bosenden Wood, the last battle on British soil takes place
The battle was reported to be the last conflict fought on British soil, although this has been disputed. The violence started in rather strange and bizarre circumstances. A detachment of soldiers from the 45th Foot had been deployed to arrest John Tom, a former wine merchant and ex-convict who had been styling himself as Sir William Courtenay and recruiting followers. On 29 May Tom organised a protest of poor agricultural labourers in Kent, agitating the local landowners who feared unrest. Two days later, a local constable called John Mears, accompanied by his brother Nicholas, approached Tom, issuing a warrant for his arrest. In response, Tom shot and killed Nicholas, creating panic throughout the county. Local leaders detached almost 100 soldiers to detain Tom, who escaped to the nearby town of Hernhill. After narrowly avoiding gunshots from some furious gentry, he was eventually cornered in Bossenden Wood. The officer commanding, Lieutenant Henry Bennett, called on Tom to surrender but was fatally shot within minutes. The soldiers then charged the group with bayonets and killed Tom. A local constable was also killed in the crossfire.

1859 Few buildings in Britain are so intrinsically associated with British culture than Charles Barry's masterpiece, St Stephens tower, which was finally completed on 31 May 1859. Less than two months later, the magnificent bell of 'Big Ben' chimed for the first time. Since 1885 the Ayrton light at the top of the tower has indicated whether either house is sitting at night. In the twenty-first century, the building underwent major restoration work and was renamed the Elizabeth tower.

June

1 June

1858-The Great Stink of the River Thames begins
London was not a city paved with gold. Outside Westminster, the grubby roads were clogged with muck, cigarettes, waste and rubbish, made worse in the sweltering summer by sewage and odious foul smells. Many city folk were so disgusted by the 'stink' that they left London altogether and retreated to the countryside. Even Charles Dickens compared the Thames to a sewer rather than an actual river. By 1 June the smell had become so bad that Parliament was forced to close early. Members of Parliament left the gilded rooms with pocket handkerchiefs pressed firmly against their noses. The severity would become so loathsome, it persuaded the government to finally improve public sanitation. Sir Joseph Bazalgette was hired to create a modern sewage system to solve the crisis once and for all.

1840 Prince Albert made his first public speech in Britain. It was hosted by the Society for the Abolition for Slavery, held at the ornate Exeter Hall in the Strand.

2 June

1840 Writer Thomas Hardy born
Much of Hardy's work reflects the disorientation and disillusionment of rapid industrialisation. His novels were situated in the semi-fictional county of Wessex, the name of the ancient Saxon kingdom. It reflected a quaint, pre-Victorian age of quiet rural simplicity, something which many feared was being eroded by the fast onslaught of modernisation. Hardy's birthplace is now preserved by the National Trust.

1857 The composer Edward Elgar was born in Lower Broadheath, a small village in Worcestershire. Elgar composed some of Britain's most popular and patriotic music, notably the *Pomp and Circumstance Marches* and the *Enigma Variations*. Knighted by King Edward VII in 1904, he died in 1934.

1893 Scotland's first black MP, Peter McLagan, resigned his seat. McLagan was the first black MP to represent a Scottish constituency. In the Commons he actively campaigned for women's suffrage and Irish Home Rule.

June

3 June

1865 King George V born in Marlborough House, London
As the second child to the Prince of Wales, his birth was not met with thunderous jubilation that greeted his older brother Prince Albert Victor. Queen Victoria was still wary of the name George, especially after her grandfather George III and her decadent, disreputable uncle King George IV. Fortunately, the young prince proved a sensible and popular member of the family. Never deemed academically gifted for the rigours of further education, George joined the Royal Navy aged twelve, serving until 1892. He became particularly close to his grandmother.

1892 Liverpool Football Club was formed. The club was established partly because of a feud. In the 1890s, the committee of Everton FC and John Houlding, the owner of Anfield football stadium, had a major disagreement over the club's premises and, in 1892, Everton moved to Goodison Park. Houlding decided to form his own club which became Liverpool FC.

4 June

1850 Alfred Lord Tennyson's *In Memoriam* is published
Tennyson had written the poem in memory of his dear friend Arthur Hallam, who died after a stroke, aged twenty-four. The death devastated and tormented Tennyson, plunging him into a long dark period of depression. *In Memoriam* was received with wide acclaim, especially from Queen Victoria who found it deeply poignant in her years of grief.

1888 James Whistler was removed as President of the Society of British Artists. Whistler had been elected president two years earlier but found his new members difficult and increasingly prickly. In 1886 an internal row erupted creating widespread tension. In May nine disgruntled members wrote to Whistler insisting on his resignation. A few weeks later, on 4 June, he was defeated as president in a humiliating by-election. Whistler claimed anti-American prejudice was a major factor in his downfall.

5 June

1861 The opening of the Horticultural Society's New Gardens
Opened in the pouring rain by the wet, shivering Prince of Wales, the grand horticultural show in Kensington was a showcase of modern gardening designs, choreographed with intense skill. Numerous politicians, peers and public figures were invited but several declined due to the bad weather. The paths were drenched in puddles and the pristine lawns waterlogged. Whereas, in previous centuries, gardening was often considered the pursuit of the very rich, by the mid-nineteenth

century middle-class enthusiasm had grown immensely. Gardening fashions were no longer dictated by the aristocracy or the wealthy, but ordinary middle-class families who shunned the traditional formal style in favour of quaint cottage gardens. This theme was very much reflected at the show.

1851 The Arsenic Act 1851 was passed. By the 1840s there was rising concern about the use of arsenic, which was killing hundreds through accidental or, sometimes, intentional poisoning. The toxic substance was frequently used for agricultural products but was easily accessible for the general public. In 1851 it was made a legal requirement to maintain a written record of customers who had purchased arsenic.

6 June

1844 The Young Men's Christian Association (YMCA) is formed
The YMCA was the result of the philanthropist George Williams, who wanted young people to thrive and excel in their communities. In 1844 he established the organisation to provide a spiritual education and steer folk away from the dangers of alcohol and gambling. The boys would pray together regularly and read the Bible. Sport also played a major role, giving some children their first encounter with swimming-pools and other facilities. Williams is the 3x great-grandfather of politician Boris Johnson.

1841 The 1841 Census took place. It was the earliest census that has survived in its entirety in England and Wales.

1896 The longest-lived man in British history, Henry Allingham, was born in London. In the First World War Allingham served in the Royal Air Force. For one month, he was certified as the oldest living man in the world, dying in July 2009, aged 111.

7 June

1881 Britain's first socialist political party, the Social Democratic Federation, is founded in London
Henry Mayers Hyndman established the federation for the sole purpose of initiating radical economic and social change. The party was not successful and was later overshadowed by the Independent Labour Party, founded by Keir Hardie. The growth of socialism arguably reflected a changing mood in British politics throughout the Victorian era which would have profound consequences for the twentieth century.

1880 *A Doll's House* by Henrik Ibsen was performed at the Novelty Theatre in London. The play explored the controversial themes of marital breakdown, blackmail and Victorian womanhood.

1. King William IV. (Courtesy of the Wellcome Collection. This work is licensed under a Creative Commons Public Domain Mark 1.0 Licence. King William IV holding a scroll of the Magna Carta in his right hand. Mezzotint by D. Lucas after R. Bowyer, 1830. Public Domain)

2. Queen Victoria. (Courtesy of the Wellcome Collection. This work is licensed under a Creative Commons Public Domain Mark 1.0 Licence. Queen Victoria. Photograph. Public Domain)

3. Prince Albert. (Courtesy of the Wellcome Collection. This work is licensed under a Creative Commons Public Domain Mark 1.0 Licence. HRH Albert, Prince Consort. Photograph. Public Domain)

4. The Prince of Wales. (Courtesy of the Wellcome Collection. This work is licensed under a Creative Commons Public Domain Mark 1.0 Licence. Albert Edward, HRH the Prince of Wales. Photograph by G. Jerrard, 1881. Public Domain)

Right: **5.** Isambard Kingdom Brunel. (Courtesy of The Metropolitan Museum of Art, New York. Public Domain. Gilman Collection, Purchase, Harriette and Noel Levine Gift, 2005. Public Domain)

Below: **6.** The Great Exhibition. (Courtesy of the Wellcome Collection. This work is licensed under a Creative Commons Public Domain Mark 1.0 Licence. The Great Exhibition in the Crystal Palace, Hyde Park, London: the transept looking north. Steel engraving by W. Lacey after J.E. Mayall, 1851. Public Domain)

7. The London Slums. (Courtesy of the Wellcome Collection. This work is licensed under a Creative Commons Public Domain Mark 1.0 Licence. London Slums. Public Domain)

8. Trafalgar Square. (Courtesy of The Metropolitan Museum of Art, New York. Public Domain. Anonymous Gift and Purchase, Alfred Stieglitz Society Gifts; 2004 Benefit Fund; W. Bruce and Delaney H. Lundberg Gift; The Horace W. Goldsmith Foundation Fund, through Joyce and Robert Menschel; Susan and Thomas Dunn and Constance and Leonard Goodman Gifts, 2009. Public Domain)

9. The Steam Train. (Courtesy of Pixabay Licence. Public Domain)

10. The underground railway. (Courtesy of the Wellcome Collection. This work is licensed under a Creative Commons Public Domain Mark 1.0 Licence. A trial journey on the first part of the underground railway in London. Wood engraving, 1862. Public Domain)

11. The Crimean War. (Courtesy of the Wellcome Collection. This work is licensed under a Creative Commons Public Domain Mark 1.0 Licence. Crimean War: Florence Nightingale going around the wards at Scutari Hospital. Wood engraving. Public Domain)

12. Queen Victoria visiting the wards. (Courtesy of the Wellcome Collection. This work is licensed under a Creative Commons Public Domain Mark 1.0 Licence. Queen Victoria visiting soldiers wounded in the Crimean War. Mezzotint by T.O. Barlow, 1859, after Jerry Barrett. Public Domain)

13. Queen Victoria in mourning. (Courtesy of the Wellcome Collection. This work is licensed under a Creative Commons Public Domain Mark 1.0 Licence. Queen Victoria in mourning for Albert, her subjects outraged at her neglect of duties. Wood engraving, c. 1861. Public Domain)

14. Prince Albert's funeral. (Courtesy of the Wellcome Collection. This work is licensed under a Creative Commons Public Domain Mark 1.0 Licence. The funeral of Albert Prince Consort, in St George's Chapel, Windsor. Wood engraving, 1861. Public Domain)

GLADSTONE'S TRIUMPHANT DANCE.
1880.

Above: **15.** Brighton Pier. (Courtesy of The Metropolitan Museum of Art, New York. Public Domain. The Elisha Whittlesey Collection, The Elisha Whittlesey Fund, 1972. Public Domain)

Left: **16.** Gladstone. (Courtesy of the Wellcome Collection. This work is licensed under a Creative Commons Public Domain Mark 1.0 Licence. Gladstone dancing with Lord Rosebery, who is wearing a kilt and a crown, celebrating the Liberal victory in the British General Election of 1880. Engraving, 1880. Public Domain)

17. The Open Fire. (Courtesy of the Wellcome Collection. This work is licensed under a Creative Commons Public Domain Mark 1.0 Licence. Queen Victoria, seated in an armchair by an open fire, day-dreaming about illustrious men of her reign. Colour lithograph by Tom Merry, 1887. Public Domain)

18. Charles Dickens. (Wikimedia Commons Public Domain Mark. Heritage Auction Gallery. Public Domain)

Left: **19.** Oliver Twist. (Courtesy of the Wellcome Collection. This work is licensed under a Creative Commons Public Domain Mark 1.0 Licence. Oliver Twist, holding a bowl and a spoon, asks for more food, while other children and a woman look surprised. Etching by George Cruikshank. Public Domain)

Below: **20.** British inventors. (Courtesy of the Wellcome Collection. This work is licensed under a Creative Commons Public Domain Mark 1.0 Licence. British inventors, politicians and military men, gathered in a room at Buckingham Palace. Engraving by C.G. Lewis, 1863, after T.J. Barker. Public Domain)

21. Charles Darwin. (Courtesy of the Wellcome Collection. This work is licensed under a Creative Commons Public Domain Mark 1.0 Licence. Charles Robert Darwin. Pen and ink drawing. Public Domain)

22. Alfred Tennyson. (Courtesy of the Wellcome Collection. This work is licensed under a Creative Commons Public Domain Mark 1.0 Licence. Alfred, Lord Tennyson. Photograph by Elliott & Fry. Public Domain)

Left: **23.** Anthony Trollope. (Courtesy of the Wellcome Collection. This work is licensed under a Creative Commons Public Domain Mark 1.0 Licence. Anthony Trollope. Photograph by Elliott & Fry. Public Domain)

Below: **24.** The National History Museum. (Courtesy of Pixabay License. Public Domain)

25. Tower Bridge. (Courtesy of Pixabay Licence. Public Domain)

26. The Royal Family. (Courtesy of the Wellcome Collection. This work is licensed under a Creative Commons Public Domain Mark 1.0 Licence. The Duke of Wellington is presenting a birthday casket to his godson Prince Arthur (later Duke of Connaught) in the presence of Queen Victoria and Prince Albert. Mezzotint by S. Cousins after F.X. Winterhalter, 1 May 1851. Public Domain)

Above: **27.** Wellington's Funeral. (Courtesy of the Wellcome Collection. This work is licensed under a Creative Commons Public Domain Mark 1.0 Licence. The funeral carriage of the Duke of Wellington. Wood engraving, 1852. Public Domain)

Left: **28.** Mr Gladstone. (Courtesy of the Wellcome Collection. This work is licensed under a Creative Commons Public Domain Mark 1.0 Licence. W.E. Gladstone represented as Samson destroying the pillars of the British Constitution by abolition of the House of Lords. Colour lithograph by Tom Merry, 24 October 1891. Public Domain)

Above: **29.** Gladstone's funeral. (Courtesy of the Wellcome Collection. This work is licensed under a Creative Commons Public Domain Mark 1.0 Licence. The coffin of W.E. Gladstone lying in state, attended by five men praying. Drawing by G.B. Scott after A. Kemp Tebby, 1898. Public Domain)

Right: **30.** Elizabeth Garrett Anderson. (Courtesy of the Wellcome Collection. This work is licensed under a Creative Commons Public Domain Mark 1.0 Licence. Elizabeth Garrett Anderson. Wood engraving. Public Domain)

31. London. (Courtesy of The Metropolitan Museum of Art, New York. Public Domain. Gift of Weston J. Naef, in memory of Kathleen W. Naef and Weston J. Naef Sr., 1982)

32. The Victoria Memorial. (Courtesy of Pixabay Licence. Public Domain)

June

8 June

1863 The politician John Archer is born in Liverpool
The son of a ship steward from Barbados, Archer was the second black mayor in British history. He defied racism, abuse and condemnation to become one of London's most respected and best-loved civic leaders. Following his mayoral career, he also became a highly successful political agent to the suffragette Charlotte Despard and the communist campaigner Shapurji Saklatvala. Despite the ferocity of criticism levelled against him, Archer refused to stoop to the low level of his critics. By the time of his death, he was a much respected political figure.

1849 A production of *Don Juan* performed by the German Opera Company opened at Drury Lane.

1889 The poet Gerard Manley Hopkins died aged forty-four. He would later achieve great posthumous acclaim.

9 June

1885 An Unexpected Summons
On 9 June, Salisbury was in his laboratory. A haven from the hideousness of political life, Hatfield was like a refuge in the summer, an oasis of tradition in the desert of democracy and a place to recharge the batteries in a rapidly confusing world. Outside, Salisbury could relax to the calming sight of the tranquil English countryside, acres upon acres of lush green fields, organised into small, neat squares and separated by high-growing hawthorn hedges. The house was airy and cool. The large Jacobean windows had been opened, breathing fresh air into the tired, dusty rooms. The gardens sparkled with life and laughter, echoed by the distant noise of a soft summer wind whistling through the air and the occasional buzz of bees.

His peace would soon be broken. Shortly after 1.00pm, a manservant clutching a telegram arrived. It was a summons from Buckingham Palace. Gladstone had resigned. The government had collapsed. Salisbury was to go immediately to London for a private meeting with the queen.

Unfortunately for Salisbury, the situation was bleak. The Liberals still remained the largest party in the Commons, making it almost impossible to achieve anything meaningful against a large Liberal majority. Arriving at Buckingham Palace later that day, Salisbury told the queen to persuade Gladstone 'to reconsider his resignation' and return. Gladstone refused. Eventually, Salisbury accepted the post as prime minister on 23 June, but only led a short government which collapsed the following year.

1865 At 3.13pm, a derailment at Staplehurst railway station, resulted in the deaths of ten passengers. Engineering work had caused a piece of track to be removed, creating a sudden and unexpected accident as the train passed over a viaduct.

Charles Dickens was among the injured. His son later claimed the accident considerably shortened his father's life. He died exactly five years to the day.

1870 Writer Charles Dickens died. No writer defined an era better than Dickens. His untimely death at just fifty-eight was mourned as a national tragedy, an immense artistic, cultural loss which could never be replaced. The writer's health had declined significantly over many years, made worse by overwork and stress. On 8 June he complained of a severe and vicious toothache. While dining with his sister-in-law the following day, he appeared notably ill and suddenly collapsed with a stroke. He died at 6.10pm.

1896 Elizabeth Garrett Anderson celebrated her sixtieth Birthday. The trail-blazing doctor was the first woman elected to a school board in British history, the first woman mayor in British history and the first dean of a medical school in British history. Her character and determination helped thousands of women to enter the medical profession.

10 June

1840 Edward Oxford attempts to murder Queen Victoria
Victoria and Albert left the secure gates of Buckingham Palace for their usual drive through Hyde Park. It was a pleasant day. The temperature was mild and warm and the crowds were characteristically cheery. Suddenly, a loud bang rang out across the park. 'Saw a little man on the footpath,' the queen recalled, 'I saw him aim at me with another pistol. I ducked my head and another shot, equally loud followed.' The man was quickly overpowered by security who dragged him forcibly to the ground. Remaining calm, Albert ordered the carriage to proceed, and they briskly departed to the Duchess of Kent's house.

Meanwhile, back at Constitutional Hill, word had broken that the queen had narrowly avoided death. Crowds looking for news descended upon the Mall; several false rumours circulated that Victoria had been hurt. As the royal party exited the Duchess's house an hour later, they were greeted by a tsunami of cheering support.

The incident was the first attempt on the queen's life and horrified royal security. Upon returning to the palace, Victoria was met by an emotional Lord Melbourne who left the meeting in tears. The would-be assassin was identified as Edward Oxford, a young lad from Birmingham whose property was promptly raided. Inside, police discovered a locked box with two pistols, a sword and lead balls. Charged with treason, Oxford escaped the death penalty on grounds of insanity after a long trial.

1854 The new Crystal Palace was opened in South London. No building seemed to epitomise the age better than the Crystal Palace. It resembled the visionary spirit of the Victorians, an era of unprecedented architectural and artistic innovation. Having been demolished in Hyde Park, the new palace was erected near Sydenham and was followed by a lavish railway station. The new location proved equally popular with tourists. Unfortunately, it burned down in 1936.

June

11 June

1879 British government launch a competition to design a piece of furniture for the American President
The desk was presented as a gift to President Rutherford B. Hayes by Queen Victoria as a goodwill gesture between both nations. Constructed from the oak timbers of a large exploration ship, it was carefully built by the masterful hand of joiner, William Evenden. The desk proved very popular with the American government. It was later moved to the Oval Office of the White House, where it remains today.

1884 The future prelate of the Catholic Church in England and Wales, Francis Bourne was ordained a priest in St Mary's, Clapham.

1896 A statue of Earl Granville was unveiled by Earl Kimberley in the Central Hall at Westminster.

12 June

1859 Lord Palmerston forms his second government
Having previously and unsuccessfully asked Earl Granville to form a government, the begrudging queen called on Lord Palmerston, the colourful Liberal peer, whom she regarded with utmost mistrust. The government was hugely consequential and controversial, both in domestic and foreign policy, but was dominated by increasing political differences with Palmerston and his chancellor, William Gladstone.

1844 John Sainsbury, founder of Sainsbury's supermarket chain, was born in Lambeth.

1858 Charles Dickens published a short note in the *Household Works*, denying allegations of marital separation from his wife. In reality, the marriage was in great crisis, so great that Dickens eventually split his house into two.

1897 Prime Minister Anthony Eden was born in Durham. His father, Sir William, was an eccentric, tough-talking landowner and dazzling watercolourist with a prodigious talent for art. His mother, Sybil Grey, had initially yearned to marry the royal courtier Francis Knolly but was deterred by the Prince of Wales.

13 June

1842 Queen Victoria becomes the first British monarch to travel by train
Victoria was the first British monarch to travel by train in a short trip from Slough to London's Paddington Station. She was deeply impressed by the new transport

and would later purchase a train of her own. Albert, however, was more dubious, arguing that the speed was dangerously fast and unrestrained.

1890 David Lloyd George delivered his maiden speech to the Commons. His address warned against the dangers of alcohol consumption, a reflection on the increasing popularity of the temperance movement, which gained traction throughout the latter nineteenth century. Lloyd George remained in the constituency until his death in 1945.

14 June

1900 Catherine Gladstone, wife of William Gladstone, dies
Although Mrs Gladstone never exercised personal political power, her influence and popularity was undeniable. An intelligent and tenacious figure, Gladstone could grasp any intellectual discussion within seconds and could soothe tension like a 'breath of fresh air'. After her husband's death in 1897, her own health declined. Upon hearing news of her imminent demise, servants at Hawarden were called into the bedroom to bid their last goodbyes. Family members followed afterwards, and she died peacefully at 5.40pm. She was granted the unusual honour of having her funeral at Westminster Abbey.

1877 Social reformer Mary Carpenter dies. Carpenter formed several ragged schools across Bristol for the poorest children. A powerful anti-slavery campaigner, she also made several trips to Asia, Europe and North America and became the first woman to have a paper published by the Statistical Society of London.

15 June

1888 Queen Victoria's son-in-law, Frederick III, the German Emperor, dies of cancer
The emperor had been severely ill for some time. He had watched his father's magnificent funeral from the window of the Charlottenburg Palace, weeping as the mournful cortege passed slowly through the densely-packed streets of Berlin. His illness was terminal, and his suffering was immense. By April, his condition had deteriorated so badly that he could no longer walk. After months of terrible pain, the emperor died at 11.30am on Friday 15 June at the age of fifty-six.

Back in London, the news was met with almost overwhelming sorrow. Business was suspended on the Liverpool, Manchester and Glasgow exchanges. In London, the bells of Westminster Abbey tolled throughout the afternoon and several mourners queued to sign condolence books. His death would have a particularly profound effect on Germany. His successor, Wilhelm II, would strike a very different tone, pursuing a notably more illiberal and rigidly conservative agenda that would spell trouble for both nations.

1850 On 15 June, Dickens published an attack on John Everett Millais's *Christ in the House of His parents*. The painting was immensely controversial and shocked society for its depiction of a youthful, ginger-haired Jesus helping his father in a conventionally untidy workshop, with dirt and detritus littering the floor. While most Victorian paintings depicted the Holy Family in a serene and peaceful light, the messy, realistic image provoked anger amongst critics, including Dickens, who compared it to a gin shop. Several argued it lacked the dignity of a religious painting. It soon proved so controversial that it was removed from the Royal Academy and transported to Windsor Castle for the queen to have a private viewing.

1877 President Ulysses S Grant of the United States was awarded the Freedom of the City of London.

16 June

1852 The Royal Family purchase Balmoral Castle in Scotland
Victoria and Albert played a major role in transforming Scotland into a popular tourist destination, overturning decades of historic criticism. The widespread misconception that Scotland was a savage, rugged and inhospitable region no longer seemed plausible. If the monarch could holiday in Scotland, then so could you. The queen loved Scotland so deeply that, in 1852, she purchased a gorgeous rural retreat called Balmoral Castle which remained a firm favourite for her entire life. Victoria was also a talented watercolourist and would frequently bring her canvases to relax in the beautiful hills.

1858 John Snow died in London. Snow was the first physician in England to establish clear links between cholera and dirty water. For years however his theory was discarded by the medical elite, including Edwin Chadwick who argued miasma, also known as 'bad air', was the central cause. In 1854 Snow personally investigated a heavily afflicted area in central London. With forensic detail, he plotted each fatality on a large map to prove that nearly all the victims lived in close proximity to a contaminated water pump. After years of overwork, Snow died of a stroke aged forty-five.

17 June

1876 Joseph Chamberlain is elected a Member of Parliament
Entering the Gothic palace of Westminster for the first time, Chamberlain represented what Herbert Asquith called 'new men, new ideas – as some thought – new era'. Chamberlain's path to power had not been easy. Critics labelled him an 'extremist', a liar and an atheist. Only a few years earlier, his anti-monarchist opinions had provoked such fury that one lady even threw dead cats in his face

when speaking on a public platform. However, despite his provocative reputation, his influence was undeniable and his legacy left a long and dominant shadow over British politics that endured into the next century.

1869 Lord Derby, who had been suffering from gout and other ailments, made his last speech to the Lords, arguably foreshadowing his forthcoming death: 'I am now an old man ... My official life is entirely closed; my political life is nearly so; and, in the course of nature, my natural life cannot now be long.'

1898 Harry Patch, Britain's last surviving soldier of the First World War and, briefly, the oldest man in Europe was born in Somerset.

18 June

1842 *Ulysses***, a poem by Alfred, Lord Tennyson is published**
Tennyson published *Ulysses* almost ten years after writing it. The poem takes the form of a dramatic monologue, spoken by the mythical character expressing his disillusionment upon returning to his kingdom after extensive travels. Tennyson later also published two other poems on 18 June, *Maud*, released in 1855, and *Idylls of the King*, the following year.

1845 The Duke of Wellington hosted his annual Waterloo Banquet at Apsley House. To mark thirty years since the battle, a large and impressive painting was commissioned by the artist John Prescott Knight. It was published in October, titled *The Waterloo Heroes Assembled at Apsley House*. The painting now hangs in the British embassy in Paris.

19 June

1849 Another assassination attempt on Queen Victoria
On the evening of 19 June, the queen, with three of her children, survived yet another attempt on her life. William Hamilton was an unemployed twenty-four-year-old bricklayer from Ireland and had arrived in London with the intention of shooting the queen. As the monarch's carriage passed Constitution Hill to Buckingham Palace, Hamilton fired a direct shot in her direction. Like the several attempts before, the bullet missed and the shooter was soon arrested. Hamilton pleaded guilty, although claimed he had only organised the murder in order to be sent to prison where he would receive regular meals. He was exiled to Gibraltar for seven years but later returned.

1899 Edward Elgar's *Enigma Variations* was performed for the first time. Elgar's composition became closely associated with British state occasions, especially *Variation IX*, better known as *Nimrod*.

20 June

1837 Queen Victoria ascends the throne
Tuesday, 20 June. The sun had not yet risen when a sombre carriage clattered into the courtyard of Kensington Palace, carrying two gentlemen, the Archbishop of Canterbury and the Lord Chamberlain, Francis Conyngham. Victoria, still unaware of the momentous event, was quietly sleeping in her bedchamber when she was suddenly awoken by a maid and ordered to get up. Still in her dressing gown, she proceeded downstairs, alone, confused, disorientated. As she entered the room, both men dropped to their knees in veneration. The king was dead. Long live the queen.

'Since it has pleased Providence,' she later wrote, 'to place me in this station, I shall do my utmost to fulfil my duty.' The king had been ill for some time, but his unexpected death still aroused shock and astonishment. At 9.00am, Lord Melbourne arrived for his first prime ministerial meeting ahead of her accession declaration. A few hours later, the new queen, accompanied by Melbourne, and her uncles, the dukes of Sussex and Cumberland, greeted the Privy Council for the first time.

At just eighteen, many worried that Victoria was simply too young for the demanding life that lay ahead. In the days following her accession, fears over her inexperience were no more vividly expressed than in parliament, with the Liberal peer Earl Russell remarking pessimistically that it was 'awful' for a girl of just eighteen to inherit such a solemn and serious responsibility. Little did people know that 22 June 1837 would begin one of the longest, most consequential and tumultuous periods in British history.

1887 The National Liberal Club, designed by Alfred Waterhouse, was opened in Whitehall. The foundation stone had been laid by William Gladstone in 1884, but it was opened early in 1887 for the Golden Jubilee. In the lobby, four stained-glass windows were installed above the porter's desk, depicting the four major Liberal leaders of the late nineteenth century, Gladstone, Harcourt, Rosebery and Campbell Bannerman. The club also boasted one of the grandest libraries in London. It remains an exuberant example of fine Victorian architecture, if not one of the greatest buildings in London.

1897 Queen Victoria celebrated her Diamond Jubilee. No British monarch had ever reached such a milestone. Unlike the Golden Jubilee in 1887, the occasion was deemed so significant that a great national celebration was required, accumulating in a glittering thanksgiving service at St Paul's Cathedral. Along the route from Buckingham Palace, large platforms had been erected for residents to get a good view of the majestic military procession. In some places, spectators even risked their lives climbing onto roofs and chimneys to get a glimpse. Unfortunately, by the late 1890s, the queen was suffering from painful arthritis and so initial plans were changed to allow the service to be conducted outside, ensuring she could remain seated in an open carriage. In parliament the following afternoon, tributes were paid by both houses, with stirring words echoed across the political spectrum.

'You will seldom find comprised within the compass of two generations,' remarked Arthur Balfour, 'so many great industrial, scientific, and literary changes ... since Her Majesty ascended the Throne.' Victoria was deeply touched by the show of emotion and pageantry, although, despite the imperial pomp, the jubilee would understandably become a source of inevitable nostalgia. Less than four years later, the queen would be dead. The colour, grandeur and glitter of the Victorian occasion would be washed away by the harsh industrial drumbeats of the First World War.

21 June

1870 Dulwich College's 'New' buildings opened by the Prince of Wales
The new buildings were designed by Charles Barry junior, son of the lamented architect Sir Charles Barry. With a healthy budget and a free artistic hand, Barry opted for an extravagant, extraordinary hybrid style of Palladian and gothic features, built with striking red bricks. Upon completion, Dulwich College was one of the most elegant and exuberant buildings in south London. Perhaps the most prominent feature was the Great Hall, decorated with a huge hammerbeam roof and barrel vault, modelled on the imposing Westminster Hall, a venue Barry visited regularly when his father was constructing the new Houses of Parliament. Barry gained the inspiration for the central lantern and half-wagon wheels from a church in Vicenza, Italy. He later claimed the building was an illustration of a style he coined 'North Italian of the thirteenth century'. To many, the college was simply revolutionary.

1898 David Fenwick, the engine driver of the Royal Train, was killed. Fenwick had climbed onto the coal tender of the royal train to fix a communication cord which had been struck by a bridge near Cove station. Tragically, he was killed instantly. A tombstone was later erected by the queen.

22 June

1895 Lord Rosebery resigns as prime minister after one year
By 1895 the Liberal government had collapsed. The Conservative opposition, eager to exploit worsening tensions within the Liberal Party, tabled a motion on 21 June to reduce the Secretary of State for War's salary by £100. It was a direct response to his alleged mishandling of cordite supplies to the army. For Rosebery, the motion was treated as a no-confidence vote against his leadership and he resigned the next day. Victoria, who had always adored Rosebery, argued he had been shamefully attacked and treated shabbily by his own cabinet. He was replaced by Lord Salisbury.

1850 The Queen's son, Prince Arthur, was baptised. He was named in honour of his venerable godfather, the Duke of Wellington, who, despite ailing health, insisted on attending the ceremony. Unlike his brothers, the christening was a relatively low key affair, hosted in the small private chapel of Buckingham palace.

23 June

1894 Birth of King Edward VIII
Perhaps foreshadowing his rebellious character, Edward was the first eldest grandchild of Victoria to break a long family tradition. It had been customary since 1841 to name the eldest son Albert in memory of the queen's lamented husband. Instead, the Duke of York decided on Edward, chosen out of respect for his deceased brother, Prince Albert Victor, commonly known as 'Eddy'. The queen accepted the decision, although reminded the young couple that Eddy's real name was in fact 'Albert'. Ironically, to make matters even more confusing, Edward was later known as David.

1887 Abdul Karim served the queen for the first time. During the last decade of Victoria's life, her close friendship with a young Indian servant called Abdul Karim ignited such serious controversy that people began questioning her mental stability. Many regarded the relationship as inappropriate, made worse by deep racial prejudice. Karim taught Victoria about India, Indian culture and even a few words of Hindustani and Urdu. Their fondness for each grew so rapidly, Victoria insisted on his presence throughout her excursions. In September 1889 the two stayed overnight at a small house near Loch Muick in Scotland. When Karim became ill the following year he was operated on by the queen's personal physician. The closeness unsurprisingly created jealousy and suspicion within the court. Courtiers tried to uncover smears and allegations on Karim's past, and even began circulating untrue rumours of corruption and scandal. The queen refused to dismiss him and grew angry at the court's hostility. After her death in 1901, Karim was subsequently sacked by the new king. He retired to India and where he died in 1909.

1898 Westminster Abbey paid homage to the artist Sir Edward Coley Burne-Jones. He was the first artist honoured with a memorial service held at Westminster Abbey, organised chiefly by the Prince of Wales. Burne-Jones was closely associated with the Pre-Raphaelite movement, famous for reviving popular and artistic interest in mediaeval stained-glass art. He was also the uncle of future prime minister Stanley Baldwin, who later opened the Burne-Jones centenary exhibition at Tate Britain.

June 24

1850 Lord Kitchener born in Ireland
Kitchener's famous poster remains an enduring image of the First World War. He was an icon, a national celebrity, hailed in some quarters as a military genius, despised in others as a harsh and brutal commander. Horatio Kitchener started

life in Ireland, raised in an austere environment by his strict, disciplinarian father who was rumoured to sleep in newspaper sheets. After his mother contracted tuberculosis, the family were uprooted to Switzerland where he was educated at Montreux. In the 1870s he relocated to England to train at the Royal Military Academy Woolwich, and then served as a volunteer in a French ambulance unit during the Franco-Prussian War. His reputation as a major military figure didn't really begin until after the Sudanese campaign. When he returned home from war in October 1898, he was greeted by a special train and a huge welcome party. His face was printed on cups, saucers, memorabilia and even biscuit tins. His controversial fame would increase throughout the twentieth century.

1851- Window Tax in Britain was abolished. The tax was infamously unpopular in England, with some families even bricking up their windows to avoid paying. The abolishment was met with approval.

25 June

1872- Lord Dufferin appointed the Governor General of Canada
Dufferin was a popular choice for governor, distinguished for his quick-witted conversations and smooth-talking charm. One favourite story he enjoyed recounting was a tale of a terrifying ghost who saved his life in Paris. One dark gloomy night in 1849, Dufferin claimed to have heard a hearse arrive outside his house in Ireland. He looked out of the window to see a man carrying a large wooden coffin on his back. The man stopped and, for a brief moment, locked eyes with Dufferin until disappearing into the mist. The following morning a woman informed him that the apparition was indeed a ghost and he would soon be dead. Several years after becoming British ambassador to France, Dufferin was about to enter a lift at the Grand Hotel in Paris but stopped. Immediately, his eyes recognised the mysterious man he saw in Ireland. Suddenly the lift crashed. All inside were killed. The Victorians, who loved a good ghost story, found the tale fascinating.

26 June

1892 William Gladstone struck in the eye while campaigning
While out campaigning during the 1892 election, an elderly lady chucked a gingerbread directly into Gladstone's face, striking him on his left eye. Gladstone made a quick witty reply but was quite evidently hurt and taken to a nearby tent for medical assistance. The attack did the party no harm. They won the election with resounding success, although Gladstone's worsening eyesight certainly was not improved.

1884 The Reform Act was passed in the Commons. The 1867 Reform Act had granted the vote to men in urban areas but had excluded those in agricultural communities. In 1884 Gladstone pushed for a new reform act that would widen the political franchise even further. The proposed bill faced bitter opposition in the House of Lords. In a private letter, the Tory peer Lord Salisbury, vowed the changes would mean the effective destruction of the Conservative Party. He need not have worried. Just two years later the Tories returned to government with an enormous majority of 393 seats.

27 June

1850 Queen Victoria assaulted by an ex-Army officer
The day had not started well. In the morning Victoria was informed that her uncle, Prince Adolphus, was terminally ill and seemed on the brink of death. Later that evening she visited him for an emotional and distressing encounter at his residence, Cambridge House. As she exited the property, a young man suddenly approached her. Without warning, he hit her violently on the forehead with his cane, creating intense panic. He was quickly arrested and taken to a nearby station for questioning. The queen meanwhile was badly hurt, yet insisted on attending the Opera as planned the same evening.

The attack was another example of the apparent failings of royal security, something which was severely criticised in the press. The assault was labelled monstrous and cowardly although many remarked privately, just how lucky the queen was to survive relatively unhurt. The man responsible was identified as a former military officer called Robert Pate. He was tried at the Central Criminal Court and sentenced to seven years' penal transportation to Tasmania.

1870 Normal political hostilities were briefly put aside on 27 June as news emerged that the Foreign Secretary, Lord Clarendon, had died suddenly. A workaholic to the bitter end, it was rumoured that he died surrounded by his papers and ministerial boxes in his office.

1870 The mortal remains of Charles Dickens were buried in Westminster Abbey.

28 June

1838 Coronation of Queen Victoria
Victoria was awoken early by the sounds of guns in St James's Park and the distant murmur of excited townsfolk arriving early for the day's event. It was a warm morning, perfect conditions for the 40,000 visitors who flocked into London from the railways, turning Westminster into a sea of euphoric spectators. Not unusually for the time, there was surprisingly little rehearsal before the coronation, creating a feeling of anxiety that persisted throughout the day. The service was so badly organised that some labelled it chaotic, offensive and even barbaric. The coronation ring was forcibly placed onto the wrong finger, and a bishop even declared the

ceremony over, hours before the end. To make matters worse, an aristocrat called Lord Rolle also suffered a fall and was badly hurt. Even the music itself was mired with controversy and attacked for its seemingly unimaginative material. Despite this, the coronation was hailed as a success in the national press. After the ceremony, the royal party was greeted with a celebratory lunch and many of the morning's mistakes were forgotten. It was fortunate that television hadn't been invented.

1843 The wedding of Princess Augusta of Cambridge on 28 June was overshadowed by the unfortunate tale of Ernest Augustus, the recently proclaimed King of Hanover who was intensely unpopular in Britain. Victoria regarded Ernest as a blabbermouth. Albert loathed him, especially for his reactionary conservative views. For many years, he had been the centre of a wild rumour that he was scheming to steal the British throne and murder Victoria.

The queen arrived at the chapel feeling ill and fatigued, having just recovered from influenza. Once inside, Ernest insisted on a superior place to Albert, arguing that, as a king, he was hierarchically more important than a mere prince. Albert settled the dispute with what he later described as a 'strong push'. After the ceremony, Ernest invited Albert for a walk in St James Park, but Albert politely declined. As the husband of the queen, Albert argued he would be flocked by crowds and onlookers, to which Ernest replied with snide remark, commenting on Albert's perceived unpopularity. The backhanded comment did much to sour relations. Ernest also managed to annoy Victoria by insisting that her jewellery was his property. Much to their private satisfaction, shortly after the wedding reception ended, Ernest fell and injured himself at Kew Palace.

1887 On the pleasantly mild evening of 28 June a seamstress called Elizabeth Cass was walking quietly along Regents Street. She had originally intended to visit an upmarket silk retailer called Jays Shop which, since the Golden Jubilee, had attracted enormous popular attention after receiving a royal warrant. Unfortunately, Cass was to be disappointed. The store was closed, and she began walking back home. Passing through the crowds in Oxford Street, she was suddenly approached by a large policeman called Constable Endacott. Placing his hand firmly on her shoulder, he calmly informed her she was under arrest. The charge was prostitution.

The incident provoked enormous controversy which spilled out into a long and much publicised legal campaign. Cass's employer, Mrs Bowman, was called to testify and declared she had been falsely arrested on inaccurate charges. Cass was acquitted but was given a stern, patronising warning by the magistrate. In the following days Bowman complained about the case. On 1 July the incident was raised in the House of Commons by the Liberal MP Llewellyn Atherley-Jones, who pushed for an official inquiry. Endacott was subsequently suspended from the police. A few days later, an inquiry was opened by the Lord Chancellor, Hardinge Giffard. Endacott was accused, but acquitted, of perjury. To some commentators, it revealed the unjust prejudicial nature of Victorian society, subjecting an innocent woman to intense and public humiliation on the basis of no evidence.

29 June

1895 Arthur Balfour appointed Leader of the House of Commons
Balfour was the nephew of the Prime Minister, Lord Salisbury, which made his appointment intensely contentious. The alleged nepotism gave rise to the popular term 'Bob's your Uncle'. Salisbury had long been criticised for appointing relatives and chums to top jobs, with nearly two-fifths of Tory MPs hailing from aristocratic backgrounds. Ironically, when Salisbury finally resigned in July 1902, the keys of power were passed once again to Arthur Balfour, who had even been living at Number 10 for several months.

1871 Trade Unions were given legal status in Britain after the passage of the Trade Union Act. Several new unions would emerge throughout the decade to protect workers' rights.

1893 The Shaftesbury Memorial Fountain was opened in London.

30 June

1860 The famous Oxford evolution debate takes place
The nineteenth century was dominated by seismic intellectual and scientific questioning, none more profoundly divisive than Charles Darwin's theory of evolution. The historic debate was fought between Thomas Huxley, a biologist known as 'Darwin's bulldog', and Bishop Samuel Wilberforce, who argued against evolution. Many other participants also contributed but it was Huxley and Wilberforce who attracted the most national attention. At one stage, the debate became taut when Wilberforce allegedly joked whether Huxley was the descendent of a monkey by his grandfather or his grandmother's line. With quick wit, Huxley replied he would be more ashamed to be connected with a speaker who used his gifts to obscure the truth. No proof actually exists that this exchange ever took place, with some arguing journalists sensationalised the words for newspaper figures. Even so, the evening was a tough battle between two intellectual heavyweights. A pillar was later installed outside the Oxford University Museum of Natural History to commemorate the debate's 150th anniversary.

1864 The Chimney Sweepers Regulation Act 1864 was granted royal assent. Throughout the nineteenth century boys as young as five were cruelly employed as chimney-sweepers. The work was extremely dangerous. Many were seriously injured or suffered with lifelong diseases. The bill was another piece of legislation championed by the social reformer, the 7th Earl Shaftesbury. After observing the appalling conditions for himself, Shaftesbury pushed for legal regulations that protected children from the devastating effects of the job.

1894 Tower Bridge was opened. At first glance, it would appear Tower Bridge looks much older than its relatively youthful age. Constructed by Horace Smith, it was created to resemble a neo-gothic symbol of London's past, an icon of British prestige. The most remarkable feature of the bridge is perhaps the lifting mechanism which allows larger ships to pass.

1897 The first typed letter from Buckingham Palace was printed. The queen could be suspicious of modern technology and insisted on handwritten correspondence. Lord Rosebery cannily observed that the ingenious typewriter was essentially paralysed by the queen's disapproval. The first typewritten letter to emerge from the royal household was on Wednesday 30 June 1897. Unfortunately, Victoria was still not impressed and commanded all officials to continue with handwritten letters until after her death.

July

1 July

1842 Edwin Chadwick publishes 'The Sanitary Conditions of the Labouring Population'
The landmark report by the social reformer Edwin Chadwick revealed that overcrowded, unsanitary and unclean urban conditions were a major contributor to the spread of disease in England. The document was published at Chadwick's own expense in 1842, and exposed deep and devastating health inequalities throughout Britain. The mood surrounding public health, however, was divisive. Many governments had adopted a policy of 'laissez faire' and would not interfere with private citizens' health. Chadwick was not deterred. His work led to the 1848 Public Health Act and the gradual awareness of the link between hygiene and disease.

1862 'The Saddest Royal Wedding in modern times' took place in Osborne House. Having only buried Prince Albert six months earlier, the wedding between Victoria's daughter, Princess Alice and Prince Louis of Hesse, was clouded by deep intense misery. The ceremony took place in the dining-room at Osborne House with only a small handful of invited guests. Emotions ran high throughout the service. While the queen tried doggedly to hold back the tears, Prince Alfred broke down in a torment of grief. As for the newlyweds, both would die tragically young, Alice in 1878 and Louis in 1892. Two of their children would predecease them.

1872 The Albert Memorial was opened in London. Following Albert's passing, Lord Palmerston announced the need for a 'permanent and substantial memorial' to commemorate the 'virtues of the great man'. The architect chosen was George Gilbert Scott, the mastermind behind the Foreign Office building in Whitehall. One of the most impressive features of the Albert Memorial was the Frieze of Parnassus, a huge, sculpted stone that encircles the podium, featuring 169 artists from history. Appropriately, the monument stands proudly overlooking the magnificent Royal Albert Hall.

2 July

1850 Former prime minister Robert Peel dies
'Are you injured?' screamed the worried voice of Miss Ellis, a longtime friend of the former prime minister. 'Yes,' came the reply, 'very much.' The Tory politician

had barely finished lunch at Buckingham Palace when he was violently thrown off his horse while riding along Constitution Hill. The queen, who was due to appear at the opera later that evening, was deeply distressed by the news. Peel died of his injuries in the early hours of the 2nd. He was only sixty-two. 'I was so upset I could not sufficiently recover myself,' the monarch recalled. 'I dropped the letter from my hands ... We felt as if we had lost a father!'

1865 The Salvation Army was formed by Charles Booth. Booth's dedication to the poor made him a firm favourite with deprived communities, especially in the East End of London, where he and his wife, Catherine, established the Salvation Army. The organisation was aimed at bringing salvation to the poor and leading an army against sin, vice and poverty.

1897 The grand 'Devonshire House Fancy dress Ball' took place, celebrating the Queen's Diamond Jubilee. No social event seemed to attract more public attention, with nearly every single member of the royal family attending, including Tsar Nicholas II of Russia.

1897 The Italian inventor Guglielmo Marconi was awarded a patent for radio communication.

3 July

1842 Queen Victoria survives another attempted assassination
On 3 July a group of young hunchbacked men were marched solemnly into a small police station in London. They were lined up in a row and inspected. One by one, police interrogated each man. Names, ages and addresses were probed. They were questioned forensically about their whereabouts at 10.00am that morning. The unusual event was the product of a strange and terrifying assassination attempt on the queen, performed by a physically disfigured but unidentified young man who had escaped the police.

Earlier that morning, Victoria had left Buckingham Palace for morning service at the Chapel Royal. The would-be assassin, William Bean, was a seventeen-year-old-son of a jeweller, who suffered from a serious spinal deformity, leaving him with the appearance of a hunchback. His suspicious behaviour had already begun to catch police attention. Officers watched him with growing unease as he loitered up and down the Mall, waiting anxiously for the queen's appearance. As he worked his way to the front of the crowd, Bean quietly drew out a gun from his long brown coat and pulled the trigger. The pistol failed to fire. Within seconds, he was tackled by furious spectators but managed to escape.

London erupted into hysterical panic. Police stormed the area, rounding up hunchbacks from across the city and drafting in reinforcements from neighbouring districts. Eventually, they located Bean at his family home, raided the property and arrested him on charges of attempted murder. Investigations concluded the gun was loaded more with tobacco than actual gunpowder. Bean argued the queen's life was hence not physically endangered. Instead of the death penalty, he was sentenced to eighteen months' hard labour. He died in 1882.

1895 Winston Churchill was enormously influenced by his friendly, large-hearted nanny, Elizabeth Everest, who died on 3 July. As a boy, Churchill's childhood was lonely and despondent, excluded from the presence of his glamorous but distant aristocratic parents, and deprived of any deep intimate affection. Everest had worked for the Churchills since the 1870s, and formed a genuinely loving relationship with Winston who grew to adore her. Unfortunately, in 1891 Everest was sacked and temporarily re-hired by Churchill's elderly grandmother in Blenheim Palace. Within a few months she was dismissed again, much to the frustration of Churchill who wrote a personal letter of appeal to his mother begging for her re-appointment. Luckily, by the 1890s his personal income was strong enough to contribute financially but her retirement would be brief. In 1895, her health significantly declined. On 2 July a mournful telegram was relayed to Churchill stating that her condition was terminal. He returned to London immediately, reaching her bedside just in time. She died in the early hours of the following morning, aged sixty-three.

4 July

1891 William Gladstone's eldest son dies
Gladstone's life was darkened by the death of his son, William Henry Gladstone, who had undergone surgery for a brain tumour. Gladstone senior, who was holidaying in Lowestoft, Suffolk, was anxious to return to London but was wrongfully persuaded to remain by his personal doctors. At eighty-one, it was feared a long journey would be equally hazardous for his health and so he remained in the countryside. The local post office at Lowestoft was kept open throughout the night to relay any updates immediately. The news unfortunately was bleak. The following morning it was clear that William's condition was critical and most likely terminal. Gladstone departed for London in despair but was too late. William Henry Gladstone died in the early afternoon, surrounded by his wife and brothers. He was just fifty-one.

1871 The inventor Hubert Cecil Booth was born in Gloucester. He was attributed for inventing the vacuum cleaner.

5 July

1839 Royal scandal hits the headlines as Lady Flora Hastings dies
Lady Flora Hastings was a youthful, unmarried Lady in Waiting to the Queen's Mother, the Dowager Duchess of Kent who, in 1839, created the biggest royal scandal in decades.

The early years of Victoria's reign were dominated by the rival courts between herself and the Dowager Duchess, creating almost two separate kingdoms within Buckingham Palace. The queen, deeply distrustful of her mother and of Sir John Conroy, suspected Flora to be a malicious spy and a gossip-stirrer who sought infiltration into the household. In 1839 things came to a head in a nasty and, ultimately, tragic tale.

Lady Flora, who was a devoutly religious woman, began suffering pain and swelling in her stomach. As an unmarried woman, rumours circulated that the pious servant was pregnant, a serious disgrace, if true. Soon her name was smeared with dishonour. 'I discovered how exceedingly suspicious her figure looked,' Victoria wrote scornfully, 'we have no doubt that she is, to use the plain words, with child!! ... the horrid cause of all this is the monster and demon Incarnate, whose name I forbear to mention.' The insinuation was that John Conroy was the secret father. A few days later, Lady Flora was subjected to a humiliating physical examination by two physicians from the royal household. She was discovered to have a terminal liver tumour and would soon be dead.

The drama seriously damaged the reputation of the palace. The queen was candidly depicted as an insensitive and judgemental bully. The scandal even damaged Lord Melbourne who, as the personal advisor to Victoria, was closely associated with the monarchy. At Lady Flora's funeral, the queen's empty carriage was stoned by angry protesters. It was an unnervingly dangerous moment for her new reign.

1841 Thomas Cook established the Thomas Cook Travel Agency. The first trip was a one-day package excursion from Leicester to Loughborough costing one shilling. The railways made it possible for tourists to travel to different previously unexplored places in Britain.

1865 Speed limits on road vehicles were established in Britain. Two miles per hour was the maximum a vehicle could travel in urban areas with a high population density. In the countryside, the speed limit was a generous four miles per hour.

6 July

1888 The Matchgirls' strike of 1888
Death, disease and despair were common features in most Victorian factories. Conditions were often deplorable, dominated by long hours, meagre wages, hazardous work and sometimes crippling long-term health effects. On 6 July a group of young women employed at the Bryant & May match factory in London decided to make a stand. They called a strike, exposing the toxic realities of modern life in all its sordid, horrid details.

The dispute had begun weeks earlier when several women were unfairly dismissed by factory bosses, prompting a mass walkout by staff. The strike gained national attention and was even debated in parliament. The crisis was finally resolved in July when managers reluctantly agreed to re-employ the dismissed workers. Working conditions, however, continued to be poor. The use of toxic industrial chemicals, such as white phosphorus, led to many serious health problems, something which continued for decades.

1887 The fifteen-year-old Charlotte Dod, known more commonly as Lotti Dod, became the youngest winner of the ladies' singles championships at Wimbledon. Her record remains unbeaten.

1892 Dadabhai Naoroji was elected a Member of Parliament. He was one of the first Indian MPs in British history, and had overcome appalling racism, snobbery and backbiting to achieve success against enormous odds. In the 1892 election, he stood as a Liberal candidate for the constituency of Finsbury Central. Known as the 'Grand Old Man of India', Naoroji argued that Britain was draining the wealth from India and causing great harm to the Indian people.

1893- The wedding of Prince George and Princess Mary of Teck took place in Windsor. The cobbled streets of the royal town thronged with a dense crowd of joyful, jubilant spectators. Carriage after carriage carried hundreds of battle-hardened fans who clamoured out of the railway station with predictable gusto, ahead of a glorious celebration. The occasion, of course, was tinged with undeniable sadness. Only a year earlier, Mary had been engaged to the queen's grandson and heir, Prince Albert Victor, who died in January 1892. Nor did the ceremony run smoothly. Contrary to tradition, Victoria accidentally arrived early at the chapel, and was seated before the other guests. To their relief, she found the error a novelty and enjoyed watching the guests arrive. Among the invitees at the reception was the dazzling parliamentarian Herbert Asquith, who would later serve as George's prime minister twenty years later.

1899 Winston Churchill was defeated at the 1899 Oldham by-election. His flamboyant persona had been somewhat tainted with controversy over allegations of egotism and 'medal hunting' in the Boer War. Others regarded him as a dangerous upstart. On voting day Churchill skilfully arranged a motor-car to drive voters to the polling station but the car broke down. The Conservatives were outnumbered by 130 to 90, with hoards of horse-driven carriages arriving every hour carrying hardened Liberal supporters. Churchill was deeply disappointed by the result.

7 July

1856 The Commander in Chief of the Army, Viscount Hardinge suffers a stroke in Buckingham Palace
The rain cascaded on London as the carriage of Viscount Hardinge, the senior military commander, clattered into the courtyard of Buckingham Palace. His visit was not a social one. Enormous losses in the Crimean War had damaged the reputation of

British senior officers, something which, as head of the army, Hardinge bore ultimate responsibility. A commission was established in 1856 to scrutinise the failings of the conflict, with its publication delivered personally to the queen.

Hardinge entered the room to greet Victoria and Prince Albert but suddenly felt unwell. His face dropped to one side. With great difficulty, the general collapsed onto the ground. Horrified, the royal couple supported him onto the coach and screamed for assistance. Slowly, he was lifted carefully and placed into a carriage to be driven home. The unofficial diagnosis was 'strain', an after-effect of years of overwork. In reality, he had suffered a paralytic stroke, news which was only conveyed to the queen a day later. Hardinge died a few months later on 24 September, aged seventy-one.

1893 The Prince of Wales hosted a glamorous garden party at Marlborough House to celebrate the marriage of his son, Prince George, to Princess Mary of Teck. Over 5,000 guests were invited. Even the queen attended, although was rather displeased to see Gladstone who inadvertently plonked himself down in the private royal tent.

8 July

1850 Prince Adolphus Frederick dies
Thirteen years after the funeral of King William IV, his brother, and Queen Victoria's uncle, Prince Adolphus Frederick died at Cambridge House. He was seventy-six. A stocky, straight-talking man, Adolphus cemented a long genealogical legacy which is interwoven into the fabric of British national life. His eldest son, Prince George, became the longest serving commander of the Army. His youngest daughter, Prince Mary Adelaide, was the mother of Princess Mary of Teck, who almost forty-three years to the day of his death, married Victoria's grandson and later became grandmother of Queen Elizabeth II.

1837 By pure coincidence, the death fell on the precise anniversary of King William IV's funeral, held in St George's Chapel. The monarch's body lay in state in the Waterloo chamber of Windsor Castle where public mourners lined to pay their respects. 'Life is short and uncertain,' Queen Victoria reflected, 'and I am determined to employ my time well, so that when I am called away from this world, my end may be a peaceful and a happy one!'

9 July

1841 Abolitionist Charles Lenox Remond delivers a keynote address in London
The renowned African American abolitionist, Charles Lenox Remond, had arrived in Britain in 1840 for an important series of lectures delivered throughout the country. His keynote speech was hosted by the British and Foreign Anti-Slavery Society in London and stressed the need for international collaboration

in abolishing slavery. His sister, Sarah, followed in his footsteps and established a hugely popular lecture tour.

1877 The first Wimbledon Tennis Championship began on 9 July. Interestingly, only 200 spectators arrived for the first tournament, a tiny number compared to the thousands who visit today. The first contest was scheduled with a short break in the middle to avoid clashing with the annual Harrow vs Eton cricket match.

1851 A Grand Ball was held to celebrate the Great Exhibition at London's Guildhall.

10 July

1877 St John Ambulance Association founded
The charity was founded by the Venerable Order of the Hospital of Saint John of Jerusalem to educate industrial workers in first aid, a skill which was deemed increasingly important. The severity of accidents on construction projects meant that victims often required immediate treatment without waiting for a doctor. Ten years later, the organisation became known as the St John Ambulance Brigade, which provided qualified volunteers to provide medical assistance at public events.

1900 Dr Edward West was awarded the Gold Medal from the Royal Asiatic Society. He was presented with the award by the Prince of Wales at Marlborough House. Guests at the reception included the influential Donald James Mackay, the 11th Lord Reay.

11 July

1900 Charlotte Cooper wins the 1900 Olympic Gold medal for Women's Single Tennis
11 July was a good day for British sport. Charlotte Cooper, a bubbly twenty-nine-year-old woman from Ealing became the first female Olympic tennis champion. She had previously won Wimbledon three times and seemed on course to become the greatest female player in the world. By coincidence, on the same day another Briton, Laurence Doherty, won the Men's Single Gold Medal, defeating Harold Mahony, followed by a further Gold in the Doubles.

1848 London's Waterloo Station was opened. The name was chosen deliberately to honour Britain's great victory over Napoleon at the Battle of Waterloo some thirty-three years earlier.

1859 The iconic bong of Big Ben chimed for the first time. The original bell weighed sixteen tons and was created by the manufacturing company John Warner & Sons. Unfortunately, the first test was a failure and the bell broke. A new, larger bell was later installed and tolled for the first time to great success on this day.

1900 A Royal zebra was presented to Queen Victoria at Windsor Castle. Although fond of animals, the monarch had no intention of having a pet zebra walking around the palace. It was moved instead to the green fields of Frogmore House.

12 July

1881 William Renshaw becomes British Wimbledon Champion
If you found yourself at the Wimbledon championship in the 1890s, you would inevitably have heard the name of William Renshaw flutter and echo in the murmur of conversation. Born in Warwickshire in 1861, Renshaw was every inch a sporting giant, like Andy Murray or Rafael Nadal. His style of play was aggressive, famous for decisive technical power and quick mobility. Renshaw shares the all-time gentleman's record with seven Wimbledon titles, a status unequalled until Roger Federer in 2017. He remained a popular figure for decades and became Britain's first President of the British Lawn Tennis Association. In 1983, 122 years after his birth, he was finally admitted into the International Tennis Hall of Fame.

13 July

1837 Queen Victoria makes Buckingham Palace her main London residence
Traditionally, St James's Palace had been the stately red-brick residence of the British sovereign. By 1837, however, the palace no longer seemed fit for purpose. It was damp, dreary and frosty, made worse by the shivering cold winters. With the accession of the young queen, things began to change. Buckingham Palace was larger and more suitable for a sprightly new monarch. Under the watchful eye of Prince Albert, the structure was modernised and redeveloped. Ventilation was improved, and the chimneys redesigned to prevent excess smoke. It remains the sovereign's principal residence and, arguably, the most famous palace in the country.

1854 Admiral John Fisher joined the Royal Navy. After embarking onboard Nelson's famous flagship, HMS *Victory*, in July 1854, Fisher's entry exam consisted of jumping over a chair naked, a medical inspection and writing out the Lord's Prayer. Despite his humble origins, Fisher became the leading figure in the Victorian Navy and a close friend of the Prince of Wales.

14 July

1884 Madame Tussauds new exhibition opens to great success
The increasing popularity of Madam Tussaud's museum persuaded the proprietors to relocate from the original premises to cope with the rising demands for modern audiences. In 1883 a new property was constructed on Marylebone Road. The first new exhibition was launched a year later in July 1884 and became a tremendous success.

July

1881 The Anarchist Congress was held in London, drawing leading anarchists from around the world including Louise Michel and Peter Kropotkin. The large, but unproductive, conference called for the formation of a new international order that advocated egalitarian socialism. A subsequent congress was scheduled for the following year but was cancelled.

1867 The chemist Alfred Nobel tests dynamite at a small quarry in Redhill, Surrey.

15 July

1837 York Poor Law Union established
Contrary to misconception, the workhouse was not a Victorian invention. The 1834 Poor Law had established the institution to provide accommodation and nutrition to the vulnerable but was kept deliberately harsh in order to deter people from entering. However, the Victorian era saw a considerable growth in workhouses, a reflection perhaps of the rising poverty inflicted by the industrial revolution. Most inmates were expected to work long hours on backbreaking labour such as crushing bones to make fertiliser. Other tasks could include stone breaking, wood chopping and weaving.

1854 The marriage of John Ruskin and Effie Gray was annulled. The separation created scandal throughout England. Gray was ostracised from society, especially royal events, but later remarried the artist John Everett Millas and became his artistic manager. Ruskin, however, emerged less battered and resumed a successful art career.

1858 Emmeline Pankhurst was born in Sloan Street, Manchester. Arguably the most influential suffragette activist of the nineteenth and twentieth century, Pankhurst was a titanic figure in national life.

1865 Alfred Harmsworth, later known as Viscount Northcliffe, was born in London. He would become one of Britain's most formidable and powerful newspaper owners.

16 July

1879 A historic Wimbledon Men Singles' Final
The match was hotly anticipated to be a climatic duel between two tennis giants, the Reverend John Hartley, a thirty-year-old-vicar from Shropshire, and Vere Thomas St Leger Goold, a charismatic, hard-drinking Irishman who was later charged with murder and finished his days on Devil's Island. The contest attracted thousands of spectators into the sleepy Wimbledon village, including several newspaper columnists and international reporters. Goold had allegedly consumed enormous amounts of alcohol and was suffering from a hangover. Hartley won the

first set with six games to two but struggled in the second. Goold came back with impressive aggression but narrowly lost with six games to four. In the third set, Hartley defeated his opponent again resoundingly, and was crowned champion.

Goold was devastated by the loss. He became an alcoholic and suffered a serious drug addiction. In 1891 he married Madame Marie Giraudin and relocated to France but lost all his money through gambling. His troubles worsened in 1907 when he accepted a generous loan of £40 from a Danish widow, Emma Levin, which he subsequently lost. After a bloody fight with Levin, he allegedly killed her. Her dismembered remains were discovered in a suitcase. Goold was sentenced to life in prison and killed himself in 1909.

1846 The London and North Western Railway was founded. The company was one of the most powerful and ruthless businesses of the nineteenth century. 'I well remember the opening,' recalled Lord Kimberly, 'that was one of the most momentous changes which has taken place, not only in this country, but in the world.' The company's rigorous pursuit of railway expansion made it a famous, but controversial, force in public life.

1885 John Evertt Millais became the first British artist in over 100 years to be awarded a baronetcy. In tribute to his artistic contribution, the Grosvenor Gallery opened a large exhibition of his work the following year.

1894 The future King Edward VIII was christened in a modest ceremony in the Green Drawing Room of the White Lodge. His full name was Edward Albert Christian George Andrew Patrick David, the last four names being a deliberate nod to the patron saints of the four nations in the British isles. Like most upper-class families of the era, Edward was raised under a strict hierarchy of nannies, governesses and domestic staff. One particularly cruel nurse was known to pinch and hurt him. As he matured, his relationship with his parents also became distant, tense and formal, something which would have profound consequences on the future of the monarchy.

1900 Alfred Ernest Tysoe won the Gold Medal in the Men's 800 metres at the 1900 Olympics, defeating the American John Cregan by three yards. The same week, Tysoe won his second Gold Medal in the Men's 5,000 metres team race. Shortly after the Olympics, he became seriously ill with pleurisy and died in 1901, aged twenty-seven.

17 July

1841 The first issue of *Punch* was published
It became famous for satirical, comical sketches depicting public and cultural events. It was formed by two men, Henry Mayhew and Ebenezer Landells. The magazine is also credited with coining the term 'cartoon'.

July

1895 The Great Wheel opened at the Earl's Court exhibition grounds. Standing at 308 feet, it was the tallest ferris wheel in the world, and became a major crowd pleaser in the area. Tourists, however, soon became bored and it was eventually demolished in 1907.

1897 *Recessional*, a poem composed for Queen Victoria's Diamond Jubilee was published. The poem was written by Rudyard Kipling, expressing pride in the British imperial power but also reminding readers that nothing lasts forever.

18 July

1895 Henry Irving becomes the first actor to be knighted
It was the pinnacle of recognition, and a testament to his prodigious talents and remarkable trajectory in bridging the class divide. Unsurprisingly, news of Irving's achievement also created gossip, especially as his wife, Florence Irving was conspicuously absent during the ceremony. Their marriage had collapsed after a catastrophic argument in a taxi carriage some years earlier. Having never approved of her husband's career, Florence accused him of making a fool of himself. Without responding, Irving exited the carriage at Hyde Park Corner and vanished. He never spoke to his wife again. Ironically, despite the break-up, Florence later styled herself Lady Irving and would talk highly of her acclaimed, if distant, husband for the rest of her life.

1848 English cricketer W.G. Grace was born in Bristol. With his bushy black beard, stocky frame and lofty height, Grace was the most recognisable Victorian sporting hero. Ironically, Grace always questioned whether he was a natural cricketer. Success, in his own words, was the result of many years' hard practice and coaching. Similarly, although passionate about the sport, cricket was not his only love. In 1879, he qualified as a doctor and practised medicine for several years. Starstruck patients were often shocked to see him.

1872 Voting by secret ballot was introduced. The landmark decision transformed British democracy, ending years of corruption and intimidation. Prior to 1872 landlords could often use their influence to unfairly force tenants to vote a certain way. Individuals found supporting rival candidates could be punished, disciplined or even evicted from their homes. Support for a secret ballot, however, was nothing new. It had been advocated many years earlier by the Chartist campaign. Some cases of voter intimidation still continued into the twentieth century.

19 July

1873 Bishop Samuel Wilberforce died in a riding accident
The charismatic Bishop of Winchester was one of Britain's most recognisable religious figures, famous for his 1860 debate against Charles Darwin. In July,

accompanied by Lord Granville, Wilberforce travelled to Holmbury St Mary to visit William Gladstone. En route, his horse apparently stumbled on a rock and threw the bishop into the road. He suffered severe head injuries and a dislocated neck. Death was instantaneous.

1837 The SS *Great Western*, Isambard Kingdom Brunel's steamship, was launched in Bristol. Constructed entirely from wood, the vessel was designed to travel from Bristol to New York in a record time and was the largest and, seemingly, greatest steam-powered ship on earth. It made its maiden voyage in April 1838.

1877 The first ever men's singles Wimbledon final took place on the grey dull afternoon of 19 July, an epic battle between the bewhiskered aristocrat Spencer Gore and the wealthy architect William Marshal. The final was initially scheduled for the 15th, but was delayed due to bad weather. Gore emerged victorious.

20 July

1837 Euston Station opened
Euston Station was named after Euston Hall, the ancestral home of the Duke of Grafton who owned the land where the station was constructed. The original building was opulent and grand, accompanied some years later by the impressive Euston Arch which was described as 'mightier than the pyramids of Egypt'. Euston was the first intercity station in London and also the first to accommodate a 'railway hotel' to host visitors into the city. It came as no surprise that many railway staff regarded Euston as the 'greatest of London stations'. In 1849 a grand hall was built to provide a visual symbol of Euston's prestige in railway life. The station was unfortunately demolished in the 1960s, and much of the Victorian elegance was lost forever.

1886 William Gladstone's 170-day government ended abruptly. It was the shortest British government of the Victorian period, lasting from 1 February to 20 July 1886. Gladstone had won the 1885 general election but, without a majority, and remained at the mercy of Irish MPs for votes. Unsurprisingly, his minority government did not survive. He resigned the following day.

21 July

1864 The Grand Brighton Hotel opens
The transformative impact of the Victorian railways was no more powerfully evident than in the Sussex town of Brighton. Previously a sleepy, mundane village, the nineteenth century saw the metamorphosis of Brighton into an epic national tourist attraction and favourite for thousands of visitors. In 1864 the architect John Whichcord was hired to create a new luxury hotel to accommodate the wealthier

visitors to the town. Suitably, it was called 'The Grand', an appropriate name for its ornate and breathtaking interior.

1867 The music hall comedian Harry Relph, also known as 'Little Titch', was born in Kent. Music halls were extremely popular by the 1880s, especially in working-class districts. Unfortunately, it also became a source of snobbery, with many theatre critics regarding 'Titch' and other music hall acts as 'inferior' to conventional theatre. The world of variety was less respected, a view expressed prominently by many judgmental newspaper reporters.

1897 Tate Britain was opened in London. Originally named the National Gallery of British Art, the Tate was created after its founder, Henry Tate, had bequeathed sixty-five priceless paintings to the National Gallery, but was turned down due to a lack of space. Instead, he founded his own gallery which showcased the best and brightest artists from the entire United Kingdom. It was later renamed in his honour.

22 July

1844 The long-serving Oxford don William Archibald Spooner is born
Spooner was a distinguished Oxford professor and vicar with a remarkable reputation for eccentricity. His comical, absent-minded, often hilarious gaffes became so famous they were later known as 'Spoonerisms', some of which were largely embellished or exaggerated for comic effect. One particularly funny story circulated that he had invited a fellow Oxford don for tea in his office, to 'welcome Stanley Casson, our new archaeology Fellow'. 'I am Stanley Casson,' the don replied. 'Never mind,' Spooner remarked, 'come in all the same.' In his capacity as a chaplain, he often remarked, 'You may now cuss the bride,' rather than kiss.

1840 The Dowager Queen Adelaide became the first British royal to travel via train. Her carriage was specially fitted with a luxurious cushioned interior and the crew drove particularly carefully. The Dowager Queen was said to have been delighted.

23 July

1847 Queen Victoria opens the new House of Lords
Barry had designed it purposefully to resemble an opulent, palatial and spectacular legislative chamber, fit for some of the highest figures in the land. The interior was dominated by the large gold throne with magnificent ornamentation and embroidery, symbolising the supreme sovereignty of the monarch. The throne was designed by Pugin, based on the coronation chair in Westminster Abbey, but on an even grander scale. Behind the chair, the carved wood panel was engraved with the Prince of Wales's coat of arms, surrounded by the chivalric Order of the Garter. Unlike the Commons, there was no speaker's chair for the presiding officer of the

chamber. Instead, the Lord Chancellor sat on a simple woolsack, as a reminder of Britain's biggest source of industry in the fourteenth century. Today his role is occupied by the Lord Speaker who is politically impartial.

In subsequent years the influence of the Lords has diminished. When Barry and Pugin designed the chamber, most Victorian premiers sat in the upper house. With the exception of Sir Robert Peel and William Gladstone, no Victorian prime minister remained in the Commons for the duration of his political career. Barry's need to reflect the significance and importance of the Lords' role was hence visually illustrated by its obvious grandeur.

1885 The royal wedding between Princess Beatrice and Prince Henry of Battenberg took place. Victoria has often been criticised by historians as a controlling, difficult mother who used her children as emotional crutches in the decades after Albert's death. Unfortunately for Victoria, Beatrice had other ideas. In 1885 she announced her engagement to Prince Henry of Battenberg. The queen was deeply unhappy with the romance. For months verbal communication stopped. She was appalled at the idea of Beatrice leaving the royal court and 'abandoning' her duties as the monarch's private secretary. Only after several weeks did she finally grant her blessing, but only with the assurance that both Beatrice and Henry would remain with her permanently in England and not pursue an independent life in Germany. Even the royal wedding itself was unusual, hosted in a small church ceremony in the village of Whippingham near Osborne House.

1866 The infamous Hyde Park riots occurred in London. From dawn, an enraged group of protesters descended upon Trafalgar Square, championing the cause of electoral reform. Exasperated by years of parliamentary inaction, their patience had simply run out. Outside the Commons, more angry crowds gathered, booing and hissing members as they scurried nervously from their carriages into the building. Unfortunately, what started as peaceful protests descended into violence, especially after being denied entry to Hyde Park by police. Protesters stormed the gates and a riot ensued. The unrest lasted for three days.

1900 The first Pan-African Conference was held in London, organised by the Trinidadian lawyer Henry Sylvester Williams, hosted at Westminster Hall (now renamed Caxton Hall). During the conference, the Bishop of London gave an address in which he pleaded for harmony and peace throughout the world between different racial and ethnic communities.

24 July

1884 Housing reforms debated in Parliament
Images of overcrowded, depilated housing were common and consistent features of Victorian Britain. Unsanitary, small, squalid, dirty and derelict houses became the heartbreaking reality for many citizens. By 1881 the population of the UK

had skyrocketed to almost thirty million. In most urban communities, an average visitor did not need to travel far to uncover slums where hundreds of families lived in appalling and distressing conditions. Three years later, the Conservative government drafted a bill to make it illegal for landlords to rent properties that were unsanitary or dirty. In his own words, Lord Salisbury argued the law 'derived from the noblest principles of philanthropy and religion'. Unfortunately, it also met with immense criticism, especially from the House of Lords. One particularly angry member condemned the government for 'strangling the spirit of independence, and the self-reliance of the people, and by destroying the moral fibre'.

25 July

1886 Lord Salisbury forms his second government
Heavy rain battered the carriage of the new prime minister, Lord Salisbury, as it skidded precariously into the courtyard of Osborne House. It was not a happy victory. The Conservatives had won the general election but did not have a majority. In a bid to form a government, Salisbury offered the premiership to the Liberal Unionist leader, Lord Hartington, pledging to serve under him as foreign secretary. Hartington declined. After intense negotiations, an unofficial agreement was reached for the Liberal Unionists to provide a confidence and supply arrangement in the Commons. Although the term 'coalition' was never actually used, the two parties formed an informal alliance which kept the Tories in office, but the Liberal Unionists firmly in the driving seat. Salisbury was especially keen to keep Hartington on good terms, consulting him on every major decision and relaying any concerns to him personally. Despite private misgivings, the government lasted until 1892.

26 July

1892 Keir Hardie elected as a Member of Parliament
Hardie caused quite a stir with his arrival. He entered the chamber dressed in a deerstalker hat, a brown tweed suit and a red flannel shirt. His hands were buried deep within his pockets. Appalled by the apparent lack of decorum, members craned their necks in shock and horror. With reluctance, Hardie slowly removed his hat but immediately engaged in conflict with the Commons Clerk. He complained that the oath of allegiance to the monarch was absurd and demanded to swear a promise instead to his constituents. It was a noteworthy start to a colourful career.

1855 The funeral of Lord Raglan took place in Bristol. The Crimean War commander had succumbed to dysentery on 28 June after battling depression. On 3 July his body was placed on board *Canada*, escorted by troops and was laid in state in the great hall of Badminton House. The mayor, civic dignitaries, clergymen and other local figureheads lined the streets outside Queen Square, where a strong body of policemen kept watch over a mammoth crowd of mourners.

27 July

1889 The Queen's granddaughter, Princess Louise, marries a former MP
It was highly unusual for a royal to marry a former politician, yet Louise broke the mould. On the humid afternoon of 27 July, she married Alexander Duff, the eldest son of the 5th Earl of Fife. For many courtiers, the romance seemed unsuitable. Duff was politically controversial. He was almost twenty years older and directly related to the illegitimate daughter of the mistress of King William IV. To the queen however, these reservations fell on deaf ears. A vast triumphal arch was erected for the newly-weds in Windsor, supplemented with mountains of colourful flowers and flags that lined the streets. All morning, thousands of fans flocked into the town, with a huge contingent of Metropolitan Police intermingled. It was, as some commentators remarked, just as grand and impressive as any other royal wedding.

1851 Thomas Grant became the first Roman Catholic Bishop of the new diocese of Southwark. Grant was a popular figure who remained in the post until his premature death in 1870. Upon hearing news of his passing, Pope Pius IX remarked, 'another saint in heaven.'

1893 The Commons has always been rowdy, but on the evening of 27 July tensions reached new heights. Two highly aggressive MPs provoked a fracas and had to be constrained by colleagues. Contrary to false rumours, however, no fist fight took place. The proceedings returned to normal afterwards, but the news made major headlines the following morning. A proposed enquiry was later established but dropped in hope of brushing the unfortunate incident under the carpet forever.

28 July

1866 The writer Beatrix Potter was born in London
Helen Beatrix Potter was born in West Brompton, the daughter of Helen Leech and Rupert William Potter, a barrister of equity law. Despite her enormous scientific talents, Beatrix struggled to fulfil her potential in a strictly male-dominated society. To supplement her income, she began printing Christmas cards in the 1890s featuring her popular depictions of rabbits and mice. In 1901, she revisited an earlier unpublished children's book which she wrote several years prior. At her own expense, she self-published the work, titled *The Tale of Peter Rabbit*. It was later taken up by a commercial publisher in 1902 and became an international bestseller. The rest, as they say, is history.

1885 Sir Moses Haim Montefiore died aged 100. Montefiore was a financier and philanthropist who became the first Jewish gentleman knighted during the Victorian era. Montefiore, who was born in Italy in 1784, celebrated his 100th birthday on 24 October. When he died in 1885, he was one of the oldest men in Britain.

29 July

1840 The Conservative Club, an influential gentleman's club, is established
Most Victorian politicians belonged to a club where the buzz and excitement of gossip, rumours and tittle-tattle could run wild, creating a complex, interconnected web of social-political interactions. In 1840 the Conservative Club was opened, located originally at 88 St James Street, until moving to number 74 a few years later. It was formed, as the name suggests, for members of the Conservative Party. Although not intending to rival the already established Carlton Club, which was the de-facto headquarters of the party, the new club became enormously influential in Victorian society and the location for many important political discussions.

30 July

1900 Prince Alfred, son of Queen Victoria, dies
Queen Victoria was no stranger to tragedy. On 30 July, after months of suffering, her beloved son Prince Alfred succumbed to throat cancer at his lodge in Coburg, aged fifty-nine. A stylish and handsome figure in his youth, Alfred's relationship with his mother was much warmer and more affectionate than her estranged older son. Alfred was the first British prince to be tattooed and exhibited quite a rebellious, charismatic temperament which endeared him to the public. Perhaps to shield the queen from the unhappy reality, his disease was kept hidden from Victoria until his death seemed imminent. She had just finished dressing when her daughters, Helena and Beatrice, informed her of the news. 'I think they should never have withheld the truth from me, as long as they did,' Victoria later remarked, 'it has come such an awful shock.'

31 July

1879 Chaos in the West End
It's every actor's worst nightmare. During a performance of the legendary Gilbert & Sullivan's *HMS Pinafore*, an enormous brawl broke out inside London's Comique Theatre, creating catastrophic disarray and chaos. The drama had begun many months earlier when the owner of the theatre, Richard D'Oyly Carte, fell out with his financial backers, leading to a bitter war of words. In July 1879, an unhappy investor, known as Water Cart Bailey, vowed to take revenge. With a group of heavy men, he stormed the theatre during the second act and seized the props and scenery from the stage. The audience reacted in hysterics, shouting and booing in utter shock and astonishment. Violence broke out. Richard Barker, the stage manager, was assaulted and thrown down the stairs. The incident was reported as a disgrace to London's theatreland.

August

1 August

1842 Children under the age of ten are banned for mining
By the nineteenth century, mining had become one of the largest sources of employment in many parts of Britain, but also extremely hazardous. The Mines Act was a response to the Children's Employment Commission report, chaired again by the famous social reformer Anthony Cooper, the future 7th Earl Shaftesbury. The reforms were supported strongly by Queen Victoria and Prince Albert, who personally congratulated Cooper on his success. It banned women, girls and boys under the age of ten from working in mining. Not everyone supported the proposals. The Anglo-Irish aristocrat Lord Londonderry objected strongly to the idea of forbidding child labour, arguing the reforms would hurt profits and decrease revenue.

1889 *Three Men in a Boat* by Jerome K. Jerome was published. Jerome originally intended it to be a travel guide but later changed it into a comic novel.

2 August

1899 The cellist Pablo Casals performs for the queen at Osborne House
Casals was the only man to have performed for Queen Victoria, President Theodore Roosevelt, John F. Kennedy, and Lyndon Johnson. Despite holding politically republican views, Casals benefitted hugely from royal patronage, especially in Britain. In 1899 he was invited to perform at Crystal Palace, followed by a royal command performance at Osborne House. The musician arrived on the Isle of Wight on 2 August and performed two pieces, the allegro from *Saint-Saëns*, followed by Fauré's *Élégie*. The queen, now in her eighties, greatly enjoyed the concert and conversed with Casals in French after the show. When the evening had finished, he was presented with a silver cigarette case inscribed with the initials VI as a memento.

1858 Charles Dickens began his first provincial reading tour. The success led to other tours, including an ambitious trip to the United States in the 1860s.

August

3 August

1867 Stanley Baldwin, the future prime minister was born
Baldwin was often called the 'epitome of the English calm', an appropriate nickname for a man born in the sanctuary and silence of Lower Park House, Bewdley, a peaceful estate in deepest Worcestershire. His father, Alfred, was a tall, resilient industrialist who became the Tory MP for the constituency in 1892 and dominated the family as an imposing, if benevolent, patriarchal figure. Stanley himself cultivated an image of a reasonable, responsible ruler, rarely angry and rarely reckless. Behind the scenes, however, he could be anxious, running on an electricity of nervous energy. Having prospered during the industrial revolution, the Baldwins were extremely wealthy and, after Alfred's death, Stanley inherited the equivalent of £22m. He became prime minister in 1923.

1891 Victor Emmanuel, later King of Italy, was awarded The Most Noble Order of the Garter. It was a reflection of the growing bonds between the UK and Italy throughout the Victorian era. The award was revoked during the Second World War.

4 August

1900 Elizabeth Bowes-Lyon, the future Queen Mother, was born
A horse-drawn ambulance is racing in abject panic through the cobbled streets of London. The passenger is Lady Glamis, a heavily-pregnant English aristocrat who is about to enter labour. Suddenly, it's too late. Absent of a midwife, a nurse or a doctor, her ladyship gave birth to a healthy baby. The child would grow up to become Queen Consort of the United Kingdom.

Alas, the famous story of the queen born in a carriage is most probably false. It appears more likely that Elizabeth started life indoors, either in England or Scotland, although the precise whereabouts remains a mystery. According to her birth certificate, Elizabeth was born in St Paul's Walden Bury, the family's rural retreat in Herefordshire, although other accounts suggest she was born in 20 St James's Square, London. One explanation is that Lady Glamis, a country woman, was so keen to escape the heat and oppressiveness of London that she returned hastily to Herefordshire after giving birth. In a daze of excitement, Lord Glamis, who was noted as an eccentric character, forgot to register the birth within the statutory six-week window, and when he finally did, recorded St Paul's Walden Bury by mistake.

1870 The British Red Cross was established. The organisation was started by Lord Wantage in hope of providing relief for injured military veterans and their families.

1895 The London School of Economics was established over a small breakfast meeting in London. The main participants, Beatrice and Sidney Webb, Louis Flood and the playwright George Bernard Shaw, joined forces to create an educational college called the London School of Economics. The driving force behind the school was socialism and to bolster the work of the Fabian Society which had been established some years earlier. The institution was partly funded by a generous donation from lawyer Henry Hunt Hutchinson, who bequeathed £20,000 in his will to the trustees of the Fabian society. Hutchinson had died in 'distressing circumstances', widely believed to be suicide, raising questions initially whether he was in a 'sound mind' when he drafted the will. Nevertheless, the money went through, and the school opened its doors just a year later.

5 August

1858 Alexis Benoît Soyer, the celebrated French chef dies in London
From the gilded rooms of the Reform Club, to the squalor of medical tents in the Crimean War, Soyer was Britain's first celebrity chef, and acclaimed throughout the world for his culinary talents and supreme abilities. Among his many achievements, Soyer is recognised for writing the first successful recipe book for the general public, entitled *A Shilling Cookery for the People*. He also introduced the Soyer Stove for the Army and, in the weeks preceding his death, planned a mobile cooking carriage for soldiers to have regular hot meals while fighting on the front. His untimely passing was met with shock. He was buried at Kensal Green Cemetery.

1843 Sarah Dazley became the last woman to be executed in public. She had previously been convicted of poisoning her husband.

6 August

1889 The Savoy Hotel opened in London
The Savoy Hotel was the product of one man's quest for excellence, luxury and culinary prowess. Richard D'Oyly Carte, a theatrical agent, composer and ambitious businessman, had achieved tremendous success in the theatrical world but now sought a challenge beyond his wildest dreams. Having observed the grandeur of international hotels abroad, Carte returned to Britain in the 1880s with the hope of creating his own establishment, preferably in London and located next to the famous Savoy Theatre. While America boasted several hotels that catered exclusively for the wealthy, there was considerably less so in Britain. The architect chosen for the colossal task was Thomas Edward Collcutt, a relatively young designer from Oxford who had recently constructed the Imperial Institute and the Palace Theatre.

The Savoy was the first hotel in Britain to be lit by electricity. It was decorated beautifully with a gilded dining-room, a magnificent lobby and several bedrooms overlooking the Thames. Despite the initial excitement, the hotel performed badly in its first six months. The directors grew wary. In one meeting, they suggested

August

Carte restructure his staff and redevelop the layout of his management. The hugely successful César Ritz was employed as the new manager and the equally renowned Auguste Escoffier was chosen as head chef. Within a few years, the Savoy became the most popular hotel in London. Famous guests included the Prince of Wales, Claude Monet and Lord Rosebery. Sadly, much of the original Victorian interior features do not survive, but its reputation for prestigious luxury remains.

1881 The scientist Alexander Fleming was born in a small farm in Ayrshire, southern Scotland. His medical ingenuity led to the discovery of antibiotics, which he named 'penicillin'.

7 August

1894 The iconic West Highland Railway was opened
Over 500 men were employed to construct the railway, many of whom had previously worked on international railways in far-flung places across the Empire. Construction was troublesome. The mountainous, rugged and remote landscape of the Highlands meant transportation of materials was arduous. In January 1889 railway surveyors came dangerously close to death in vicious wet weather. Nonetheless, the iconic road was eventually opened in 1894 and boasts some of the best lines in Scotland.

1874 After 7 August all births and deaths that occurred within England and Wales had to be registered officially. Those who did not comply could be fined. This also ensured greater accuracy for genealogists tracing their Victorian ancestors.

8 August

1886 Admiral Beresford is appointed the Junior Lord of the Admiralty
By the 1880s Beresford was a leading celebrity, affectionately nicknamed by the press 'Charlie B'. After personal intervention from the Prince of Wales, the prime minister appointed Beresford as the Junior Lord of the Admiralty, a role which he unfortunately came to despise. Despite knowledge of naval affairs, Beresford felt sidelined by the higher authority of the First Lord of the Admiralty, Lord George Hamilton, a man who had never served in the Navy. He became especially critical of the government's shipbuilding policy. After less than two years he resigned.

9 August

1844 Imprisonment for debt is abolished
Many Victorians had been jailed for debt, including the father of Charles Dickens who was incarcerated for three months. By the late 1830s, the law was deeply

unpopular and regarded increasingly as ineffective. Several debtors left prison bankrupt, thus starting a new cycle of poverty and misery. In 1844 it was abolished. However, the wider problem of relieving poverty still remained unsolved.

1870 The Elementary Education Act 1870 was granted royal assent. It was arguably the first major piece of legislation relating to education in the UK. It created a new system of school boards which were elected locally but did not establish compulsory education.

1875 Composer Albert Ketèlbey was born in Birmingham. After studying at Trinity College of Music, he surprised his contemporaries by becoming the musical director of London's Vaudeville Theatre, specialising in popular 'light music'. Many of his works were later used in silent films.

10 August

1895 The first ever Promenade concert is held in London
The first Promenade concert was held, not in the Royal Albert Hall, but the equal grandeur of the Queen's Hall in Langham Place, a venue tragically destroyed during the Blitz. Organised by the legendary composer Henry Wood, the evening was unusual for allowing audience members to eat and drink during the performance. It was also more joyful than previous concerts with a greater emphasis on audience participation and laughter.

Wood was dedicated to finding, promoting, and encouraging young musicians throughout his life, but was similarly prodigious in his high expectations of professionalism and hard work. In order to raise orchestral standards, he abolished the system where musicians could bypass rehearsals, insisting that everyone practised together as a team. The first concert opened with the national anthem, followed by pieces from Chopin, Wagner, Leoncavallo and Kistler. It was described subsequently as the very 'first night of the proms', a musical tradition which continues to this day.

11 August

1892 Vote of No Confidence in Lord Salisbury
When the results of the 1892 election were finally counted, the Conservative government had lost seventy-nine seats but remained the largest party. The Liberals on the other hand made limited gains, but not enough to form a government. Gladstone tasted blood. In a special meeting with Irish Party leaders, he agreed to table a motion of no confidence in the government and topple Salisbury once and for good. This was dangerous. The debate sprawled over three days, finally reaching its conclusion at midnight on Thursday 11 August. The Commons was so crowded that staff had to bring extra chairs into the chamber. Of a total of 655 MPs,

only five were absent. Even the ninety-year-old Liberal Charles Villers arrived: although rather against Gladstone's wishes, he voted in favour of the government. The Conservatives were defeated and Salisbury dually resigned.

1892 The poet Hugh MacDiarmid was born in Langholm, Dumfriesshire. He would become one of Scotland's most famous writers.

12 August

1865 Lister performs historical surgery
In 1865 James Greenlees, an eleven-year-old child, was injured in an accident and rushed to Glasgow Royal Infirmary. The local surgeon, Joseph Lister, a handsome, dark-haired thirty-eight-year-old from Essex, had watched with growing alarm the escalating death rates in post-surgery care. Greenlees was administered chloroform. With the use of carbolic acid, Lister cleaned the wound. It was washed again several times each day for the next six weeks. Finally, it had healed and the young lad was declared fully recovered. It was arguably a milestone in British medical history.

1848 George Stephenson, 'The Father of the railways', died. His work was inextricably linked with the emergence of the British railway system that heralded one of the most profound social changes in history. Stephenson was born into a poor family in Northumberland and was illiterate until the age of eighteen. He is credited with constructing the first public line in Britain that employed steam locomotives, and later opened the famous Liverpool and Manchester Railway. His career was a rare example of self-made Victorian success.

1854 *Hard Times* by Charles Dickens was published. The novel was a striking critique of the industrial revolution where citizens were moulded from emotional and imaginative human beings, into products of a great industrial machine. The work also highlighted the growing problem of pollution in urban cities, depicting Coketown as physically disfigured by the poison of satanic smoke. Dickens dedicated *Hard Times* to his friend Thomas Carlyle.

13 August

1846 Buckingham Palace undergoes refurbishments
Every house has its flaws, even Buckingham Palace. Despite being the largest property in London, Queen Victoria was not satisfied with her new residence. The building was dingy and dark, especially in the winter. The floorboards were creaky and the interior was increasingly dowdy. In 1846 she proposed plans for renovations, including the removal of the large triumphal arch outside the main entrance. Sensitive to public opinion, Prime Minister Robert Peel was reluctant to agree. He remembered the extravagance of George IV, whose reckless spending

on lavish projects created much hostility towards the monarchy. On 13 August, parliament finally agreed and granted the queen a generous sum of £20,000. To quell any anger, however, money was generated through selling the Royal Pavilion in Brighton and opening it up to the public.

1888 John Logie Baird was born in Scotland. He is recognised for creating the first working television in 1925 and, later, the development of colour television. His technological inventions changed the world in ways few Victorians could ever have imagined.

1899 The pioneering director Alfred Hitchcock was born. He started life above a small grocer's shop at 517 High Road in Leytonstone, East London.

14 August

1889 London Dock strike begins
In 1889 a group of discontented, overworked, underpaid dockers from the Wharf, Riverside and General Labourers' Union walked out on strike. It was the biggest example of industrial action in Britain for decades and ignited considerable commotion. The dispute had started several months earlier after complaints were raised by the union leader, Ben Tillet, about the appalling working conditions dockers suffered on a daily basis. The drama also raised national awareness of the daily torments of dockers, most of whom endured backbreaking poverty. The strike would continue for four, long agonising weeks until finally being resolved with a pay increase.

1850 For the first time, local boroughs were allowed to create their own public libraries, providing universal access to books and educational resources for all aspects of British society. Many Victorians hoped they would become a beacon of education and self-improvement for poorer communities. Others, however, worried that libraries would become a 'meeting place' for political purposes.

1870 The actor Bransby Williams was born in Hackney. With his thick black hair, strong jaw and distinctive East London accent, Williams was a successful stage performer, known for his impersonations of characters from Dickens's novels. He made his professional debut in 1896 at the London Music Hall in Shoreditch. In 1957 Williams remarked on *Desert Island Discs* that one of his earliest memories was listening to William Gladstone speaking on a cylinder.

15 August

1875 The composer Samuel Coleridge-Taylor is born in London
In 1975 the great Victorian composer was finally honoured with a blue plaque outside his home in South Norwood, a testament to his lasting significance to

classical music. Coleridge-Taylor started life in Holborn, the son of Daniel Taylor, a doctor from Sierra Leone and Alice Martin. After studying at the Royal College of Music, he became a noted and popular classical composer. Coleridge-Taylor was also a passionate activist against racial prejudice, something which he suffered throughout his life. He died young of pneumonia in 1912 but lives on with a large and respected body of work.

1842 The Duke of Wellington was appointed the Commander in Chief of the Army. Robert Peel nominated the duke on account of his restless energy since leaving politics. Some critics argued the move was strategic, removing a potential leadership rival from the political mainstream.

16 August

1858 Queen Victoria communicates with President Buchanan of the United States
What became known as 'The Special Relationship' between both nations arguably had its roots in the Victorian era. In 1858 a telegraphed message was sent from Buckingham Palace over the transatlantic cable to American President James Buchanan. It was a remarkable experiment of a technological innovation which would transform communication. Victoria would never meet a serving US president, but enjoyed many official correspondences.

1888 T.E. Lawrence, also known as Lawrence of Arabia, was born in Carnarvonshire, Wales. He was the illegitimate son of the Anglo-Irish landowner Thomas Chapman and Sarah Lawrence. Chapman had previously been married to a Mrs Edith Hamilton, but deserted her with his daughter's governess, Sarah, in the 1880s. T.E. Lawrence's life would later be famously depicted in David Lean's film *Lawrence of Arabia*.

17 August

1896 Bridget Driscoll becomes the first person in the world to be killed in a car accident
On the horrifying afternoon of 17 August, a young woman called Bridget Driscoll accompanied by her daughter and close friend, was walking quietly along Dolphin Terrace in Crystal Palace, London. Without warning, a motor-car driving at a fast and reckless speed emerged, knocking her down and killing her. She was the first pedestrian in Britain killed by a car. The coroner remarked at the inquest that he hoped such a tragedy would 'never happen again'.

1837 John Kent became the first black police officer in British history, serving in the Carlisle Constabulary for seven years. He later became a court bailiff in 1844. He died in 1886.

1884 Dorothy Jewson was born in Norwich. In 2018 a Norfolk Theatre Company produced a play called *All Mouth, No Trousers*. The synopsis focused on a series of rebellious women who defied social prejudice and adversity to make significant contributions to society. One of the main characters was Dorothy Jewson, a now relatively unknown Labour politician and feminist campaigner, who became one of Britain's first women MPs.

18 August

1855 Queen Victoria visits Paris
The historic state visit was organised by both governments to celebrate the Anglo-French alliance during the Crimean War. The trip did not begin well. The queen arrived in Paris three hours late, creating serious discontent among the crowds. Fortunately, none of the public disapproval was depicted in the officially commissioned painting by Eugene Guérard which was given to Victoria by the French government. The queen was also keen to visit the tomb of Napoleon Bonaparte at les Invalides, but Napoleon's brother, Prince Jerome, was less than enthusiastic and refused to turn up. Luckily, the visit began to improve after Emperor Napoleon III hosted a magnificent reception for the royal visitors at the Palace of Versailles. It was a huge and powerful recognition of the improving relations between the two powers.

1882 The Electric Lighting Act was passed. With the use of electricity increasing throughout the century, the government eventually passed Britain's formal regulations. The Board of Trade was granted powers to facilitate electricity supplies in any areas across Britain and to terminate its supply to any household, business or individual who had not paid for its services.

1882 Castlerigg stone circle in the Lake District was registered as a scheduled monument

19 August

1897 Electrically-powered cabs introduced in London
The cabs were operated by the London Electric Cab Company who wanted a new and exciting mode of transport for the capital. The vehicles could drive at a whopping 9 miles per hour and boasted great interior luxury. However, a stipulation by the police meant they had to be driven by professional drivers in order to prevent accidents. They also proved extremely expensive and were discontinued three years later. The company blamed its failure partly on an orchestrated smear campaign driven by horse-drawn cab drivers. London would not see electric cabs on the streets again until 2019.

1890 The funeral mass of Cardinal John Henry Newman took place in Birmingham. The celebrated figure was canonised by Pope Francis in 2019.

1899 Lord Walter Talbot Kerr became the first Roman Catholic First Sea Lord. In an age of colossal national pride in the Royal Navy, the position held enormous respect and reverence in British society, as well as considerable power. Kerr was also the last First Sea Lord of the Victorian era. After his retirement in 1904, he became the President of the Catholic Union of Great Britain.

20 August

1854 A major cholera outbreak in London
The dreaded cholera returned in full fury in August 1854, inflicting misery and mayhem throughout London. Two years earlier, a cartoon labelled 'The Court for King Cholera' was published by *Punch*, highlighting the terrible realities of Victorian urban poverty. Unsanitary conditions, infected water and poor hygiene meant diseases spread rapidly throughout poor communities but were met with little meaningful solutions by central government. The widespread consensus was that 'miasma', or 'bad air' was the chief cause, a theory eventually disproven by John Snow. Even then, however, his findings were subjected to criticism and mockery. Outbreaks continued for several years.

1868 The Abergele rail disaster, one of Britain's deadliest accidents took place. The sad event occurred in the Welsh town of Abergele, when a mail train heading to Holyhead collided with a derailed goods train loaded with paraffin. Two carriages exploded. Thirty-three people were killed and many more badly burned.

1896 The painter John Everett Millas was buried in Painter's Corner at St Paul's Cathedral.

21 August

1876 Benjamin Disraeli is made Earl of Beaconsfield
By the late 1870s, Disraeli was beset by almost constant illness. In one session he complained of agonising pain and discomfort, made worse by the long laborious debates which drained his energy and worsened his mobility. Doctors advised he retire from the Commons or risk a serious health crisis. The queen, fearful of his illness, begged him to take a peerage, which he reluctantly accepted. In August 1876, Disraeli became the Earl of Beaconsfield and Viscount Hughenden. Despite the congratulations, his ennoblement signalled trouble for the Conservative party. His elevation removed one of the most charismatic Commons performers in history. No figure could emulate his quick wit or masterful parliamentary speeches. It would prove detrimental for future Conservative success.

22 August

1893 Prince Alfred becomes Duke of Saxe Coburg and Gotha
Alfred's accession to the Dukedom had been mired with controversy and intense family arguments. Since the late 1860s, it seemed inevitable that the incumbent Prince Ernest of Saxe Coburg, brother of Prince Albert, would die without an heir. Alfred was chosen as the designated successor but had not received a German education, nor ever lived in Germany. Ernest wanted Alfred to attend schools in Coburg, but Victoria refused. Relations between the two families soured. After Albert's death in 1863, Ernest began spreading gossip about the British royals, published in an anonymous pamphlet accusing Victoria of hostility towards Germany. The queen replied that the document was 'monstrous' and deeply disrespectful. By the time of Ernest's death in 1893, relations had healed, and Alfred enjoyed a relatively smooth transition. The elevation of course was more than just a title. Until 1918 Saxe Coburg and Gotha was a small duchy. The new position meant radical changes to Alfred's life and the stewardship of Rosenau Palace. Victoria deeply and intensely missed her son's presence. He died in Germany seven years later.

23 August

1868 The artist William Granville Hastings is born
Hastings was born in Kennington, Surrey, the third child of William Hastings senior and Williamina MacKay. As a child, his artistic abilities were recognised by insightful teachers and he enrolled at Lambeth Art School, followed by the Royal Academy in London. Unfortunately, opportunities for artists were often limited in nineteenth-century Britain, prompting Hastings to emigrate to the United States in the 1890s where he carved an enormous reputation for himself as a sculptor. Through much of the decade he designed numerous well-regarded statues including the famous 'Liberty Arming the Patriot'. Tragically his young life was cut short by stomach cancer in 1902, aged only thirty-four.

1900 The Mentmore Flower show was hosted on the estate of Mentmore Towers, the residence of Lord Rosebery.

24 August

1900 The Prince of Wales visits Germany
The Kaiser's prickly and unpredictable personality ruffled the feathers of many senior royals, especially the Prince of Wales. The prince found his nephew arrogant, argumentative, boastful and brash. Alexandra similarly loathed him, especially since the Prussian annexation of Schleswig-Holstein from Denmark in 1860, and found his loud, salty sense of humour 'common'. The growing tension

was mirrored by the kaiser, who secretly craved the acceptance of his British relatives but was also increasingly hostile. He was particularly angry that his uncle treated him as a mere nephew instead of a reigning monarch. Accompanied with his eldest son, the Prince of Wales travelled to Homburg to the castle of Friedrichshof to meet the kaiser but the meeting was fraught with anguish and the two returned home with seething bitterness. Poor relations would worsen significantly after Victoria's death.

1846 Patrick Bronte, father of the Bronte sisters, travelled to Manchester to undergo surgery for cataracts. The operation was performed painfully without anaesthetic.

1856 The English inventor Henry Bessemer developed a remarkable method of converting iron into steel, known subsequently as the Bessemer Converter. The results were revolutionary. For the first time, steel could now be produced in large quantities and used for numerous manufacturing industries across the country.

25 August

1875 Matthew Webb becomes the first man to swim the English Channel
The swashbuckling twenty-eight-year-old Matthew Webb swam the Channel in a time of twenty-one hours and forty-five minutes. He returned to England a national hero and received immeasurable media attention. Webb had previously attempted the challenge a few days earlier but was forced to withdraw after bad weather. With the safe escort of three boats, his second attempt proved more successful, although he was unfortunately stung by a jellyfish midway. This didn't delay his timings. When he arrived on French soil on the 25th, enthusiastic crowds gave him a hearty welcome. Webb sadly died in 1883 while swimming in the Niagara River.

1861 The Clayton Tunnel rail crash took place. The tragedy occurred in the morning of Sunday 25 August when two trains collided in a tunnel five miles from Brighton. Twenty-three passengers were killed and over 170 people were injured. Following an inquest, it seemed that communication errors were responsible for the disaster. For years, the crash was the deadliest railway disaster in British history. It is said the tunnel is still haunted by the screams and torment of terrified victims.

26 August

1859 Prince Albert celebrates his 40th birthday at Osborne House
The day started with music, performed by a superb choir at Osborne House, followed by a long line of congratulatory messages from friends and family. In the afternoon, Albert planted a tree in the palace grounds and had dinner accompanied with the band of the Rifle Brigade. In the evening, the royal couple enjoyed a

stupendous firework display. The nearby yachts in the sea illuminated their lights to create a fanfare of colour and celebration.

1880 For the first time, school attendance became compulsory, but only between the ages of five and ten. Most poor children were often forced to find employment to supplement their struggling parent's income.

1889 The Protection of Children Act was granted Royal Assent. The new law introduced penalties for the mistreatment of children.

27 August

1855 The Queen returns from her trip to France
Victoria arrived from the sunshine of France to predictably wet English weather. The mud roads were thick and solid, marked by the faint indentations of horse hooves and footprints, made worse by the sporadic splashing of cold rain and hail. The queen had enjoyed a historic visit and received genuine praise in the national press for her diplomacy and charm. She adored French food, loved French scenery, the people and the weather, although often found the temperatures oppressively hot and unbearable. Albert, meanwhile, relished the opportunity to drive independently through the famous Bois de Boulogne, which also coincided with his thirty-sixth birthday. The British government expressed their appreciation to the royals for helping strengthen Anglo-French relations.

1896 The Anglo-Zanzibar War was declared. The conflict was one of the shortest in history, lasting just thirty-eight minutes. The war ended in British victory.

28 August

1884 Peter Fraser, Prime Minister of New Zealand, is born in Scotland
Like many Victorians, Fraser emigrated from the poverty and pain of working-class Britain in hope of a better life in the mountainous haven of New Zealand. He was born in Hill of Fearn, a tiny village in the Highlands. His parents were poor, and his education was limited. Fraser later became a politician, and eventually the twenty-fourth prime minister of New Zealand.

1857 The Matrimonial Causes Act was granted royal assent. The new law sparked intense controversy for allowing men to divorce their wives for adultery, sparking backlash from the Church of England. Bishop Samuel Wilberforce was a particularly fierce critic, as was Gladstone who warned it would signal the breakdown of society.

1837 Worcestershire Sauce was invented by Lea & Perrins. It proved extremely popular with the Victorian public.

1900 Philosopher Henry Sidgwick died. Sidgwick was distinguished for co-founding Newnham College, an educational institution exclusively for female students. Together with his wife, who later became the college principal, Sidgwick worked hard to promote female education throughout Britain. He is also remembered for the publication of a philosophy book, *The Methods of Ethics*. Sidgwick was diagnosed with cancer and died in 1900, aged sixty-two.

29 August

1892 William Gladstone is attacked by a 'Mad Cow'
On 29 August, Thomas Bailey, an estate worker at Hawarden, was sitting peacefully in his office. It was a pleasant morning. Sunlight smiled on the window, as rays of light beamed softly through the glass, bouncing across the walls. The air was smooth and calming, perfect conditions for a nice summer's day. The peace was about to be disturbed.

Suddenly, a sweaty, exhausted figure stormed into the room. A 'mad cow' had attacked Prime Minister William Gladstone, who had almost been killed in a bizarre accident. Gladstone had been walking the fields of his country estate when he suddenly encountered a large and very angry cow. The cow rushed towards the premier, piercing her horns into Gladstone's body.

Bailey immediately took his rifle and ran into the estate. Spotting the cow from afar, he fired two shots. The cow was killed instantly and Gladstone was saved. Later, the dead animal was sold to a butcher in Chester. The story, however, had become famous and frequently embellished by local townsfolk. Recognising the financial appeal of the story, Bailey travelled again to Chester and repurchased the cow's head, which he later mounted in a large presentation case and placed on display in his local pub.

30 August

1841 Sir Robert Peel forms a Conservative government
Unlike his dazzling predecessor, Peel seemed a dull and dour replacement. Unusually for the time, Peel was no aristocrat. His family had made their fortune from the textile industry and Peel entered Parliament at just twenty-one for an Irish constituency which was later abolished. His government was perhaps most famous for the controversial abolition of the corn laws, and a number of reforms including the 1844 Factory Act, the 1844 Railway Regulation Act and the Income Tax Act 1842. Although contentious within his own party, his supporters were proud and often deeply protective of their leader. In later years, they became known as 'Peelites'.

1895 The Marquess of Queensberry was questioned by French police in Monte Carlo for challenging Lord Rosebery to a duel.

31 August

1888 The first of the Whitechapel murders occurs
No killer had inflicted as much horror, disgust and despair on Victorian Britain as Jack the Ripper. His identity was unknown, but his crimes became famous throughout the world for their brutality and cruelty. The murders created both a terrifying sense of mystery and morbid fascination. The first murder associated conclusively with Jack occurred on the grim evening of 31 August 1888 in the gloomy back streets of Whitechapel. The body of a forty-three-year-old woman named Mary Ann Nichols was discovered at 3.45am in Bucks Row. She had been stabbed multiple times. As news spread of the killing, a large crowd of spectators gathered on the scene. Police arrived afterwards and moved the body to a nearby street for investigations. By the time her official inquest was concluded, three other women had been killed in the area. Panic swept the nation.

September

1 September

1893 Winston Churchill enrols at Sandhurst
Churchill's enrolment at Sandhurst came after two previous rejections, yet he received little congratulations from his family. In a shatteringly harsh letter, his father, Lord Randolph, accused Winston of laziness and sloppiness, living an idle life with little meaningful direction. He even accused him of acquiring enrolment through 'uncredible' means. The letter was deeply wounding and entrenched Winston with a deep-rooted desire to please his father, an ambition which was ultimately never achieved.

1877 The scientist Francis William Aston was born. He later won the Nobel Prize for chemistry after discovering isotopes in several non-radioactive elements.

2 September

1870 Claude Monet arrives in London
Monet escaped the chaos of the Franco-Prussian War to live in London, where he found refuge in a tiny flat near Piccadilly Circus. Monet was unimpressed with London. Compared to the grandeur and flamboyancy of France, England seemed considerably duller and less vibrant. With limited English, Monet became friends with the French community, especially Camille Pissarro and Paul Durand Ruel, who proved a steady influence on his work. While in England, he produced one of his most famous pieces, *The Thames Below Westminster*, which was exhibited by Ruel in 1873, providing a much-needed financial boost. Overall, however, the visit was unproductive and, in 1871, he relocated to the Netherlands. In later, more successful years, Monet returned to Britain, and frequented the luxurious Savoy Hotel. His favourite room was renamed 'The Monet Suite'.

1898 The Battle of Omdurman took place. It was the final stage of the Anglo-Egyptian Mahdist War. Among the participants was Winston Churchill.

3 September

1878 The Thames shipping disaster
The sinking of the SS *Princess Alice* was the greatest inland waterway tragedy in British history, leading to between 600 and 700 deaths and multiple serious injuries. The steamer was sailing in the Gallions Reach between Woolwich and Thamesmead when it suddenly collided with a large cargo ship, the SS *Bywell Castle*. Hundreds of terrified passengers threw themselves into the Thames and drowned. For weeks, corpses of victims were washed up onto the shore. Local watermen were paid £2 a day to search for dead bodies and five shillings for each corpse they recovered. Anxious family members gathered for days outside Woolwich Dockyard waiting for any news of their loved ones. Over 20,000 people donated money to a fund for the victims.

4 September

1839 The First Opium War is declared
The origins of the conflict had begun several years earlier. The Chinese government had long complained that several Chinese citizens were becoming addicted to a dangerous opium drug which the British exported throughout the eighteenth and nineteenth century. In 1839 the Chinese government confiscated the drug from British dealers and publicly destroyed much of its surplus. In response, the British government, heavily influenced by Lord Palmerston, despatched a naval force to China and declared war. The conflict was controversial with many opponents highlighting the immorality of the opium trade. William Gladstone was a particularly vocal critic, labelling the conflict as 'Palmerston's War', smearing Britain's reputation with disgrace.

1860 The first weather report appeared in *The Times*. Ironically, the historic moment occurred by chance. Vice Admiral Robert FitzRoy had been studying British weather for decades but only decided to publish his findings in 1860. Unknowingly, he created the world's first weather forecast and started a trend which continues to this day.

1884 The British government ended its policy of transporting criminals to New South Wales in Australia.

5 September

1856 The overheated Birmingham Music Festival
The final day of Birmingham's Music Hall Festival finished with a bang, although not necessarily for the right reasons. Although seen as a masterpiece of Victorian architecture, the hall struggled with ventilation, something which hadn't become

September

apparent until 5 September when the building was crammed to full capacity. The heat was extremely intense and intolerable.

1882 Tottenham Hotspur Football Club was established by a fourteen-year-old child called Bobby Buckle and a group of schoolboys. The lads were already members of a cricket club but wanted to play sport during the winter months and so established the 'Hotspur football club'. Buckle served as the first captain, and their bible teacher; John Ripsher, became the club's first president. It was later renamed Tottenham Hotspur and played its debut match on 30 September.

6 September

1844 The christening of Prince Alfred
Alfred was baptised precisely a month after his birth in the small private chapel at Windsor. His godparents included Prince George of Cambridge, the Duchess of Saxe-Coburg and Gotha and the Queen's half-brother, the Prince of Leiningen. Unfortunately, Leiningen couldn't attend the ceremony, and was represented by the Duke of Wellington.

1853 Writer George Bradshaw died. Bradshaw was the author of the *Bradshaw Guide* of railway travel, covering many miles of railway lines and timetables across Britain. Having contracted cholera in Norway, he died in Oslo aged fifty-three. His guides continued to be printed years after his death.

1880 W.G. Grace made his international test debut. Few cricketers have enjoyed more popular and posthumous acclaim as William Gilbert Grace. He made his international debut at The Oval in September 1880, competing against the formidable Australian team in a tense match.

7 September

1858 Leeds Town Hall opened
Propositions for a town hall had begun in 1852, with an open competition established to find the most appealing proposals to reflect Leeds' rising status within the country. The judging committee was advised by Charles Barry, but a premium of just £200 was offered for the winning candidate, a relatively small amount in light of the task. The eventual winner, Cuthbert Brodrick, was a thirty-one-year-old Yorkshireman who submitted a Roman-style design with an ornate decorative interior. The project commenced in 1853 but was plagued with problems and stress.

Recruitment for the Crimean War meant many workers enlisted in the Army, leading to a builder shortage and an increase in wages. Construction was slow. Brodrick grew disappointed at the quality of work and faced escalating costs which eventually left him bankrupt. On one occasion, he physically took a hammer and destroyed part of the brickwork to protest about its quality. His regular revisions of plans also created frustration with workmen. The hall was finally opened by Queen Victoria in 1858. Its enduring popularity is a testament to Brodrick's work and innate perfectionism.

1890 The Southampton Dock strike took place. The 1880s were a time of festering industrial unrest, epitomised by the famous London dock strike of 1889. A year later, a similar strike occurred in Southampton with representatives of the Dockers' Union proposing better wages for workers. The industrial action did not prove successful. Just a week later, the strike ended and the Southampton branch of the Dockers' Union collapsed.

8 September

1888 The second victim of Jack the Ripper is murdered
On 8 September the second official victim of Jack the Ripper was discovered in the backyard of 29 Hanbury Street. Annie Chapman, a forty-seven-year-old mother of three, was found brutally murdered, sending London into yet another wave of hysteria and panic. Jack the Ripper's presence cemented a horrifying feeling of unease in London, unleashing unprecedented national attention.

1893- The Second Home Rule Bill was defeated by the House of Lords. Gladstone was deeply disappointed and resigned as prime minister a year later.

9 September

1845 The Irish Famine begins
In 1845, a devastating humanitarian disaster took place on the doorstep of the richest nation on earth. A blight in the potato crop created one of the worst famines in modern Irish history and killed about a million people. The British government's response was slow and inadequate. To make matters worse, many smallholders were forcibly evicted from their homes by landlords, including the military leader the Earl of Lucan who dislodged thousands of tenants from his estates. Approximately two million people left Ireland, with the principal destination being England or Scotland. Many others relocated to the United States and Canada.

1885 The sculptor Clare Sheridan was born. A self-confessed communist, Sheridan was the cousin of Winston Churchill but differed enormously in her political views. She is particularly well known for creating a large bust of the Bolshevik leader, Vladimir Lenin.

September

10 September

1855 Over 40,000 people witness the funeral procession of Feargus O'Connor in London
The funeral of the Irish politician Feargus O'Connor attracted some of the largest crowds seen in London for decades. O'Connor was a passionate political and controversial radical who led the Chartist cause to huge national prominence. In the 1850s his once strong health declined and, in 1852, he was arrested for assaulting three members of Parliament. Suffering from severe stress, he relocated to an asylum until dying in Notting Hill in 1855. His Roman Catholic funeral service was held in Kensal Green Cemetery. Two men were later arrested for pickpocketing mourners during the service.

1897 A London taxi driver, George Smith, became the first Briton convicted of drunk-driving. He was fined £1.

11 September

1869- The National Wallace Monument is opened
The reassuring sight of the Wallace Monument is an icon of Stirling, a visual architectural tribute to one of Scotland's most famous figures. Calls for a permanent memorial had spread across Scotland since the 1840s, but it took twenty years until something was actually done. The monument was erected suitably near Wallace's victory at the Battle of Stirling Bridge and the foundation stone was laid in 1861, appropriately on the 547th anniversary of the Battle of Bannockburn, followed by a poignant inaugural ceremony on 11 September 1869. A large procession of local leaders from the Stirling Corn Exchange proceeded to the monument where the official opening took place. In 1886 a 'hall of heroes' was also opened with several busts of famous Scottish characters, including Robert the Bruce.

1878 A terrible mining tragedy took place in the small Welsh town of Abercarn. Over 300 workers, including children, were underground when an explosion tore through the Prince of Wales Colliery. The mine was filled with smoke and 268 people were killed. A verdict later stated that the tragedy was caused by firedamp ignition.

1885 The writer D.H. Lawrence was born in the deprived town of Eastwood, Nottinghamshire. His powerful descriptions of working-class life interweaves throughout his novels, providing a rich and lasting illustration of the Victorian era for future generations.

1895 Panic hit the town of Birmingham on 11 September when the iconic FA Cup was mysteriously stolen following Aston Villa's victory over West Bromwich Albion. After a sensational game held earlier that afternoon, the trophy was triumphantly displayed in Mister William Shillcock's football shop in Birmingham. Unfortunately, a rogue customer stole the cup and seemingly vanished into thin air. It was never seen again.

12 September

1846 Elizabet Barratt marries Robert Browning in secret
By the mid-1840s Barratt had become one of Britain's most respected and popular poets, crowned with a legion of devoted fans and supporters. One such supporter was the thirty-four-year-old writer Robert Browning who, in 1844, wrote a letter to Barratt, praising her latest collection of works. They met for the first time on 20 May 1845 and quickly fell in love. Unfortunately, the Barratt family were deeply disapproving of the relationship and regarded Browning as a gold-digger who would use the romance for personal profit. In defiance of her parents, on 12 September 1845, Barratt married Browning in a private ceremony at Saint Marylebone Parish Church. She told nobody of the event and, a week later, eloped with her husband to Pisa, Italy. Barratt's father was furious and disinherited her. She never returned to England.

13 September

1877 Manchester Town Hall is opened
Many Victorian architects felt it was their duty to stamp their mark on Britain, none more so than Alfred Waterhouse. As was common for the era, in 1863 a competition was launched to construct a town hall in the great city of Manchester. Over 100 entries were submitted but only eight were chosen as finalists. Curiously, Waterhouse's initial design did not meet with immediate acclaim. The judges, Thomas Leverton Donaldson and George Edmund Street, both found his drawings bland compared to other proposals and he was eventually placed fourth in terms of aesthetics. Nevertheless, in actual quality and layout, it was deemed far superior by providing meticulous professional detail which eventually won him the contest.

As many Victorian properties had become damaged by smog over the years, Waterhouse adopted a uniform stone exterior, which would cope better with Manchester's heavy industrial backdrop. The centrepiece included a large Gothic clock tower, inscribed with the line from Tennyson's famous poem *Ring Out, Wild Bells*: 'Ring out the false, ring in the true'. Initially it was hoped that the building would be opened by Queen Victoria, but she refused. Instead, the honour was passed to the radical mayor, Abel Heywood, creating local controversy.

14 September

1852 The Duke of Wellington dies at Walmer Castle
'One cannot think of this country without the duke,' scrawled a mournful Queen Victoria, 'our immortal hero … His loss will be quite irreparable.' Victoria was in Scotland when the news broke, by which point plans for a state funeral were already in motion. His body lay in state in the Great Hall of the Royal Hospital Chelsea, covered entirely by enormous black drapery that formed a protective tent

September

over his coffin. Before the public were admitted, the emotional queen visited for a private viewing, followed by Chelsea in-pensioners. The public queue eventually became so long that it stretched back towards Victoria station. Two women were tragically crushed to death in the wait.

1852 On the same day the architect Augustus Pugin also died suddenly at his home. Forty-three years younger than the duke, Pugin had suffered severe mental and physical exhaustion after years of overwork. In February he had a mental breakdown while travelling on a train. After a four-month stay in an asylum, he was moved to Bethlem Royal Hospital, commonly known as Bedlam, followed by convalescence in a private house. In September, he was moved back to his residence, 'The Grange', in Ramsgate where he grew dangerously ill. Just a few days before his death, Pugin was visited by Charles Barry who presented him with drawings of the proposed parliamentary clocktower. He died shortly afterwards, aged forty. Despite his untimely passing, Pugin's historical profile has risen in recent years. He now receives the just architectural appreciation he deserved in life.

15 September

1859 Isambard Kingdom Brunel dies
Overwork eventually had its toll on Britain's most iconic engineer who breathed his last on 15 September. He was fifty-three-years old. After decades of relentless stress and heavy smoking, Brunel suffered a stroke onboard the SS *Great Eastern*. He was driven back to his London residence in Duke Street, but declared dead shortly after arrival. In 2002, a public poll organised by the BBC placed Brunel as the second greatest Briton of all time. His innovative structures, vessels, buildings and bridges left a long and powerful legacy for future generations. He remains unquestionably the most recognisable Victorian engineer, perhaps the greatest in British history.

1871 The Army and Navy store was established by a group of military officers with the aim of providing goods and clothes for officers at low costs. The shop eventually became a successful department store.

1890 The writer Agatha Christie was born in Torquay. Christie's father died in 1901, the same year as Queen Victoria. For the rest of her life, she regarded the year as heralding the end of her childhood and the dawn of her adult years.

16 September

1858 Andrew Bonar Law is born in Canada
While most Victorian conservative parliamentarians emerged from the striped-lawn sanctuaries of aristocratic estates, Bonar Law was born in a tiny, draughty house overlooking the raging Richibucto river in New Brunswick. His father was

a fiery minister of the New Church of Scotland and had originally hailed from Ireland. His mother, Eliza, initially wanted to name him Robert after a favourite preacher, Robert Murray M'Cheyne, but decided on Andrew Bonar instead, the name of another tough Victorian clergyman. Life was hard for Bonar Law. He relocated to Scotland in 1861 and joined the Conservative Party as a young man. He was elected to parliament just three months before Queen Victoria's death.

1847 William Shakespeare's birthplace was purchased by the Shakespeare Birthplace Trust. The American millionaire Phineas Barnum had originally hoped to buy the iconic sixteenth-century property in Stratford upon Avon, demolish the building and then rebuild it in the United States. Fortunately, a group of Shakespeare enthusiasts clubbed together and formed the Shakespeare Birthplace Trust. Donations were received from the likes of Charles Dickens and other influential figures. Eventually, they raised £3,000 and purchased the house on 16 September 1847.

1889 The London Dock Strike was concluded. The crisis was resolved partly thanks to the work of Cardinal Henry Manning who served as a mediator between the dock owners and workers. Manning was later awarded with £160 from the thankful strikers in recognition for his conduct.

17 September

1895 Fears of an Anglo-American war
Relations between Britain and the United States were often fraught with controversy, epitomised no more vividly than a major argument in 1895. A border dispute between Venezuela and British Guiana had dangerously escalated into a full-blown crisis. The United States intervened to take Venezuela's side, creating fury in Whitehall. President Grover Cleveland demanded British withdrawal from the region and threatened military conflict. War was averted but relations remained strained for several years.

18 September

1893 Lord Stanley resigned as Governor General of Canada
Stanley created the Stanley Cup which even now is presented to the National Hockey League champion. It is regarded as the oldest trophy awarded to a professional sports franchise in North America. Unlike his father, former Prime Minister Lord Derby, Stanley was a prodigious and passionate sports enthusiast. He is also credited for raising awareness of hockey throughout Canada, Britain and beyond.

1879 The Blackpool Illuminations were switched on. Known initially as 'artificial sunshine', the illuminations were made from eight carbon-arc lamps. It has since become a tradition to have the lights turned on in an annual light festival.

September

19 September

1881 Britain shocked by the death of President James Garfield
The violent and cruel death of the American President Garfield, which shocked both sides of the Atlantic, created an unprecedented display of grief and horror throughout Britain. The British public were stunned that another sitting president had been murdered. Throughout London and other major cities, flags were flown at half-mast and many shops were closed early. Queen Victoria sent a colossal wreath, along with a personal telegram. Prayers were offered for the president in St Paul's Cathedral. Some remarked that the death even helped strengthen Anglo-American relations.

1839 The chocolate manufacturer George Cadbury was born in Birmingham. He was the son of the legendary businessman John Cadbury, founder of the Cadbury chocolate brand. George took over the company in 1861, working alongside his brother Richard to radically improve the welfare of his workers. As devout Quakers, both brothers believed passionately in helping the poor and worked to build an ideal Victorian model village where their employees would live and work. The company even organised leisure and built a swimming pool.

20 September

1862 One of London's oldest housing associations, the Peabody Trust, is founded
Slum housing was an unattractive and painful feature of poor communities in Victorian Britain. Shocked by appalling urban poverty, in 1862 the American financier George Peabody launched the Peabody Trust to provide adequate housing for some of London's poorest citizens. The first property was opened in Commercial Street, Spitalfields, costing a colossal £22,000 to construct. In line with Victorian morality, residents were expected to adhere to a strict moral code. Heavy drinking, gambling and swearing were discouraged. Punctual rental payments were expected and a night curfew was also established to prevent 'vice' and 'moral impropriety'. Despite the initial strictness, the trust provided vulnerable citizens a clean and comfortable place to live.

1860 The Prince of Wales departed for the first royal tour of the United States of America. It was a source of momentous Anglo-American interest.

21 September

1856 Queen Victoria meets Florence Nightingale
The meeting did not run smoothly. The usually gregarious Victoria found herself lost for words with Florence Nightingale who seemed different, almost detached from her public persona. The Victorian image of Nightingale commonly focused

on her motherly, compassionate qualities, overlooking her enormous academic and organisational abilities. She was an intellectual, one of the first individuals to incorporate data and statistics into medical practice and a highly intelligent administrator. She wanted medical reform and was prepared to pursue her case, even with the government. Desperate to break the awkward silence, the queen called Albert into the room and intellectual conversation flowed freely.

1866 The celebrated author H.G. Wells was born in Kent, the youngest son of Joseph Wells, a professional cricketer, shopkeeper and once gardener at the grand Sussex home, Uppark, now owned by the national trust. His mother, Sarah, also worked at Uppark. His parents had married in 1853.

1874 Gustav Holst, the legendary composer, was born in Cheltenham, Gloucestershire.

22 September

1890 Russian flu outbreak in England
In September an explosion of flu burst across the Russian city of Petropavlovsk and spread halfway across the world in a matter of months. The illness was no respecter of rank, wealth or power. Thousands of well-known people were infected, including Gladstone, Salisbury, the Prince of Wales, Tsar Alexander III, Alfonso XIII and several others. Princess Augusta of Germany died of the disease, as did the former king of Spain. Many shops in London temporarily shut. Courts were closed and railway lines disrupted. Despite appeals from doctors to downplay hysteria, the epidemic spread fear across the country.

23 September

1842 The queen's beloved former governess, Louise Lehzen, was dismissed from the royal court
Lehzen was dedicated to Victoria. She was a generous lady who held a deep affection for the queen, especially during her unhappy and restrictive childhood. Lehzen long boasted of never taking a day off work in eighteen years, something which unfortunately did not secure her position. Albert regarded Lenzen as noisy, interfering and 'crazy'. Despite Victoria's personal intervention, she was dismissed on 23 September under the guise of 'ill-health', but granted a generous pension of £800 a year. She continued to communicate regularly with the queen until her death in 1870.

1896 Queen Victoria surpassed King George III as the longest-reigning British monarch. Celebrations were delayed until June 1897 when the country came together for the spectacular Diamond Jubilee. The occasion also marked a period of reflection, notably on the transformative changes that had taken place during her reign.

September

24 September

1888 The Royal Court Theatre is opened
The Royal Court was a majestic explosion of colour and Victorian vibrancy. Having originally opened in 1870 as the New Chelsea Theatre, the building was closed on 22 July 1887 for major renovations under the guidance of Bertie Crewe and Walter Emden. The new design was constructed in an exciting Italianate style with bold red bricks. The interior was bright, cheerful and immensely popular.

1842 Writer Branwell Bronte died aged thirty-one. Perhaps the least famous member of the illustrious clan, Branwell suffered a turbulent life of artistic disappointment and personal misfortune. In the 1840s he was plagued with tuberculosis, alcoholism and delirium and reportedly died standing up as a physical illustration of the human will. His untimely death devastated the family, especially Emily, who succumbed to the same disease later the same year.

1853 England's first provincial daily newspaper, Liverpool's *Northern Daily Times* was established.

1863 William Debenham, the founder of Debenham's department store died in London

25 September

1889 The Frome Cheddar Cheese Festival took place
Over 193 cheeses were entered into the festival. Twenty-six ladies also competed in a tough butter-making contest. The show attracted colossal crowds of battle-hardened cheese enthusiasts, with the first prize going to a Mr J. Hall from Swindon. In the afternoon, contestants sat down for a lunch presided over by the Marquis of Bath. Cheese was appropriately first on the menu.

1871 The earliest recorded snowfall occurred in London. Even by British standards, September was an early month for frosty weather. The unseasonably cold temperatures were deeply unpopular with Londoners who, only a few months earlier, had been basking in a long hot summer.

26 September

1875 The Prince of Wales departs for India on an eight-month tour
The trip was no holiday. Every day included excursions to various places across the beautiful country, followed by several formal dinners in the evening and the occasional diplomatic reception. Accompanying the prince on the trip was the naval officer, Charles Beresford, who quickly became exhausted by the prince's tiresome demands. Ever fashionable, the prince demanded his entourage dress for

dinner with a formal bow tie and tails, even in the extreme heat. The prince was also appalled at the nasty treatment of Indians by many British officers.

1881 Godalming in Surrey became the first town in Britain to have its streets illuminated by electric light. More sceptical commentators remarked that the invention would be expensive and costly to run.

1900 The last, and arguably most divisive general election of the Victorian era, was called on 26 September. Rising nationalism and anger, coupled with the backdrop of the Second Boer War, combined to create an aggressive atmosphere of sectarian political differences. The Conservative government, led by the ailing Lord Salisbury, was increasingly dominated by the energetic Joseph Chamberlain who led a vicious campaign against the Liberals. The election resulted in a large Conservative victory.

27 September

1871 Rochdale Town Hall is inaugurated
The hall was praised by various critics as one of the greatest municipal buildings in England. Success, however, did not come cheaply. At a cost of approximately £160,000 (the equivalent of over £15million today), it was designed by the young Henry Crossland, previously a pupil of George Gilbert Scott. The building was so popular, it was said that even Adolf Hitler was a fan and wanted to transport it brick by brick to Germany in the event of a successful invasion of Britain.

1880 The Guildhall School of Music and Drama was established. It was the first municipal music college in Britain and opened with just sixty-four part-time students. Future alumni included the playwright Noel Coward.

1899 *King John* became the first Shakespearean film adaptation in British history. The central role was performed by Herbert Beerbohm Tree, with Dora Senior as Prince Henry. Since 1899 there have been numerous big screen adaptations of Shakespeare's works, but ironically few modern depictions of *King John*.

28 September

1869 Hilda Runciman, a campaigner for cancer care and later member of parliament, is born in Durham
Hilda Runciman began life as Hilda Stevenson, fifth daughter of James Cochran Stevenson, a Scottish Liberal MP, and Eliza Ramsey Anderson. Runciman was among the first women magistrates in British history, a charity campaigner, founder of the Westminster Housing Trust, Member of Parliament, chairwoman of the Westminster Housing Association, President of the Women's National Liberal Federation, and the Women's Free Church Council. She was also a prominent campaigner for cancer care, a

somewhat taboo subject in the nineteenth and early-twentieth century. Her achievements were frequently overlooked by her more famous husband, Walter Runciman.

1852 John French, the first commander of the British Expeditionary Force during the First World War was born. Unlike many of his military colleagues, his childhood was not privileged or especially wealthy. His father was a military man who died when French was young, leaving the family heartbroken. His mother later suffered a nervous breakdown and was admitted to an asylum. As a young man, French joined the Royal Navy but suffered seasickness and moved into the Army. After surviving many scandals, including allegations of adultery, he became a leading commander of British forces during the First World War.

1884 Michael Mark' opened a small, unassuming market stall in Leeds. It would eventually evolve into Marks and Spencer, one of the biggest department stores in Britain.

29 September

1850 The Pope re-establishes Roman Catholic diocesan hierarchy in England
Universalis Ecclesiae was a landmark Papal Bull that re-established Catholic dioceses in England for the first time since the reign of Queen Elizabeth I. Within a few years, several Catholic churches emerged across Britain. Plans also began for the construction of a new cathedral in Westminster, the heartland of London. A charismatic forty-eight-year-old Spaniard, Nicholas Wiseman, was appointed as first Archbishop of Westminster. His arrival in England, however, was hostile, tarnished by allegations of 'papal aggression' in the press.

1885 The world's first electric tramway was opened in Blackpool. While railways had transformed travel in Britain, the experience was not always comfortable, particularly for those in third-class carriages. In 1885 Blackpool opened its first electric tramway which promised to bring comfort and speed for the everyday commuter.

30 September

1850 A Political scandal
The chartist leader Feargus O'Connor was apprehended by police on charges of sedition and inciting riots, strikes and general unrest against the British government. The summer of 1849 had been dominated by a wave of chartist protests, including the famous Plug Riots. At 6.30pm, O'Connor was taken from his house in Hampstead and escorted to a police station where he was duly arrested.

1888 Jack the Ripper's victims, Elizabeth Stride and Catherine Eddowesis, were discovered dead in London's East End.

October

1 October

1868 St Pancras Station is opened
The Victorians were fascinated by history. The construction of St Pancras, like the Houses of Parliament, was designed partly to resemble the majestic mediaeval buildings of England's past. Its facade was bold, visionary and magnificent. In 1873 the Midland Grand Hotel was added which stands as further testament to the vibrant neo-Gothic style which defined the era. In the 1960s the hotel fell into despair but was faithfully restored in the twenty-first century to recapture its true Victorian essence of stately grandeur.

1885 The Victorian philanthropist the 7th Earl of Shaftesbury died in Kent. The celebrated figure had previously been diagnosed with inflammation of the lungs and died after midday. The date is commemorated annually by the Church of England. He is also remembered in the liturgical calendar of the Episcopal Church.

1890 Oscar-winning actor Stanley Holloway was born in Essex. He is best known for playing Dr Doolittle in the 1964 film *My Fair Lady*.

2 October

1870 Sir Francis Knollys appointed the Prince of Wales's Private Secretary
Francis Knollys was often described as the 'most powerful' man in Britain. A shrewd, tenacious former soldier, his appointment came after weeks of damaging scandal that threatened the reputation of the Prince of Wales. Sometimes referred to as the Victorian Thomas Cromwell, Knollys was a gifted, canny and hardworking operator who would stop at nothing to protect his master's reputation. After the death of Prince Albert in 1861, Victoria blamed her 'decadent' son for hastening her husband's death. She pleaded with Knollys to inject a sense of sobriety into her young son's life. He improved his finances, curtailed his lavish spending and provided sound and constructive advice. His association with the prince would last a lifetime and, after the queen's death, he became the Private Secretary to the Sovereign.

October

1899 The London School of Hygiene and Tropical Medicine was founded. The institution was formed thanks to a generous donation by Bomanjee Dinshaw Petit. The school's aim was to perform medical research. Today it has grown into one of the world's leading public research universities.

3 October

1845 The Queen purchases Osborne House on the Isle of Wight
The royal family would often holiday at Osborne during July, soaking up the calming views of the sea, an asset unmatched by any royal residence in England. Much of the property was designed by Prince Albert who wanted a visual representation of an Italian renaissance palace, an embodiment of British imperial craftsmanship in the modern era.

While at Osborne, the royal children were encouraged to engage in outdoor pursuits such as gardening and vegetable growing, while, at the same time, learn the basics of mathematics and economics by selling their produce to their father. Unusually for the time, they were also expected to cook and even clean. The house had a private beach where the family would swim and relax. The Queen hoped that Osborne would be passed down to subsequent generations but her wishes were ignored. Having never liked the property, Edward VII bequeathed the house to the nation on his coronation day in 1902.

1896 Queen Victoria was captured on film for the first time. In the age of digital phones and affordable cameras, it's quaint to think that most Victorians treated the camera with either suspicion, awe, or confusion. On 3 October 1896, John Downey, son of the professional photographer William Downey, recorded film footage of Victoria at Balmoral Castle. Although the total length runs to just over a minute, it is a fascinating and treasured historical source. Victoria was intrigued by the device, although in private remarked it was unlikely to take off.

1896 The British artist William Morris succumbed to tuberculosis after many years of declining health. In July 1896 he was taken seriously ill in Norway after suffering hallucinations. He returned to England incapacitated and died at his house in the early hours of 3 October.

4 October

1896 Journalist Dorothy Lawrence is born
During the First World War Lawrence disguised herself as a soldier to join the Army. Operating under the false name of Private Denis Smith, she travelled to the Somme in France but was quickly horrified by the vicious realities of trench warfare. Her health suffered and, after just ten days, she revealed her true identity. Lawrence

was arrested on false charges of espionage but was released after assurances that she would never reveal the drama. She later wrote an autobiography describing the experience which was published posthumously.

1837 Queen Victoria visited Brighton for the first time as monarch but was not impressed. She found the locals 'indiscreet and troublesome' and was unhappy with the town's architecture. She visited again for the last time in February 1845.

5 October

1895 The first individual time trial takes place
Cycling became almost a national craze in the late nineteenth century. Even ardent traditionalists like Lord Salisbury approved and could be spotted regularly riding his penny-farthing through the dusty walkways of St James Park. In 1895, the first time trial for cyclists took place on a gruelling fifty-mile course in North London. It was organised by the North Road Cycling Club after a formal ban on cyclists racing in residential roads. The trial required contestants to compete against the clock on an individual basis in tough battle of fitness.

1900 Early in the morning of 5 October, an enormous fire broke out at Welbeck Abbey, the rural residence of the 6th Duke of Portland. One wing of the building was completely destroyed.

6 October

1866 The West Pier in Brighton is opened
Construction on the great West Pier started in 1863 but wasn't completed for three years. The brain behind the project was Eugenius Birch, a prominent local engineer who wanted to attract visitors to the peaceful seaside town, which he felt was painfully unappreciated by English tourists. The pier itself was built in a rather simple structure, using dozens of sturdy iron threaded columns that were screwed tightly into the seabed. The pier did not survive. Like many Victorian buildings in the twentieth century, it fell into disrepair and disuse, made worse by heavy conservation costs. In 2003 it suffered a devastating fire and was destroyed.

1891 The Irish politician Charles Stewart Parnell died aged forty-five. Parnell was an electric, almost unstable, force in politics and exhausted himself through years of stress and personal turmoil. In 1889 he was named in a scandalous divorce case and was accused of fathering three illegitimate children. The allegations were shocking and ruined his career. In September 1891 the physically and mentally fatigued Parnell was soaked in torrential rain and contracted pneumonia. He died on 6 October.

October

7 October

1871 Field Marshal Sir John Burgoyne dies
The impregnable Tower of London was cast into mourning on 7 October 1871. Sir John Burgoyne, the elderly constable of the tower and a figure of huge military respect, died aged eighty nine. Notably, he was one of the rare officers to have served under four monarchs: George III, George IV, William IV and Queen Victoria. His funeral was presided over by the Chaplain General of St James's Piccadilly.

1884 The Peterborough by-election took place. The election had been called in tragic circumstances following the shocking death of the MP, John Wentworth Fitzwilliam, who was killed in a horse-riding accident aged thirty-seven. The seat was unexpectedly won by an architect, Alpheus Morton.

8 October

1844 Louis Philippe I, king of France, arrives in Portsmouth
The French monarch arrived in England onboard the elephantine paddle-steamer *Le Gomer*, one of the largest ships seen in Portsmouth for decades. After a short presentation with local leaders, Louis was met with the warm handshake of the Duke of Wellington and Prince Albert, who travelled especially on the royal train from Windsor. Unknown to Louis, just four years later he would relocate permanently to England after the 1848 revolution. He died in Surrey in 1850.

1885 The 7th Earl of Shaftesbury's memorial service was held at Westminster Abbey. Shaftesbury's philanthropy left a lasting legacy on London, epitomised by the massive crowds that gathered for the ceremony.

9 October

1851 The Queen visits Liverpool
Victoria loved Liverpool. She particularly adored St George's Hall which she compared to the wonders of ancient Greece. The inclement weather did nothing to dampen the spirits of thousands of well-wishers who gathered in the pouring rain to see her. Later in the afternoon, Victoria travelled via boat on the Bridgewater Canal to Manchester, where the Earl of Ellesmere had erected a temporary landing stage. The trip left a deep impression on the monarch who later described it as 'fairylike'.

1897 Henry Sturmey started his 929-mile journey from Land's End, the southern point in England, to John O'Groats in Scotland. He succeeded.

1900 Actor Alastair Sim was born. Sim enjoyed an accomplished career as a gifted comic actor, especially famous for his portrayal of Ebenezer Scrooge in Dickens's *A Christmas Carol*. He started life at 94 Lothian Road in Edinburgh, the son of Isabella McIntyre, a native Gaelic speaker from the Scottish Highlands, and clothier Alexander Sim.

10 October

1884 Electric light is installed in Downing Street
Although it may seem implausible in the twenty-first century, in 1839 plans were drafted to demolish Downing Street and other neighbouring buildings. Thankfully, the idea was rejected. Out of all of Victoria's prime ministers, few personally lived in or even liked Downing Street. Lord Palmerston used the cabinet room for weekly meetings but preferred his private townhouse. Disraeli, Derby, Melbourne and Salisbury similarly found Downing Street dull and dowdy. In 1884, however, Gladstone decided a change was due. Electric light was installed for the first time, bringing about much needed modernisation. The house was redecorated and improved. Telephone lines were later also installed, although most politicians would often prefer communicating via letters in case of eavesdroppers.

11 October

1896 The Archbishop of Canterbury is found dead
Normally an oasis of calm, on 11 October 1896 the tranquillity of William Gladstone's rural estate was ruffled with sombre tragedy. Edward Benson, the sixty-seven-year-old Archbishop of Canterbury and guest of the former premier, was found dead in his bedchamber. The cause was heart failure. Gladstone was shocked by the discovery and immediately dispatched a telegram to Balmoral informing the queen of the sad news. Benson was succeeded by Archbishop Frederick Temple.

1872 Suffragette activist Emily Davison was born in Roxburgh House, Greenwich. Emily gained a first-class degree at Oxford University but was forbidden to graduate because she was a woman. The injustice later inspired her to join the suffragette movement. She was famously killed after throwing herself in front of the king's horse at the 1913 Derby.

1899 The Second Boer War began in South Africa. The conflict was vicious and bloody, inflicting widespread death and terrible suffering for civilians. The war was particularly associated with the Secretary of State for War, Joseph Chamberlain. It even became known as 'Joe's War'.

12 October

1866 The first Labour prime minister, Ramsay MacDonald, is born
MacDonald started life in a modest rural cottage in Moray, Scotland. He was the illegitimate son of labourer John McDonald and servant Ann Ramsay. As a young boy he watched his mother struggle and suffer under the harsh economic realities of Victorian rural poverty and later became a Labour politician to fight social injustices. In 1923 he was elected as Labour's first prime minister. The social stigma of illegitimacy was a major burden throughout MacDonald's life and his rise from a poor working-class family to the highest office in the land was both remarkable and unique.

1869 Lord Derby was accidentally declared dead in the British press. Flags at his local town hall were prematurely lowered to half-mast and a crowd of mourners began gathering outside his home. Luckily, Derby was still alive but would die a few weeks later.

1878 The University of London became the first in Britain to admit women on equal terms with men.

13 October

1844 Nathan Marcus Adler is elected Chief Rabbi of the United Kingdom
Adler succeeded Solomon Hirschell as the Chief Rabbi in 1844 after a short contest. Only thirteen candidates were shortlisted and Adler emerged as overwhelming victor. His tenure was historic, overseeing the emancipation of Jews in the UK and the election of the first Jewish member of parliament. He is also credited with helping numerous charitable initiatives. Adler remained in the role for over forty-five years until his death in January 1890.

1853 Actress and mistress of the Prince of Wales, Lily Langtry was born in Jersey. At the height of her affair, the couple would regularly dine in the fashionable London restaurant called Rules in Covent Garden. A secret door was created to allow Langtry and the prince to escape without detection. As a mark of thanks, she gave a signed portrait of herself to the restaurant; it still hangs proudly there today.

1864 Queen Victoria visited Aberdeen in her first public engagement since Albert's death. She unveiled a large statue of her husband but later remarked that the appearance was both painful and upsetting.

1894 The first Merseyside football match took place in Goodison Park. Everton stormed to victory against Liverpool with a comfortable 3-0 result.

14 October

1878 The first floodlit British football match takes place
We can thank the Victorians for floodlit football matches. In the comfort of the twenty-first century, floodlights are an indispensable component of modern football, yet in previous years, matches that extended into darkness would either be postponed or cancelled, creating much annoyance to fans. The first floodlights were powered by lights behind two goals in Sheffield on Monday 14 October 1878. The experiment was well received and eventually became a regular feature for most clubs in England.

1881 The Scottish town of Eyemouth was battered by a fierce, brutal storm, costing the lives of over 189 fishermen. The tragedy left a painful mark on the community. For many years, 14 October was annually referred to as 'Black Friday'.

1892 Arthur Conan Doyle published *The Adventures of Sherlock Holmes*. The book was a success and led to further novels. Interestingly, Doyle also enjoyed a successful sporting career as a footballer, golfer, boxer and cricketer. He even became a judge in the world's first bodybuilding competition.

15 October

1839 Queen Victoria proposes marriage to Prince Albert
In the 1830s it was universally considered improper for a prince to propose to a reigning monarch. Instead, the question was asked by Victoria on the afternoon of 15 October at Windsor Castle. Albert accepted and their union was celebrated in a glittering ceremony the following year. After the wedding, Albert was officially known as the Prince Consort, much to the queen's displeasure who wanted him proclaimed king. He also acquired his own personal coat of arms which, unusually, was distinctively unique in heraldry tradition. In 2016 a slice of Victoria's wedding cake was sold at auction at £1,500.

1895 The foundation stone of the Mar Lodge was laid by Queen Victoria. The sumptuous property was built four miles west of Braemar, overlooking miles of Caledonian pine forests, constructed by the personal request of Victoria's granddaughter, Princess Louise. Unfortunately, much of the beautiful property was destroyed in a fire in the early 1990s but over 2,000 stag heads survived.

16 October

1847 *Jane Eyre*, Charlotte Bronte's iconic work was published
The novel followed the infant Jane Eyre through a brutal childhood and a tough adulthood, fighting against the injustices of a class-structured society until defying social conventions by marrying the wealthy Mr Rochester. The book was a huge,

if controversial, success with many objecting to the political subtext within the text. The prominent critic Elizabeth Eastlake labelled the work 'anti-Christian' and rebellious, while others regarded it as an artistic and literary masterpiece.

1888 George Lusk received the famous 'From Hell' letter. The note claimed to be from Jack the Ripper, and was delivered to the house of George Lusk, chairman of the Whitechapel Vigilance Committee on 16 October 1888. Lusk had patrolled the streets of Whitechapel in pursuit of the killer but was increasingly concerned about his safety. The note was accompanied with the remains of a human kidney. The horrifying discovery was quickly published in the press, leading to a further wave of letters, most of which were considered fake.

17 October

1894 The Bath Club is founded in London
By the 1890s, all was not well within the chummy world of clubland. Many younger folk were growing tired of the stuffy, venerable establishments which seemed overwhelmingly dominated by crusty old men. In 1894 the Bath Club was formed to provide a fashionable and flamboyant place for rich young chaps to congregate, providing state-of-the-art access to a luxurious swimming-pool, Turkish baths and sporting facilities. The pool, measuring seventy-five-feet long and thirty-five-feet broad, was one of the most popular in England. Among future members included King Edward VIII.

1860 The world's first professional golf tournament took place in Prestwick, southern Scotland.

18 October

1865 Prime Minister Lord Palmerston dies
It was alleged that Palmerston died on a kitchen table while making love to a maid. The truth is probably less interesting. Having turned eighty the previous year, the elderly prime minister contracted a fever in early October but remained doggedly determined to the end. A workaholic even on his deathbed, his last reported words were related to diplomatic treaties. The following morning, he was discovered dead by his valet.

Britain awoke to astonishment. The usually robust night life of London's West End was deserted. In Whitehall, throngs of spectators arrived to pay their respects, with large crowds gathering outside parliament and Downing Street. The queen, who had for so long disliked and distrusted Palmerston, expressed personal sadness at his passing, although in private admitted he had often worried and exasperated her. He was the last prime minister to die in office. Having avoided constitutional reform for years, his passing also heralded a change in political history, beginning the slow march towards electoral reform. Within two years, the landmark 1867 Reform Act was passed which redefined the nature of British politics forever.

1872 The suffragette Edith Rigby was born in Preston. Rigby was a stalwart campaigner who participated in numerous hunger strikes, marches and even militant action to further the cause of female suffrage. In 1913 she was arrested for placing a bomb in the Liverpool Corn Exchange, and later claimed to have set fire to an MP's house. Rigby was also the first woman to ride a bicycle in Preston, something which attracted scandal throughout Victorian Britain. Furious pedestrians reacted by shouting and even throwing vegetables as she rode past. Undeterred, two years later, she rode 200 miles to Leicester while visiting a friend. In later years she founded a girls' school and died in 1950.

1884 Labour politician Manny Shinwell was born. After his death, one MP remarked that Shinwell's 100-year life spanned 'the most fascinating period in our history. In the year of his birth, in 1884, Victoria ruled securely, Mr Gladstone was prime minister, and the Fabian Society was founded. Karl Marx also died in that year.'

19 October

1839 Artist Jane Morris is born
Morris was arguably one of the most remarkable artists of the nineteenth century but is little remembered today. As a foremost embroiderer in the Arts and Crafts Movement and wife of William Morris, many regarded her as the female personification of Pre-Raphaelite beauty, yet this overlooked her independent abilities which made her an accomplished artist in her own right. Morris was born into a working-class family in Oxford and had a limited education, but was ambitious, intelligent and determined to improve her situation. Morris may also have been the inspiration behind the character Eliza Doolittle in George Bernard Shaw's *Pygmalion*.

1856 The Queen dined with Prince Victor of Hohenlohe, a well-regarded sculptor of the famous statue of King Alfred the Great in Oxfordshire. The queen was so impressed with Victor's work, that she offered him a private suite of studio apartments in St James's Palace, after which his career reached new heights.

1858 Zoologist George Boulenger was born. The British-Belgian zoologist named over 2,000 new species and was also a renowned botanist. He worked for several years at the National History Museum.

20 October

1842 Grace Darling dies aged twenty-six
Darling had come to national attention in 1838 after courageously rescuing victims of a shipwreck near the coast of Northumberland. A daughter of a lighthouse-keeper,

her quick thinking turned a potential tragedy into a heroic rescue operation and made her a national heroine. Her fame became so huge that over £700 was raised for her, the equivalent of over £60,000 today. Even Queen Victoria donated. Tragically, Darling's newfound status was short lived. She died of tuberculosis in 1842 aged twenty-six, casting the country into despair and heartbreak.

1858 Trade unionist and politician John Burns was born in Vauxhall, London. Burns helped co-found a branch of the Social Democratic Federation and stood unsuccessfully for parliament in 1885. A year later, he was arrested during the infamous 1886 West End Riot and later played a central role in the 1889 London Dock Strike. By the time he emerged as a government minister in 1905, he was a widely-known and controversial political name.

21 October

1854 Florence Nightingale departs England for the Crimean War
Together with thirty-eight volunteer nurses, Nightingale left Southampton for a field hospital at the Scutari Barracks in Constantinople. Her aims were simple. Firstly, to help injured and disease-stricken British troops. Secondly, to provide assistance to other struggling nurses who were overwhelmed with the immensity of casualties. Nothing could prepare her for the horrifying scenes she witnessed. Wards were disgustingly overcrowded, unhygienic and dirty, made worse by a dangerous lack of medical equipment. Men slept in dirty, filthy beds with unclean, thin blankets. Food was short and clean water was scarce. Within a few months she set about re-organising and restructuring the hospital system. Her work and dedication to soldiers' welfare gave her the nickname 'lady of the lamp'. It would also make her a national icon and an international celebrity. Crucially, pioneering work was also undertaken by a group of Irish nuns of the Sisters of Mercy, although their role is often overlooked and underappreciated.

1885 The eightieth anniversary of the Battle of Trafalgar was celebrated with predictable gusto on 21 October. All throughout the country, dinners were hosted to commemorate the occasion, including an exclusive banquet at Admiralty House. By the evening, hundreds of people descended upon Trafalgar Square which was covered in colossal Union flags. HMS *Victory* was also decorated with garlands of laurels and flags.

22 October

1877 Scotland's worst ever mining disaster takes place in Blantyre
The Blantyre mining disaster was one of Britain's greatest mining tragedies, costing the lives of 207 victims. The morning had started peacefully. At around 4.40am, No. 2 Pit at the William Dixon's Blantyre Colliery was inspected by firemen. No dangers or concerns were reported and miners began to descend as normal.

At approximately 9.00am, however, a huge explosion was heard from the nearby No. 3 Pit. The area was engulfed by smoke. Several men were trapped and many others dead. Volunteers from local areas were quickly enlisted to form a rescue party to search for victims. The wailing noise of the pit horn screamed across the town to alert family members of the crisis; they soon scrambled to the scene. The heartbreaking search for victims continued into the night. By 23rd it was apparent that over 200 people had been killed. Many bodies were later transported to a temporary mortuary, where families had the sad responsibility of identifying loved ones. One casualty was just eleven. In a grim twist, it was later alleged that William Dixon evicted thirty-four widows from their tied cottages just two weeks after the tragedy.

1895 Charles Hallé, founder of the Hallé orchestra, conducted the last concert of his life on Tuesday 22 October in Liverpool. He appeared in fine form and received several ovations. Three days later Hallé was discovered unresponsive in bed. He died of a cerebral haemorrhage aged seventy-six.

23 October

1869 Former prime minister Lord Derby dies aged seventy
Derby, who had long suffered a painful battle with gout, died in Knowsley Hall at 7.00am. To the toll of the mournful bells of his modest parish church, the former premier was buried six days later with tenants forming a guard of honour. A motion of sympathy was passed in London with a small memorial service held at St Margaret's Church, Westminster conducted by George Granville Bradley and Archdeacon Farrar, grandfather of the future Field Marshal Montgomery of Alamein. Another memorial service was held in Liverpool.

1844 Poet Robert Bridges was born in Walmer, Kent. He would succeed Alfred Austin as Poet Laureate in 1913.

24 October

1857 Sheffield Football Club is formed
Widely regarded as the oldest existing football club in the world, Sheffield was co-founded by two gentlemen, Nathaniel Creswick and William Prest, who initially established the club in a small greenhouse on East Bank Road. For the first few years, the club operated upon 'the Sheffield Rules', which had a profound influence on the formulation of football laws. This included free kicks for fouls and injuries and the corner kick. It was recognised as a member of the Football Association six years later but did not adopt the formal FA football code until 1878.

1895 The actor Jack Warner was born. Warner started life, Horace John Walters, in Bromley-by-Bow. His father, Edward Walters was a master fulling marker who nurtured a passionate love of the arts. After a career in the music halls, Horace adopted the stage name 'Jack Warner' and became an actor in his mid-thirties but did not receive professional success until his role of George Dixon in the popular series *Dixon of the Dock Green*. He reprised the role he had played in the popular film *The Blue Lamp*. His sisters were also well-known comedians.

25 October

1854 The Charge of the Light Brigade
On 25 October, 670 tired and exhausted cavalrymen under the command of Lord Cardigan attacked Russian artillery stationed in 'the valley of death'. Over 100 men were killed. The disaster left a bitter taste in British public life for generations. A poem by Alfred Lord Tennyson was later released in December commemorating the tragedy. A second poem was published in 1891 by Rudyard Kipling, exploring the hardships of veterans of the war in their old age.

1848 On 25 October, the usually drowsy Oxfordshire town of Wantage became the scene of immense celebrations, commemorating the 1,000th birthday of King Alfred, the legendary monarch of Anglo-Saxon England. Shops were closed and the streets embellished with enormous flowers, flags, bunting and banners. After divine service in the local church, a morning lecture was delivered by a local historian, followed by a joyful procession to King Alfred's Well. Many quaint and eccentric traditions were resurrected, including a greasy-pole climbing contest. Meat was handed to the poor and a colossal dinner was held for local civic dignitaries. Ironically, Alfred's precise birth date is unknown, but this didn't stop the townsfolk from having a jolly good time.

26 October

1843 The Queen visits Cambridge
The monarch's visit had created such a commotion that Cambridge was brought to a standstill. By midday, the density of crowds had become so dangerously thick that royal carriages were unable to move and traffic temporarily came to a halt. Various stands had been erected along the highways with enormous assemblages of hysterical people, desperate to get a glimpse of the illustrious visitor. Victoria was escorted by approximately 5,000 horsemen, passing under an enormous arch, with the word 'welcome' interwoven in red roses and decorated by an imperial floral crown. The following day, Victoria visited Wimpole Hall where she enjoyed a huge ball with over 800 guests. The trip was regarded as a resounding success.

1897 The Victoria Medal of Honour was established to celebrate outstanding British horticulturists in memory of Victoria's 'glorious reign'. The first sixty recipients included Gertrude Jekyll and Michael Foster.

27 October

1865 The state funeral of Lord Palmerston
Although not as magnificent as Wellington's enormous funeral thirteen years earlier, Palmerston's service was a major event and attracted crowds of over half a million spectators to the frostbitten streets of London. His solemn coffin was carried into Westminster Abbey to the haunting sound of William Croft burial sentences, 'I am the Resurrection'. As the former premier was interred, the sun, which had shone sporadically all day, suddenly faded amidst an empire of thick clouds, dominating the Abbey with darkness. In this gloomy, immersive atmosphere, the *Dead March in Saul* was played, and the ornate wooden coffin disappeared from view into the earth.

28 October

1882 Six Benedictine monks return from France to rebuild Buckfast Abbey
The ecclesiastical elegance of Buckfast Abbey had been destroyed during the English Reformation under King Henry VIII but was unexpectedly re-established 300 years later in October 1882. The first six monks who arrived at Buckfast had been exiled from France and yearned to create a new religious community in England. The abbey was constructed suitably in the 'Norman Transitional' style of the eleventh century, designed by the Roman Catholic architect Frederick Arthur Walters. Unfortunately, building work was painfully slow and it wasn't until 1932 that the abbey was finally consecrated.

1844 Queen Victoria opens the New Royal Exchange in London. The previous exchange had been destroyed by a fire.

29 October

1900 Queen Victoria's grandson, Prince Christian Victor, dies
The public knew relatively little of Prince Christian Victor, the eldest son of Prince Helena, who had served in the Army since 1880, eventually rising to the rank of major during the Second Boer War. In October 1900, Christian contracted malaria, and died two weeks later in the South African city of Pretoria. He was only thirty-three.

1843 The first-ever telegram was sent from Paddington to Slough. The invention proved popular and grew in prominence throughout the decade. It was particularly useful for governments and embassies to communicate quickly with other ministers. Even as late as the 1980s, telegrams were still being sent.

1860 The actor Thomas Cook gave his last public appearance at a charity event hosted for the Royal Dramatic College, a retirement home for actors. Cooke was,

October

by Victorian standards, quite an elderly man himself and died four years later aged seventy-seven. His will bequeathed £2,000 to the college.

30 October

1841 A terrible fire breaks out at the Tower of London
The fire broke out originally in the historic Bowyer Tower after a flue had accidentally overheated. By the time guards had been alerted, the flames had already spread to other parts of the fortress. Within minutes, the Martin Tower, which stored the Crown jewels, was engulfed. Panic-stricken firemen desperately tried to force their way inside, only to face further complications and danger. The Keeper of the Jewel House held the key to the outer room but the other key to the barred cabinets was stored by the Lord Chamberlain. The jewels were also protected by large metal bars which could not be broken. Whilst battling against the inferno, policemen attempted to bend the bars with crowbars. News of the tragedy created immense sadness across Britain. It wasn't until 3.00am that the mayhem was finally brought under control. By a huge stroke of luck, most of the castle was not damaged and, more importantly, no one was killed.

31 October

1864 Cosmo Lang, future Archbishop of Canterbury is born
Lang's childhood was inexplicably shaped by the Church. He was born in a tiny church manse in the rural parish of Fyvie, north Aberdeenshire. His father, the Reverend John Marshall Lang, was the local Church of Scotland minister, and later Moderator of the General Assembly. His early years were dominated by change and travel. In 1865 the family relocated to Glasgow, followed by Edinburgh, followed again by Glasgow and, later, Aberdeenshire. Lang was ordained a vicar in May 1891 and played a crucial role in British history, especially during the abdication crisis of 1936.

1881 Anthony Trollope finished writing *Mr Scarborough's Family*.

November

1 November

1895 The Duke of Cambridge resigns as Commander in Chief of the Army
Critics often described the duke as a pompous bumblebee. Having served in the role for thirty-nine years, he had come under fierce criticism as a cankerous, belligerent dinosaur, dogmatically refusing to accept any reforms to his beloved Army. To his supporters, he was a tough stalwart of traditional military values, the likes of which were forged during the Napoleonic Wars. His close relationship with Queen Victoria also meant his removal risked offending the palace. Nevertheless, by 1895 the government had grown wary of his bombastic presence. Perhaps to appease the disgruntled monarch, Victoria's son, Prince Arthur was initially rumoured to be a strong successor, but this came to nothing. The role instead passed to the sixty-two-old year Garnet Wolseley.

1848 WH Smith opened its first book stall at Euston Station. The business was astute in recognising the emerging market of the Victorian railways, which presented thousands of potential customers each day. Several travellers would flock to the store to purchase new books to read on their journeys. As their success grew, the firm opened shops in Birmingham and Liverpool and later expanded across the whole country.

1887 The artist Laurence Lowry was born in a tiny terrace house in Manchester. His depiction of industrial city life was unique and made him one of Britain's most popular twentieth century painters.

2 November

1895 General Sir Garnet Wolseley kisses Queen Victoria's hand
Wolseley's tenure as Commander in Chief of the Army was short, stressful and dominated by power struggles within the government. On 2 November the newly-appointed commander arrived at Balmoral to pay respects to Victoria, who was quick to remind him of the grave and difficult responsibilities that lay ahead. Wolsey had developed a strong reputation for efficiency and organisation in military circles, leading to the popular catchphrase 'Everything's all Sir Garnet'. His tenure, however, was characterised by the Second Boer War which exposed the

painful inadequacies of the Army and the dangerous divisions between the military and the War Office. He was dismissed from his post just five years later.

1877 William Robertson was a distinctive and remarkable soldier who served in every rank from private to field marshal. He began his career on 2 November 1877, enlisting in the 16th Queen's Lancers aged seventeen, three months before his eighteenth birthday. Having lied to the sergeant, his age was incorrectly recorded for the rest of his life.

3 November

1843 Nelson's statue is placed on Nelson's Column in Trafalgar Square
In 1838, a group of eager parliamentarians grouped together to organise a memorial to England's greatest seafaring hero, Horatio Nelson. The estimated budget was between £20,000 and £30,000, a considerable sum, with the deadline set for the last day of January 1839. The sub-committee was chaired by the Duke of Wellington, one of the last surviving figures who had actually met Nelson in the flesh. Several designs were submitted, but the eventual winner was William Railton, a thirty-nine-year-old architect from Clapham, who had earlier been rejected from designing the new Houses of Parliament. The statue was placed on Nelson's column on 3 November 1843 and has remained a re-assuring icon of London ever since.

1888 The Mysterious Oxfordshire Sheep Panic of 1888. At around 8.00pm, a small group of walkers in Oxfordshire discovered hordes of terrified sheep rushing from their fields into the roads and lanes of the county. The next morning, farmers discovered thousands of sheep scattered across the county, with some even cowering under hedges. The mystery dumbfounded experts who could not find a logical explanation.

4 November

1839 The Newport Rising takes place
The Newport Rising was the last armed protest in British history and sent shivers down the spines of the British establishment. By the late 1830s Chartists had grown frustrated by the continual refusal of the Commons to reform the political system. In 1839, a group of hungry, disillusioned and disgruntled protesters marched through the Welsh town of Newport in the hope of releasing some Chartists prisoners from the local jail. The demonstration turned ugly. Brawls and fights broke out with the police, and soon the military were called in. Fearing that a revolt was taking place, troops fired at the protesters, killing several men and injuring approximately fifty. Chartist leaders were rounded up, arrested and charged with treason. They were later sentenced to transportation. For the British government, the event looked terrifyingly like a precursor of rebellion.

1852 Journalists were allowed in the House of Commons for the first time to record debates. Not all members welcomed the new arrangement. Some parliamentarians regarded journalists with intense suspicion, disdain and disapproval. Always with an ear for publicity, however, Lord Palmerston recognised the potential benefits of befriending, even dazzling, newspaper editors with his characteristic charm. He began cultivating a reputation as a tough guy, something which the media loved and readily helped construct.

1900 Britain's first driving lesson in a motor car was taken.

5 November

1854 Nineteen Victoria Crosses are awarded for valour in the Battle of Inkerman
The Battle of Inkerman was a major clash during the Crimean War in which nineteen soldiers were awarded the Victoria Cross. Among them was Private John Byrne, of the 68th Durham Light Infantry, a colourful character whose post-war life was mired with intense scandal. Byrne, who originated from County Kilkenny in Ireland, was awarded the VC for two acts of gallantry. According to reports, after leaving the military, Byrne found employment for the Ordnance Survey in Newport, but became embroiled in a furious dispute with a colleague whom he felt disrespected his Victoria Cross. In a fit of rage, Byrne allegedly killed him, and later committed suicide. Over 160 years later, a metal detectorist found a Victoria Cross on the shore of the Thames, dated from 5 November 1854, a strong indication that it belonged to one of the nineteen. Only two Victoria Crosses of the nineteen are unaccounted for: John McDermond and John Byrne.

1883 While celebrating Guy Fawkes' Night in 1883, four young men from Hanley, Staffordshire, were seriously injured by an explosion of fireworks.

6 November

1871 Charles Dilke criticises the monarchy
Not all Victorians were royalists. On 6 November, the firebrand Liberal MP Charles Dilke lit the flames on a volcanic fire by publicly denouncing the British monarchy, and even the queen herself. Victoria understood the danger of losing support, especially after the unpopular reigns of her uncles, George IV and William IV. For the last decade, however, she had remained hidden from public affairs, separated from the mainstream of court life. No politician could persuade the 'Widow of Windsor' to return to London, precipitating rising frustration among her courtiers and subjects alike. Some likened her to a 'absentee landlord'. More critically, others began to question the very concept of monarchy. What was the point of having a sovereign if she never appeared in public?

November

1856 Mary Ann Evans submitted her debut novel *Scenes of Clerical Life* for publication. Evans, better known by her professional alias, George Elliot, feared her own name would deter some Victorian readers who disapproved of women pursuing independent careers.

7 November

1876 Cricketer Charles Townsend is born
Townsend was a popular and successful sportsman of the late Victorian era but a largely forgotten figure in British history. He started life in Bristol, the son of former cricketer and headmaster, Frank Townsend who encouraged all three of his sons into the profession. Charles made his debut aged sixteen in 1893 and joined the English national team a few years later. Having enjoyed a distinguished career, he retrained as a lawyer in the 1900s and lived peacefully until his death in 1958.

8 November

1866 Herbert Austin, founder of the Austin Motor Company, is born
Austin started life in Little Missenden, a small rural village in Buckinghamshire, but later relocated to Yorkshire and Australia. Upon returning to Britain, he formed his own motor company, Austn, which became one of the most successful brands of the twentieth century.

1898 Birmingham Chrysanthemum Show was held at Bingley Hall, the first purpose-built exhibition hall in Britain. Although not in attendance personally, the queen sent a huge collection of fruit which was handed to the Lady Mayoress at the close of the show and distributed among the various charities in the city.

1862 Sir Benjamin Hall celebrated his sixtieth birthday in style. Hall is best remembered as the civil engineer who oversaw the final completion of the new Houses of Parliament. It is rumoured that 'Big Ben', is named in his honour.

9 November

1841 The Prince of Wales is born
Ever since the untimely death of George IV's celebrated daughter, Princess Charlotte, who died in childbirth in 1817, fears of a similar tragedy rocked England with horror and apprehension. For Victoria, the pregnancy was a tiresome and difficult experience. Four physicians were present during the labour, as well as a midwife called Mrs Lilly. Albert's calm and re-assuring presence throughout the pregnancy became a model for Victorian husbands who were previously aloof and absent from the event. At 10.48am, a healthy baby boy arrived. He was named Albert in tribute to his revered father, and

appointed Prince of Wales just three days later. The prince even enjoyed his first royal engagement just a few hours after his birth, taken by his father to greet the various ministers lined up outside the room. As the first-born son to the reigning monarch, he automatically became the heir to the British throne. The prince became so fashionable in high society that he is credited for introducing Yorkshire puddings and horse-radish sauce to Sunday meals. He would later become King Edward VII.

10 November

1871 Henry Morton Stanley meets David Livingstone
'Dr Livingstone I presume.' The immortal line was uttered by Henry Morton Stanley on 10 November at an iconic meeting. The event has become so famous, the phrase is now indelibly etched into national memory. The thirty-year-old Stanley had arrived in Africa as a journalist working for the *New York Herald* in a quest to find the lost British explorer David Livingstone. The two met in Ujiji, near Lake Tanganyika. Ironically, there is no concentre proof that the famous line was ever spoken, with some asserting that Stanley added the phrase to generate more interest and raise newspaper figures. As a mark of thanks, nevertheless, the queen presented Stanley with a personal letter and a snuff-box.

1843 At approximately 8.20pm a terrible fire broke out in Paradise Street, Lambeth. The fire spread quickly, destroying many buildings in its path and creating enormous panic. An army of firemen battled the blaze for hours, but several properties were destroyed beyond repair.

1855 David Salomons became the first Jewish Lord Mayor of London. Salomons had previously served as the first Jewish Sheriff of London in the 1830s.

11 November

1892 The Duke of Marlborough inquest
A significant inquest was concluded on 11 November concerning the mysterious death of Winston Churchill's uncle, the Duke of Marlborough, who died unexpectedly aged forty-eight. The duke, who had shown no apparent signs of illness, was found unresponsive in bed by a valet on the 9th. Having entered his bedroom twice that morning, the valet attempted to wake him by banging the door. A doctor was called quickly and pronounced the duke dead. The inquest concluded that no foul play was involved, and that the duke succumbed to sudden heart failure while also suffering the pre-existing condition of calcareous degeneration.

1866 Pioneering chemist Martha Annie Whiteley was born. Whiteley fought tirelessly for women's equality in chemistry. She also campaigned for cloakroom facilities for female members of staff in academic departments throughout England.

November

12 November

1900 Lord Salisbury retires as Foreign Secretary
Ironically for a man who had been so reluctant to take office in his early years, by 1900 Salisbury was jealously guarding his power. Supporters were quick to point out that age was no obstacle to good government. Several Victorian public figures were of venerable ages, not least the queen. Palmerston had been elected as prime minister in 1855, aged seventy, and went on to lead the country for another ten years. Earl Russell was seventy-three when he formed his last administration, not to mention Gladstone who was eighty-two, a whopping forty years older than the average life expectancy. In November, however, Salisbury finally relented, handing the baton to the younger Lord Lansdowne.

13 November

1887 Bloody Sunday
On the morning of 13 November, a large group of protesters gathered in London's Trafalgar Square to demand the release of the Irish nationalist MP William O'Brien, who had recently been arrested under the Coercion Act. The marchers soon encountered a counter-demonstration and violence ensued. Over seventy people were injured seriously and one man was stabbed with a bayonet. Two policemen were also stabbed and over 400 people arrested.

1856 The Queen was informed that her beloved half-brother Prince Carl died of a stroke in Germany, aged fifty-two. The news was devastating for the royal family, especially as his mother, the Duchess of Kent, was still alive. Carl had briefly served as prime minister of the German Empire in the 1840s and was influential in Anglo-German relations.

1899 The statue of Oliver Cromwell was unveiled outside Parliament. Having been proposed several years earlier by Lord Rosebery, the statue proved intensely controversial. Situated in the garden adjoining St Stephen's entrance, some MPs were deeply uncomfortable with his presence. Because of the controversy, the statue was not unveiled with a formal ceremony.

14 November

1850 *David Copperfield* by Charles Dickens is published
The book was Dickens's personal favourite and undoubtedly one of his most successful. The novel weaved fiction with autobiographical elements that mirrored Dickens's own, often complicated life, but it also drew attention to prevailing questions in Victorian society, including class struggles, child labour, the justice system and exploitation.

1883 Robert Louis Stevenson published his iconic book *Treasure Island*. Stevenson had originally devised the idea for an adventure story based on an imaginary map he created during a holiday. Upon its release, the book played a profound influence in embedding pirates and pirate stories back into the public consciousness.

15 November

1897 Labour politician Aneurin Bevan is born in Wales
'Bevan's supreme qualities were superb, unflinching moral courage, deep sincerity, and complete selflessness,' remarked the Liberal politician Clement Davies, 'he was upright; he was downright; he was forthright. Statesman, administrator, Parliamentarian, orator.' Born in a modest terraced house in the mining town of Tredegar, Monmouthshire, Bevan's childhood was hard and tough. Like many Victorian miners, his father worked long, exhausting hours, starting work at 5.30 am and returning home, tired and dirty, in the evening. In his youth, Bevan supported the Liberal Party, until joining the Labour Party and becoming an MP in 1906. He is best remembered today as the founder of the National Health Service.

1849 A Thanksgiving service was held at St Paul's Cathedral to celebrate the end of a dreaded cholera outbreak. In reality, the disease was not gone and would re-appear in the city shortly afterwards.

16 November

1898 The first stepless escalator in Britain is installed at Harrods department store
The escalator was known initially as Britain's first 'moving staircase', although it proved quite controversial. Many customers disliked the invention, complaining of its 'scary' and intimidating nature. It was alleged some people were even offered alcohol to de-stress after the torment of using it.

1899- The Wyndham Theatre was opened in London. The theatre was the product of Charles Wynham's desire to construct a flourishing and exciting theatrical hub in London, something he finally achieved in 1899. Opened in the presence of the Prince of Wales, its first play was the 1856 comedy *David Garrick*.

17 November

1887 The military commander Bernard Montgomery is born in Kennington, London
Montgomery was the son of the strict Reverend Henry Montgomery and Maud Farrar who raised their children with stern Victorian discipline. As a young military

cadet, he could be unpredictable, rebellious and mischievous. While at Sandhurst he was reprimanded for setting fire to the shirt-tails of a fellow cadet, causing serious burns. In later years he became the most recognisable British officer during the Second World War, and one of Britain's most famous modern generals.

1887 In November 1887, the Earl of Meath delivered an important address titled 'The Importance of Open Space' at the Parkes Museum of Hygiene. The speech called for more green areas, gardens and playgrounds for city dwellers and children. Crucially, it warned that, if overcrowded living conditions continued, the effect would be disastrous for the health and wellbeing of the nation.

18 November

1852 Funeral of the Duke of Wellington
Under a grey and dour November sky, the body of the late duke was borne through the densely packed streets of London in an enormous, gilded hearse, drawn by six sombre horses. The funeral was to be the grandest ceremonial occasion for decades and, at a cost of £100,000, remains one of the most expensive in British history.

The event was the first state funeral for a non-royal since 1806 and promised to attract large crowds. The duke's coffin, covered by the Union flag, was transported from Clapham Common to Vauxhall Station, where it was later carried by members of the Royal Horse Artillery and placed on a large funeral cart.

Like the man himself, the funeral was not devoid of controversy. The special hearse considerably divided public opinion, with Charles Dickens describing it as monstrous, cumbersome and inappropriate. When the procession reached the Mall, one of the cart's six wheels seized. Up to sixty policemen were called to release it, creating huge embarrassment. By the time the vehicle had finally reached St Paul's Cathedral, the hearse once again stopped due to another mechanical problem. It took over an hour for the coffin to be lifted into the cathedral, by which point many guests had grown restless. It would be the last of such state funerals until Winston Churchill's in 1965.

1870 The Surgeon Hall Riot took place. On the crisp autumn morning of 18 November, a group of female medical students were strolling quietly into Edinburgh's Surgeons' Hall to attend an anatomy exam. As the women approached the building, a large gang of violent, confrontational male students gathered outside and encircled them. They began chanting abuse, spat at them and threw mud into their faces. Soon an even larger crowd had gathered. After several minutes of terror, the women entered the hall but were confronted by further scenes of unrest. Finally, after several students had been evicted, the exams proceeded, but more mayhem was unleashed. A sheep, known as 'Poor Mailie' walked into the hall through a back door. As the examination came to an end, the women were escorted safely by a group of Irish students who were heavily abused as they walked out. If the protesters had hoped to discourage female medical students, they were mistaken. The event made international headlines and increased public opinion in favour of female doctors. In the twenty-first century, a plaque was installed to mark the occasion which has since became known as 'The Surgeon Hall Riot'.

19 November

1850 Alfred Tennyson is appointed Poet Laureate of the United Kingdom
Tennyson enjoyed immense success in the role, gaining adulation and praise from, among others, Queen Victoria. Unlike his predecessor, William Wordsworth, Tennyson was highly active as Laureate and composed some of his best known works, such as *The Charge of the Light Brigade* and the *Ode on the Death of the Duke of Wellington*. Tennyson was also the first poet laureate to record some of his material, courtesy of the American soldier Edward Gouraud, who introduced the phonograph cylinder-audio device to Britain in 1888. Tennyson was also the longest serving poet laureate, remaining in the role for forty years until his death.

20 November

1874 The Grand Sandringham House Ball takes place
The Prince of Wales was famously generous with his friends, although on some occasions his chums would take his generosity too far. At a large Sandringham ball, a very drunk Sir Frederick Johnstone caused a scene in the billiard room. The prince advised him to stop drinking, to which Johnston rudely replied 'tum tum, you're very fat', patting the prince's stomach as he said it.

1887 Another protest in Trafalgar Square demanding the release of the Irish nationalist MP William O'Brien turned nasty when a young clerk named Alfred Linnell was knocked over and killed by a police horse.

1886 Arthur Conan Doyle signed a publication deal for *A Study in Scarlet*, marking the debut appearance of the legendary detective Sherlock Holmes. The novel would distinguish Doyle as a major British writer, whose work transcended national borders.

21 November

1840 Queen Victoria's first child, Victoria, is born at Buckingham Palace
It was the first of Victoria's many pregnancies, and national apprehension was extremely high. After confirmation that the queen had finally entered labour, the palace exploded into a mass of manic activity. Sir James Clark, the principal

medical attendant, was roused from his bed and hurried in a carriage to relay the news to the prime minister. Meanwhile, Prince Albert marched frantically through the corridors to find the Duchess of Kent. Clergymen were called on standby. Thankfully the ordeal would be a short one. At 2.10pm, a healthy baby girl was born. She was named in honour of her illustrious mother, Victoria. Until the birth of her brother, she was briefly the heir to the throne. Had legislation similar to the Succession to the Crown Act 2013 been in force, she would most likely have become monarch..

1895 Arthur John Bigge becomes Private Secretary to the Sovereign. He was the first private secretary to have been born during Victoria's reign, twelve years after her succession. He would also be her last private secretary.

22 November

1869 The *Cutty Sark* is launched
Upon its launch in Dumbarton, the Cutty Sark was among Britain's last tea clippers. At a considerable cost of over £16,000, no expense was spared for this elaborate and decorative ship which departed Britain in 1870, transporting wine and spirits to China in return for over 600,000 kilograms of tea. Despite its initial popularity, the *Cutty Sark* emerged during a time of real economic uncertainty in British shipbuilding. Steamships, not clippers, were increasingly favoured as the modern alternative of sea travel, championed especially by ambitious and forward-thinking businessmen. In the 1890s the ship fell into decline but was thankfully preserved and restored for public viewership. The *Cutty Sark*'s motto was 'When there's a Willis a way', an affectionate nod to the builders, Willis and Sons who had constructed the ship.

23 November

1896 A hugely successful Royal Command performance for Queen Victoria takes place
Contrary to the misconception, Queen Victoria was quite frequently 'amused', especially during visits to the theatre and the opera. The 1896 Royal Command show was so hilarious, the royals were apparently roaring with laughter. It is now a regular entertainment tradition and a source of enjoyment for monarch and subjects alike.

1837 The Queen attended a lavish performance of Gaetano Donizetti's opera *L'elisir d'amore* at the Lyceum Theatre. Victoria travelled incognito to avoid the crowds and thoroughly enjoyed the evening. Unfortunately, she also took an intense dislike to the performer, Franceschini, whom she found 'a fat and rather ugly person, and a detestable singer'.

1852 Britain's first four pillar-boxes came into service. The idea originated from Anthony Trollope who, before his literary career, worked for the General Post Office in London. The first box came into operation in the Channel Island of Jersey, and later spread across the UK.

24 November

1859 Charles Darwin published *On the Origin of Species*
The landmark scientific paper proved both extremely influential and intensely controversial. Core to Darwin's argument was that humans, like other species, evolved over time, directly challenging traditional Christian teaching that God created humans in His own image. Having started the project in the 1830s, Darwin openly described the book as a 'living hell'. He delayed publication for several years due to fear of social exclusion. On its initial release in 1859, the book cost 15 shillings and only 1,250 copies were printed. Nevertheless, it had an immensely profound effect on scientists throughout the world and continues to provoke debate.

1879 The famous Midlothian Campaign started in Edinburgh. Ever since his retirement in 1875, Gladstone had grown restless with the backbenchers and yearned for a spectacular return to contest the Scottish Midlothian constituency, organised by Lord Rosebery. The campaign is sometimes described as the first modern rally in British history. As an experienced traveller, Rosebery adopted American style techniques such as open-deck trains, catchy slogans and huge rallies to drum up unprecedented national interest.

25 November

1896 The first parking fine is handed to Mr William Marshal in the City of London
25 November was a bad day for Mr William Marshal, the unlucky first Briton to receive a parking fine. Marshal had made the error of leaving his car in Tokenhouse Yard, in the City of London. Thankfully, the case was later dismissed, and Marshal was not required to pay the fine.

1871 The first performance of *The Bells*, starring Henry Irving took place at the Lyceum Theatre. The opening night was exceptionally successful, leaving the audience physically stunned by the power of his performance. One lady even fainted. It further solidified Irving's reputation as a theatrical great.

1898 The Duke of Connaught visited the Elysee Palace as a guest of President Felix Faure of France. The trip would be one of the last examples of good Anglo-French relations which declined massively during the Second Boer War. Anti-British feeling eventually became so high that, in 1900, the Prince of Wales's trip to France was cancelled due to alleged security concerns.

26 November

1867 Lily Maxwell becomes one of the first women to vote in a British election
Lily Maxwell was a strong advocate of women's voting rights and had worked closely with the campaigner Lydia Becker for wider political enfranchisement. In the 1867 general election Maxwell's name was mistakenly placed on a list of voters in Manchester, something which was later discovered by the Liberal candidate and suffragette supporter Jacob Bright. Egged on by Becker and Bright, on 26 November Maxwell proceeded to the polling station at Chorlton Town Hall and cast her vote in front of a stunned audience. As her name was officially published on the list, the returning officer had no choice but to accept her vote. The crowd allegedly reacted with a huge cheer. Contrary to misconception, Maxwell was probably not the first female voter in British history, but certainly the most famous of the Victorian era.

1865 *Alice's Adventures in Wonderland* by Lewis Caroll was published. Two years earlier, Caroll met with the famous Scottish publisher Alexander Macmillan and agreed to a publishing deal. To maintain greater editorial influence, Caroll decided to finance the original print run which gave him greater creative powers over the project. On release in 1865, the story was extremely popular. It became an enduring classic of the Victorian age.

27 November

1867 The radical MP Jacob Bright wins the Manchester by-election.
Bright was regarded by the Liberal hierarchy as an 'advanced radical'. A passionate, persuasive former mayor of Rochdale, he was an unapologetic advocate of universal suffrage and was not afraid to ruffle feathers. The by-election victory was a great success, but his career would neither be long nor particularly famous. He was almost completely overshadowed by his more dominant, influential brother, John Bright.

1897 Horticulturist James Bateman dies. Bateman designed the first public park in England, Derby arboretum. He also created the magnificent gardens at Biddulph in Staffordshire. Having suffered from chronic bronchitis, he relocated to Worthing in the 1880s and died there aged eighty-six.

1897 On medical advice from doctors, William Gladstone spent much of November 1897 in France where the warmer weather was deemed more suitable for the ailing prime minister. Gladstone was also suffering from facial neuralgia.

28 November

1898 The Duke of Marlborough opened the Primrose League conference in Bristol.
The league was formed after Disraeli's death to commemorate his legacy and advocate Conservative principles in public life. Curiously, the name 'Primrose' was chosen specifically as a nod to the late premier who famously adored primroses. Throughout the latter Victorian era, the league grew from strength to strength and even opened its own gentlemen's club. Winston Churchill boasted that by the early twentieth century, it had over one million members, but it declined after the First World War.

1888 Henry Irving was graced with a prestigious banquet held at the newly-completed Edgbaston Assembly Rooms in Birmingham. Among the guests were actress Ellen Terry, Marion Terry and politician Austen Chamberlain.

1893 Writer Talbot Baines Reed died. Reed was a formidable, if now overlooked, presence in children's literature, recognised for his fictional works aimed at young boys. His books were a particular favourite of the young P.G. Wodehouse, although sadly his life was cut short by tuberculosis. He died aged only forty-one.

29 November

1843 Gertrude Jekyll is born
Jekyll left a legacy of horticultural greatness which survives to this day. Born in Mayfair to a wealthy military family, her passion for gardens started early. She studied at the South Kensington School of Art and travelled extensively to explore different variations of gardens across the country. It was said that Robert Louis Stevenson, a friend of Gertrude's brother, borrowed the surname Jekyll for his famous 1886 novel, *The Strange case of Dr Jekyll and Mr Hyde*. She is credited for designing over 400 gardens.

1898 By coincidence, 29 November was also the birthday of another famous writer, Clive Staple Lewis, born in Ulster, fifty five years later. His father, Richard, was a Welsh lawyer who had moved to Ireland in the mid-nineteenth century. Lewis achieved worldwide fame for the publication of *The Chronicles of Narnia*, released between 1950 and 1956.

30 November

1900 Oscar Wilde died in poverty
Increasingly sick with meningitis, Oscar Wilde spent his final days in Paris, living in the squalor and misery of the Hôtel d'Alsace. Having been largely ostracised by

November

British high society, Wilde suffered a lonely existence without regular or consistent income. On 25 November, he was baptised into the Roman Catholic Church by the Irish priest, Father Cuthbert Dunne. A few days later he died aged forty-six.

1872 England and Scotland played each other in the first international Association Football match. The venue was Hamilton Crescent in Scotland. The result was 0-0.

1874 Winston Churchill was born. Contrary to misconception, Winston was not born in a bathroom but a former cloakroom in Blenheim Palace, his grandfather's palatial ancestral home. Winston would often talk about the Victorian era with nostalgia and affection, yet he suffered an unhappy and austere childhood.

December

1 December

1844 Princess Alexandra is born in Denmark
Alexandra started life in the Yellow Palace, Copenhagen, the daughter of the future Danish king, Prince Christian, and Princess Louise. Despite their wealth, Alexandra had an austere childhood. She shared a cold bedroom with her sister Dagmar and even had to make her own clothes. Fortunately, by the time she came to Britain in 1863 her family's fortunes had much improved. Her popularity in England was so immense that fashionable women frequently emulated her style, even mimicking her famous limp which she suffered since a bout of rheumatic fever. Her birthday would be marked with the bells of St George's Chapel each year until her death in 1925.

1858 Lord Lyons was appointed the UK Ambassador to the United States. He took office in a contentious time for Anglo-American relations, made more complicated by his poor relationship with President Buchannan. He remained ambassador throughout the Civil War and the assassination of Abraham Lincoln.

1868 London Smithfield Meat Market was opened

2 December

1849 The Dowager Queen Adelaide dies
Adelaide died on 2 December at her residence, Bentley Priory in Middlesex, surrounded by family members, medical attendants and a vicar. A well-respected figure in British society, Adelaide's marriage to William IV was darkened by the deaths of her five children and dominated by political upheaval. As the first Queen Dowager since 1719 her funeral, held at St George's Chapel Windsor, was marked by an official day of mourning in the royal court. The British Museum, National Gallery and other public institutions in London were closed. Business was suspended and many theatres also shut. Bentley Priory was later sold to the Air Ministry and became the headquarters of RAF Fighter Command during the Second World War.

1877 The National Dog Show was opened in Birmingham. The show was hosted at Curzon Hall in Birmingham with 975 dogs taking part.

1898 The Bicentenary of St Paul's Cathedral was celebrated to mark 200 years since the completion of Sir Christopher Wren's iconic landmark.

1898 The Golden Jubilee of Franz Joseph of Austria-Hungary was celebrated with a small ceremony hosted at St Mary's Roman Catholic Church in Chelsea. Telegrams of congratulations were also sent from Queen Victoria.

3 December

1891 Prince Albert Victor and Princess Mary announce their engagement
The engagement came to the great delight of the British public, although few knew the sad and sorrowful tale that had preceded the announcement. In the 1890s Albert Victor had fallen madly in love with Hélène of Orléans, the daughter of Prince Philippe of Orléans, the disputed King of the French. Hélène was a Roman Catholic and under the rules of the Act of Settlement 1701, no heir to the British throne could marry a Catholic without disqualification from his inheritance. Despite the ramifications, Albert was determined to maintain the relationship and even promised to renounce his position to the throne. Meanwhile, Hélène declared that she was equally willing to convert to the Church of England. Queen Victoria was largely supportive of the romance, but Philippe was less sympathetic. In a desperate attempt to save the courtship, Hélène travelled to Rome to intercede with Pope Leo XIII. Her hopes were to be disappointed. The relationship was over. On 3 December, Albert was engaged to the assuredly sensible Mary of Teck, with a wedding arranged for the following February. Despite the apparent jubilation of the news, his sisters Maud and Louise were deeply saddened by the verdict and claimed that Hélène was the one true love of his life. Albert died in January 1892, one month before the wedding.

1897 McEwan Hall was opened in Edinburgh. Constructed in an Italian Renaissance style, the building was officially unveiled by Arthur Balfour.

4 December

1882 Queen Victoria opens the Royal Courts of Justice in London
In 1866, a large architectural competition was launched to construct a grand testament to British judicial power. Surprisingly, the winning candidate was the relatively unknown ecclesiastical architect, George Edmund Street. Construction began in 1873, undertaken by the building company Bull & Sons of Southampton, whose workers later walked out on strike. Work was stopped and international builders were hired, creating major tension with the strikers. The court wasn't finished until eight years later and was opened by Queen Victoria.

1865 The British nurse Edith Cavell was born. She is most remembered for her dedication during the First World War, nursing thousands of injured and disease-stricken soldiers. In 1915, Cavell helped several servicemen escape from Belgium, but was arrested and executed by the Germans. The Church of England and the Episcopal Church in the USA commemorate her life annually on the anniversary of her death where she is listed in the calendar of saints.

1868 Archibald Campbell Tait was appointed Archbishop of Canterbury. A few months earlier, the only recently appointed archbishop, Charles Longley, had died suddenly of a stroke, triggering an unexpected search for a new candidate. At fifty-seven, Tait became the surprise successor and was the youngest appointee in over sixty years.

5 December

1865 The engagement is announced between Princess Helena and Prince Christian of Schleswig-Holstein
Fifteen years her senior, Christian was a tall, commanding and controversial choice for a royal suitor. The announcement brought particular disappointment to Princess Alexandra, who was still reeling from anger after the Prussian-Danish War. Schleswig and Holstein were two regions that had been fought over during the conflict, with Prussia emerging victorious. Alexandra was furious at the relationship and dismissive towards Christian. Fortunately for Helena, the marriage had the backing of the queen. She became the only child of Victoria to celebrate a golden wedding anniversary in December 1915.

1859 Admiral Sir John Jellicoe, commander of the Grand Fleet at the 1916 Battle of Jutland, was born in Southampton. After Jutland he served as First Sea Lord and reluctantly introduced convoys in 1917. This arguably helped save the UK from defeat.

6 December

1879 The Duke of Portland dies
It was alleged that the eccentric duke would often employ several hundred workmen on his various gardening projects, but insisted that no one communicated, talked or even acknowledged his presence in any way. The same instructions were issued to the local vicar, doctor and community figures who were told to pass him by, as they would a tree. One man was unfortunately fired after ignoring the rules and raising his hat to the duke as a form of deference. Bizarrely, it was also alleged the duke lived a strange double life as a London upholster who faked his own death.

1882 The esteemed writer Anthony Trollope died at a nursing home at 34 Welbeck Street in London at the age of sixty-seven. Just a few weeks earlier, Trollope had

December

suffered a stroke while reading Anstey's *Vice Versa: A Lesson to Fathers*. It was alleged he died laughing, although this was never officially certified. Trollope was buried in Kensal Green Cemetery.

1897 The first motorised taxi-cabs begin operations in London. In 1829, the first horse-drawn omnibus service had started in London, almost seventy years before the motorised cabs began operation.

7 December

1837 Benjamin Disraeli's maiden speech
Not all prime ministers begin their parliamentary careers with success. Disraeli's maiden address was a failure of epic proportions. His words were so poorly received that, towards the end of the speech, he even received heckling and barracking. 'I sit down now,' he concluded, 'the time will come when you will hear me.'

1868 Gladstone was defeated in a shock election disaster. Having been widely expected to win the Southwest Lancashire constituency during the 1868 general election, Mr Gladstone found himself upstaged by a young Tory barrister called R.A Cross.

1889 Gilbert and Sullivan's successful play *The Gondoliers* opened in London. *The Gondoliers* is sometimes regarded as Gilbert and Sullivan's last great success. It ran for 554 performances and received huge plaudits.

8 December

1864 Clifton suspension bridge in Bristol opened to the public
Isambard Kingdom Brunel had begun construction on the bridge in 1831 but was thwarted by a host of unforeseeable problems. Only a few months after commencing the project, Bristol was rocked with ferocious riots, reducing commercial confidence in the city. Funding for the project evaporated and, in 1837, the contractors went bankrupt. Construction resumed the following decade but was hampered again by a lack of money. The project was further delayed in 1859 after Brunel's death and resumed under a new direction. It was finally completed twenty-three years later and opened to acclaim on 8 December 1864.

Like most of Brunel's works, the Clifton suspension bridge was ambitious, forward thinking and visionary. Spanning 214 metres, and 76 metres above the river Avon, it was the longest bridge in the world at the time. It is regarded as an architectural icon of Bristol, if not the entire country.

1863 The first heavyweight boxing championship took place on a small farm near Wadhurst in Sussex, fought between the American John C. Heenan and the London docker, Thomas King. King won the match in the twenty-fourth round. He stands among the greatest English heavyweight champions of the nineteenth century.

1900 Winston Churchill embarked on his first lecture tour. He had returned from South Africa as a national celebrity and was keen to capitalise on his money-earning potential. Before 1911, members of parliament did not receive a formal salary, meaning that many were forced to pursue secondary careers, such as journalism, to supplement funds. The tour was a resounding success.

9 December

1854 ***The Charge of the Light Brigade*** **by Alfred, Lord Tennyson is published**
The work commemorated the devastating military disaster in the Crimean War. Tennyson had composed the poem several days earlier on 2 December and completed it within just a few minutes. Unusually for the time, Tennyson later recorded the poem onto a wax cylinder, a copy of which survives today on YouTube. Unfortunately, the audio quality is poor, but it is still fascinating to listen to his voice.

10 December

1871 The Prince of Wales suffers typhoid
In a strange and terrifying parallel to her late husband, in 1871 the queen's eldest son fell seriously ill with typhoid. On Sunday 10 December, his condition deteriorated. He had become delirious, with heavily laboured breathing and incoherent muttering. The following day even bleaker news emerged that the prince had suffered a 'spasm' and appeared close to death. Victoria ran from her private quarters into his room, where she found her desperately sick son gasping for air. In the following hours, his condition continued to decline, reaching a devastating low on the 13th, just one day before the anniversary of Prince Albert's death. 'Alice and I said to another in tears, there can be no hope,' the queen remarked, 'this really has been the worst day of all.' Prayers were offered for the prince in every cathedral throughout England, including a special service at Westminster Abbey. The prayers were answered.

The following morning, doctors discovered the prince sitting up in bed, smoking a cigar. His pulse was better and his breathing recovered. His health continued to improve and he eventually made a full recovery. Victoria was so relieved that she ended her period of mournful isolation and slowly returned fully to public life. A service of thanksgiving was later held at St Paul's Cathedral.

1868 The first traffic lights in Britain were installed. The concept, however, had been initiated several years earlier to prevent the traffic collisions. The intention was to create greater safety for drivers and pedestrians, something still used today.

December

11 December

1877 The Stanford horse bet
The millionaire American governor Leland Stanford won a longstanding bet proving that horses' feet leave the ground simultaneously once in every stride. To help him prove the case, Stanford hired the English photographer Eadweard Mubridge who used several cameras around Stanford's track to take pictures of horses. The bet was won.

1844 A statue of King William IV was unveiled. It was the first granite statue to be erected in London, situated close to London Bridge, which was opened by the king in the 1830s. The statue took three years to create due to the difficulties of carving granite.

1896 Elizabeth Garratt Anderson published a letter in *The Times* advocating for female medical training.

1898 Queen Victoria presented the composer Henry Wood with a special conductor's baton surmounted with a gold crown inscribed with the initials VRI.

12 December

1849 Engineer and creator of the 'Thames Tunnel', Marc Isambard Brunel died in Westminster following a stroke
Brunel enjoyed a fascinating trajectory of successes and heart wrenching failures throughout a long and eventful career. Born in France in 1769, he made his fortune in the United States but relocated to London in 1795 where he initially struggled to adjust to British engineering. After suffering several disappointing projects in the early 1820s, Brunel found himself incarcerated in a debtors' prison and even considered emigrating to Russia. Fortunately, his career improved considerably during the Victorian period and, by the time of his death, he was widely regarded as an engineering giant. He is most famous today as the father of Isambard Kingdom Brunel.

1895 While shooting on the estate of Sir Edward Lawson, the Prince of Wales found himself in a dreadfully painful situation. While aiming at a bird above him, a few grains of gunpowder fell directly into his right eye, causing severe agony. A doctor was immediately called onto the scene and administered cocaine to ease the pain. The prince returned to Marlborough House later the same day but did not recover fully for some time.

1872 A rare meteorite strike allegedly hit a wall near the sleepy town of Banbury in Oxfordshire. It attracted considerable local interest.

1889 Writer Robert Browning died in Venice, Italy, aged seventy-seven. Browning had been staying at his son's house in Italy during the autumn and was preparing to return home when he was suddenly seized with bronchitis. Despite his illness, he continued working and seemed in high spirits but died later on 12 December from heart failure.

13 December

1867 The infamous Clerkenwell explosion
The explosion was described as the most startling attack since the Gunpowder Plot, although unlike 1605, did not receive widespread fame. The attack was carried out by the Fenian Brotherhood, designed to rescue one of their members held at Clerkenwell Prison. A group of armed men arrived and detonated a bomb outside the complex, killing twelve people. The attack was not successful, and no prisoners escaped.

1880 The 25th Earl of Crawford died. After his coffin was interred in the family crypt his body was scandalously stolen by grave-robbers, creating national alarm. A poacher was eventually convicted of the crime.

1884 Another violent attack occurred on 13 December, this time at London Bridge. The culprits were again the infamous Fenians, organised by two Americans with Irish ancestry. With the goal of destroying London Bridge, the men hired a boat and rowed out into the river. The bomb exploded prematurely, killing both and creating major damage to nearby buildings overlooking the Thames.

14 December

1861 Prince Albert, husband of Queen Victoria, dies
Britain awoke to a thick sea of grief. The prince was only forty-two. Energetic, intelligent, full of life, vigour and promise, his death seemed almost like an improbable dream. The Prime Minister Lord Palmerston remarked, it felt as if every Briton 'had themselves lost some dear friend or near relation'. In December 1861, doctors diagnosed typhoid, although the prognosis was not initially bleak. The Queen was hopeful for a full recovery. His pulse was improving, his breathing was no longer laboured. The following day, however, his condition deteriorated gravely. At 11.10am, Albert breathed his last. No journal entry was written by the queen that night. Her grief was so dark, so deep; in the immediate moments after his death she allegedly ran howling through the corridors in an almost frenzied state, seizing her daughter Beatrice from the nursery and carrying her into the bedroom.

In the years after his death, Victoria entered into an inconsolable mourning which continued for decades. Every anniversary, she would lead her children into the bedroom and remind them, in gushing candid detail, about his memory. He became a saint, a figure of impenetrable superhuman virtue, qualities which the children were consistently reminded of but struggled to emulate. A photographer

December

was hired to take pictures of his deathbed. Almost every aspect of his bedroom was kept as it had been when he was alive. He was a continually living presence in Victorian society, perhaps even more so than when he was alive.

1878 On the anniversary of Albert's death, Queen Victoria suffered another tragedy with the death of her second daughter, Princess Alice. Ever since her marriage, Alice had resided in Darmstadt, Germany, living with her husband and seven children. In November 1878, her eldest daughter Elizabeth contracted diphtheria, which spread across the household. Almost every member of the family contracted the illness, including her other daughter Marie, who died on 16 November. Alice was soon afflicted and succumbed to the disease aged thirty-five. For the rest of her life, the queen would refer to 14 December as her 'terrible anniversary', a painful yearly reminder of the two great tragedies of her life.

1895 Several years later, the future King George VI was born in the small, rather austere York Cottage, a few hundred yards from Sandringham House. A more inauspicious date in the royal calendar would be hard to find, but his grandmother luckily regarded his birth as a positive omen. In February 1896, the future king was baptised at St Mary's Church in Sandringham. Almost fifty-six years later to the day his coffin returned to the church as the shortest-lived monarch in over 200 years.

1860 Yet another morbid event took place on 14 December with the death of the former premier, Lord Aberdeen. Aberdeen had suffered poor health for several months, exacerbated by the stress of political office. Being the Christmas recess, no official tributes were paid to him in the Commons.

15 December

1881 Leadenhall Market re-opens
As one of London's oldest and most popular markets, by the 1870s Leadenhall had become intensely overcrowded and increasingly dirty. In 1880, the premises were closed to the public and redesigned under the stewardship of Sir Horace Jones who wanted a grander, more imposing façade to rival the great markets of Europe. Having travelled extensively in Italy, Jones took his inspiration from the Victor Emmanuel Galleria in Milan, especially for its elaborate roof that protected visitors from the rain. The market reopened in 1881 at a cost of £99,000.

1899 The Olympic runner Harold Maurice Abrahams was born in Bedford. He is best remembered for his outstanding athletic performances at the 1924 Olympic games, gloriously depicted in the 1981 film *Chariots of Fire*. Abrahams was the son of Jewish parents from the Russian Empire and Wales. After a short stint in the Army, he enrolled at Cambridge University and became a successful sprinter. With the assistance of his sports coach, Sam Mussabini, he took part in the Paris Olympic games in 1924 and won the gold medal for the men's 100 metres.

16 December

1897 The Adelphi Theatre murder
It has long been claimed the Adelphi Theatre in London is haunted by the ghost of a young actor, William Terriss, who was viciously murdered in cold blood by a jealous and disgruntled performer. The tragedy occurred in December 1897, when Terriss, who regularly assisted unemployed actors to find work, encountered a young man called Richard Archer Prince. Terriss helped Prince get employment in his production of *The Harbour Lights* at the Adelphi, but the two men quarrelled and Prince was eventually fired. On 13 December, Prince was physically removed from the Vaudeville Theatre and, the following day, visited Terriss in his dressing room, resulting in another heated argument. On the 16th, Prince, armed with a knife, decided to get revenge. After waiting silently in the doorway near the Adelphi's stage door, he stabbed Terriss viciously several times in the chest. He died in the arms of his shocked, heartbroken girlfriend, Jessie Milward. The appalling murder horrified London. Prince was later discovered to have suffered from alcoholism, made worse by destitution and poverty. The verdict was guilty but insane, and he spent the rest of his life at Broadmoor Hospital where he died in 1937. The perceived leniency of the case angered many actors, including Henry Irving.

17 December

1875 Louis Bruce, Britain's first black Olympian, born in Scotland
Bruce's full name was listed as Louis Bruce McAvoy Mortimore, born in Newington, Edinburgh to unmarried parents. The word 'illegitimate' was scrawled across his birth certificate in striking bold ink, an indication of the deep social stigma that illegitimacy provoked in conservative nineteenth-century Britain. Having moved to England in the 1880s, Bruce found employment as a tram driver, and joined the Hammersmith Amateur Wrestling Club. In 1908, he represented Great Britain in the Summer Olympic Games, finishing fifth in the men's heavyweight division. Additionally, he is believed to be one of Britain's first black tram drivers.

1852 Herbert Beerbohm Tree, founder of the Royal Academy of Dramatic Arts (RADA), was born in Kensington, London.

18 December

1892 Biologist Sir Richard Owen dies
Owen is credited for coining the term 'Dinosaur' and doing extensive work to enrich the academic understanding of prehistoric fossils for future generations. As a founding father of the National History Museum, his work was lauded for reigniting public interest in science. In private however, he proved a controversial, sometimes even maligned figure who attracted enormous criticism. Many complained of his

prickly, allegedly egotistical, personality that would take credit for other people's projects for his own gratification. Charles Darwin found him intolerable, although others complained he was possibly the victim of a smear campaign fostered by rivals. When he died in December 1892, tributes were paid from around the world.

1887 In a sign of improving relations between the Church of England and Roman Catholics, in December 1887 the queen's special envoy, led by the Duke of Norfolk, arrived in Rome to offer a personal message of congratulations to Pope Leo XIII for his ecclesiastical Jubilee.

19 December

1843 *A Christmas Carol* by Charles Dickens is published
'Bah Humbug': the iconic snarling line uttered by the greedy miser Ebenezer Scrooge in the iconic Dickens's novel, *A Christmas Carol*. The acclaimed tale tells the story of a bitter man who experiences a profound spiritual change on Christmas Eve after being visited by three spirits. Like many of Dickens's works, the novel had a profound political message, but also a powerful social effect as well. It's no exaggeration to say that Dickens reinvigorated, if not re-invented Christmas in British national life; something which had arguably declined throughout the 1830s. After Dickens's death in 1870, one girl asked her father, 'Daddy, does this mean there will be no more Christmas?' *A Christmas Carol* remains a bedrock of Christmas reading material even today.

1848 The writer Emily Brontë was devastated by her brother's death from tuberculosis in September 1848. In a tragic twist of fate, Emily would also succumb to the disease on 19 December 1848. She was only thirty.

1851 The legendary British painter Joseph Turner died of cholera at his home in Chelsea. Regarded as one of the greatest artists in history, Turner achieved enormous acclaim early in his career, but suffered a deterioration in popularity during the Victorian era. By the mid-1840s, his work was no longer fashionable, and increasingly criticised as 'outdated' and dull.

20 December

1852 'Disgraceful scenes' at the Carlton Club
Mr Gladstone's presence had already created alarm. Earlier that afternoon, his unmistakable figure had been seen plodding up the grand staircase of London's Carlton Club, the bastion of British Conservatism. Unsurprisingly, the Grand Old Man was not universally popular in the premises, especially since defecting to the Liberals in 1846, making his appearance intensely controversial. Gladstone had just begun to relax in a comfy leather armchair when a group of young, hot-headed

members approached him. They were aggressive, taunting him as a traitor and threatened to throw him over to the nearby Reform Club. After many curt words, one gentleman threatened to chuck Gladstone out the window. Several newspapers labelled the incident 'disgraceful'. The drama temporarily damaged the club's reputation for civility and sobriety.

1863 Society hostess Lady Margaret Grenville was born. Grenville was born Margaret Anderson, the illegitimate daughter of the millionaire brewer William McEwan and his mistress, Helen Anderson. Helen was a cook from Scotland, who at the time of Margaret's birth, was already married to a porter working at McEwan's brewery. Grenville is best known today as the owner and hostess of the legendary Polesden Lacey estate in Surrey.

21 December

1842 Pentonville Prison is opened
Construction on the new prison began in 1840 and took two years to complete. Like most Victorian prisons, discipline was brutally harsh and strictly enforced. Speaking was forbidden, as was smoking, drinking and swearing. Prisoners were forced to attend daily church services, but were isolated in tiny cubicles, known sarcastically as 'coffins'. Food was meagre and bland. Prisoners were expected to work thirteen-hour days from 6.00am to 7.00pm. Famous Victorian inmates included Oscar Wilde, who was interned briefly, before his transfer to Wandsworth, and the infamous murderer Charles Peace.

1846 Anaesthetic was used for the first time in a British operation. A small blue plaque outside 24 Gower Street, London commemorates the occasion.

1880 Widows and unmarried women were granted the right to vote in the Isle of Man, but only if they owned property annually rated at £4 or more. Universal suffrage would not emerge until the 1920s.

22 December

1886 Lord Randolph Churchill resigns as Chancellor of the Exchequer
Churchill's resignation shocked the nation. Having been appointed as Chancellor only in August 1886, his blend of radical excitement and impatience proved a combustible mixture for his conservative and reserved leader, Lord Salisbury. Churchill had demanded large cutbacks to public expenditure. Salisbury was willing to compromise but soon grew wary of his controversial, uncompromising colleague. In an act of extraordinary brinkmanship, Churchill demanded cutbacks to the armed forces or threatened to resign. The threat backfired: Salisbury accepted his resignation.

The Queen was particularly angered by the news, summoning her private secretary, Sir Henry Ponsonby, to Hatfield for urgent clarification. 'Randolph Churchill had the audacity to write his letter of resignation from Windsor,' she gasped, 'the night he dined!' In Westminster, the reaction was of similar astonishment. The overwhelming feeling was that the youthful Churchill had been outmanoeuvred by the canny, older man. In later decades Winston Churchill would describe the resignation as Randolph's greatest political mistake.

1843 The foundation stone of the Victoria Tower was laid. It took almost twenty years to be finally completed, by which point it was the tallest square tower in London, a gleaming illustration of British gothic architecture. At over 300-feet tall, the tower was designed to store the rich collection of parliamentary archives, many of which had survived the October 1834 fire. Suitably, Charles Barry installed eight fireproof strongrooms which were further protected by a sturdy iron staircase.

1880 Mary Ann Evans, known professionally as George Elliot, died on 22 December, only a few months after her marriage to John Cross. Partly because of her rejection of the Christian faith, Evans was not offered a burial at Westminster Abbey. She was interred instead at Highgate Cemetery in London, situated next to her lover, George Henry Lewes. Karl Marx's grave is nearby.

23 December

1861 The funeral of Prince Albert
Albert's death could not have come at a worse time. With an economic crisis looming, and fears of an Anglo-American war, the feeling in Britain was one of doom and despair. The fact that the funeral occurred so close to Christmas similarly created an extra sense of misery that hovered over the year. Pantomimes and festival productions were cancelled. In London, the frosty streets were lined with mourners gathering into churches for memorial services. Like the Dowager Queen Adelaide, Albert's funeral was not a state event, but held in the pomp and privacy of St George's Chapel at Windsor. Ever determined to keep Albert's memory alive, Victoria had his private rooms at Osborne, Windsor and Balmoral kept just as they were in his life. His clothes were laid out daily, and a jug of hot water was placed in his dressing room. Even his shaving equipment was kept intact. Lord Clarendon, who visited in 1862, was struck by how she spoke of her husband continually in the present tense, as if 'he was in the next room'.

24 December

1848 Queen Victoria's Christmas
Henry Cole is often described as the 'inventor' of the Christmas card, a trend which swiftly gathered momentum, even with the royal family. Indeed, the Victorians are

also credited for introducing Christmas trees to Britain, although the custom had been around for a while longer. Even so, the illustration of the royal family huddled around a warm and cosy tree, printed in *Illustrated London News*, led to a huge upsurge in both Christmas cards and Christmas trees across the country. By the end of the Victorian era, they had become almost an archetypal image of the Christmas tradition. Even in the age of the internet, the Christmas card remains as popular as ever.

1840 Queen Victoria's beloved dog, Dash, died. Dash had originally been purchased by John Conroy for Victoria's mother but later transferred to the young princess as a companion for her lonely childhood. Victoria adored Dash. He was buried at Adelaide Cottage in Windsor.

1863 The writer William Makepeace Thackeray died shortly after returning home from dinner on Christmas Eve. The following morning, his unresponsive body was discovered in bed by staff. He was fifty-two.

1880 The first festival of Nine Lessons and Carols was performed. The festival was devised by Bishop Edward Benson to attract new parishioners into the church and to deter locals from a night of heavy festive drinking. Prior to the nineteenth century, carols were rarely performed in Anglican churches, something which Benson hoped to change. The popularity of the festival became so huge that it was soon considered a Christmas tradition and remains immensely popular even today.

25 December

1875 Golfer 'Young Tom' Morris dies
When the swashbuckling figure of Thomas Morris lifted the trophy of the Golf Open Championship in 1868, a legend was born in the history of sport. The youngest winner in the tournament's history, 'Young Tom' was a dazzling legend in his own lifetime, a player blessed with unique skill and distinctive charisma which made him one of Britain's biggest sporting stars. Unfortunately, beyond the golf course, Morris's life was short and sad, dominated by heartbreak, untimely loss and tragedy. In 1875 his wife and new-born son died. Devastated by the news, Morris suffered a pulmonary haemorrhage and died on Christmas Day 1875. He was only twenty-four years old.

1881 The politician Willie Gallacher was born in the icy backstreets of Paisley, Scotland. His father was an alcoholic Irish immigrant who had travelled to Scotland in the hope of a better life, but soon found himself disappointed. Gallacher later became a Socialist member of parliament.

1900 To celebrate the last Christmas of the nineteenth century, the Queen's Hall hosted a large Christmas concert with the Concert Trombone quartet and the Guildhall Glee Singers. Most countries recognised 1 January 1901 as the first day of the new century, echoing in a feeling of excitement and renewal.

December

26 December

1871 Boxing Day is formally recognised as a Bank Holiday
It was a historic tradition that servants of aristocratic households were permitted to visit their families on the 26th after working throughout Christmas Day. Some even more generous employers would hand out boxes containing gifts or food as a means of gratitude. The decision to recognise 26 December as a bank holiday was well received by most citizens. It subsequently became known as 'Boxing Day'.

1877 The Christmas festival for Barnardo's children's homes took place in London. The charity, Doctor Barnardo's, was formed after a tragic tale several years earlier in the 1860s. One night, a young boy allegedly knocked on the door of Thomas Barnardo, an Irish doctor living in London. The boy asked for a room to stay but Barnardo refused. To his horror, Barnardo discovered the boy dead the following morning. The calamity distressed him so badly he later created his own charity dedicated to caring for homeless, or orphaned, children. The institution became known as 'Dr Barnardo's'.

27 December

1867 William Gladstone is nearly killed in a tree accident
Tree cutting was a hazardous hobby of Gladstone who had avoided death on numerous occasions. On 23 December 1867, his eye was pierced by a wooden splinter causing serious pain and a short period in bed. By the 27th, however, he was back on his feet and determined to cut more trees. Accompanied by his fifteen-year-old son, he had begun to slash a large trunk when the tree suddenly collapsed, almost killing both of them. Gladstone was undeterred by the incident and would continue cutting trees even into his late eighties.

1864 Queen Victoria issued a letter to several major British railway directors enquiring about the frequency of fatal accidents. Since 1837, Britain had suffered over forty serious railway disasters, killing hundreds of innocent passengers. Like many others, the queen had grown troubled by the regular news stories of safety concerns arising from British railways. On 27 December 1864, she wrote a personal note to several British senior railway directors urging improved safety requirements for travel.

28 December

1879 The Tay Bridge disaster
The tragedy was perhaps the most infamous railway catastrophe of the nineteenth century. The Tay Bridge had been constructed over the mighty Tay river by the eminent engineer Sir Thomas Bouch and was considered a modern landmark of

Scotland. On the evening of 28 December, a train from Edinburgh to Aberdeen was passing over the bridge at the usual speed when the structure suddenly collapsed. The train was plunged into the freezing water below, killing over seventy-five people. The cause of the accident was later registered as structural damage.

1858 The abolitionist Sarah Parker Remond left the United States for a tour of England. In January, she delivered a historic address titled 'Slave Life in America' in London, highlighting the barbaric treatment of enslaved people in the United States. Her charisma won her huge supporters. In 1859, she enrolled at Bedford College and joined the London Emancipation Society. She is believed to be the only black woman to have signed the 1866 petition urging female suffrage in Britain.

1886 Dan Leno, the acclaimed comedian, began his pantomime career in *Jack and the Beanstalk* at London's Surrey Theatre. He later transferred to the Royal Drury Lane Theatre Company where he remained for sixteen years, playing his acclaimed performances of the pantomime dame. By the 1890s he was the highest paid comedian in Britain.

29 December

1860 HMS *Warrior* launched
HMS *Warrior* was the UK's first ironclad warship, an enormous vessel built by the Thames Ironworks and Shipbuilding Company in London. Unfortunately, the launch did not run to plan. Being December, London was covered in thick blankets of snow. As the ship left the yard, it froze in the ice and needed six tugs to move it into the river. Thankfully, the *Warrior* wasn't seriously damaged and went on to have a long career in the Channel Squadron. Despite threats of destruction, *Warrior* was later purchased by the Ships' Preservation Trust in 1983 and enjoyed a sensitive restoration.

1861 Musician Walter Galpin Alcock was born. Alcock holds the distinction of playing at the coronations of three British monarchs.

30 December

1871 Illustrator George Cruikshank publishes a letter in *The Times*, claiming credit for the plot of *Oliver Twist*
The accusation was deeply unpopular, not least because Dickens had been dead barely a year. Unfortunately, Cruikshank himself would die just a few years later in 1878. Heavily burdened with debt, his last few months were plagued by ill health and financial problems. Cruikshank's last words were allegedly, 'O, what will become of my children', a seemingly strange remark considering he and his wife were supposedly childless. In reality, it was later revealed, he had fathered eleven

illegitimate children by his long-term mistress, something which did not emerge until after his death.

1865 Rudyard Kipling was born in Bombay, India. Kipling's posthumous reputation has changed and evolved through time, but in the Victorian era he was a lionised and respected literary giant. Born in Bombay in 1865, his father was a pottery designer and principal of an art school. Many of his most famous works, such as *Jungle Book*, and *The Man Who Would Be King* were set in Asia.

1878 Henry Irving's legendary production of *Hamlet* opened in London.

31 December

1842 The first instalment of *Martin Chuzzlewit* by Charles Dickens is published
The novel focused upon greed, pride, and romance, with the young protagonist, Martin Chuzzlewit, denied the prospects of marrying his love because of the strict disapproval of old Martin Chuzzlewit, his elderly grandfather. Dickens regarded the novel as one of his greatest works, although the public didn't agree, and the reception was disappointing. The following year, he published the critically acclaimed *A Christmas Carol*, which became an international hit.

1857 Queen Victoria, under heavy pressure from her ministers, selected Ottawa as the capital city of Canada. The decision was not spontaneous. From a strategic perspective, Ottawa's position on a cliff face, plus the large forest that surrounded it, created a natural protective shield from attacks. Secondly, the city was also blessed with a modern, fully functioning railway system. Ottawa remains the Canadian capital today.

1884 The St James Cabmen's Shelter was opened by the Bishop of London. Despite London's booming wealth, St James lacked provisions for the cab drivers who were often left cold and hungry on the doorsteps of the richest families in England. In 1884, the daughter of John Jackson, Bishop of London, gazed from her gilded house in St James's Square and observed the regular sights of poor, weary drivers huddled around like birds in discomfort and hunger. With her father's backing, she helped raise over £150 to construct a shelter for the drivers in the area. Her generosity was rewarded by a vote of thanks from the Cabmen's Shelter Fund. You can still see a handful of these shelters around London today.

Selected Bibliography

Aldous, Richard, *The Lion and the Unicorn: Gladstone and Disraeli* (London: Vintage Digital, 2012)
Bedford, Barbara, *Oscar Wilde: A Certain Genius* (New York: Random House, 2000)
Blake, Robert, *Disraeli* (London: Eyre & Spottiswoode, 1966)
Bond, Brian (1961), 'The Retirement of the Duke of Cambridge', *Royal United Services Institution. Journal*, 106:624, 544-553, DOI: 10.1080/03071846109420729
Brookes, Pamela, *Women at Westminster* (London: Peter Davies Publishing, 1967)
Brown, Colin, *Whitehall, The Street that Shaped a Nation* (London: Simon and Schuster, 2009)
Cheltenham Examiner, 14 April 1869
Clark, Christopher, *The Sleepwalkers: How Europe Went to War in 1914* (London: Penguin, 2013)
Dorset County Express and Agricultural Gazette, 26 January 1858
Dundee Evening Telegraph, 4 March 1891
Dundee, Perth, and Cupar Advertiser, 15 April 1864
Edinburgh Evening News, 27 January 1896
Freeman, Richard, *The Great Edwardian Naval Feud: Beresford's Vendetta Against 'Jackie' Fisher* (Barnsley: Penn and Sword Military, 2009)
Gash, Norman, *Politics in the Age of Peel: A Study in the Technique of Parliamentary Representation, 1830-1850* (London: Longmans, 1953)
Gough, Barry, *Churchill and Fisher: Titans at the Admiralty* (London: Seaforth Publishing, 2017)
Hansard. HC Deb 17 February 1845 vol 77 cc529-30. Contains Parliamentary information licensed under the Open Parliament Licence v3.0. https://api.parliament.uk/historic-hansard/commons/1845/feb/17/title-of-king-consort
Hansard. HC Deb 23 April 1863 vol 170 cc601-602. Contains Parliamentary information licensed under the Open Parliament Licence v3.0. https://api.parliament.uk/historic-hansard/commons/1863/apr/23/supply-memorial-to-thelate-prince#S3V0170P0_18630423_HOC_78
Hansard. HC Deb 20 May 1867, vol 187 cc779-852. Contains Parliamentary information licensed under the Open Parliament Licence v3.0.
Hansard. HL Deb 17 June 1869 vol 197 cc40-41. Contains Parliamentary information licensed under the Open Parliament Licence v3.0.

Selected Bibliography

Hansard. HC Deb 3 March 1884 vol 285 cc393-466. Contains Parliamentary information licensed under the Open Parliament Licence v3.0

Hansard. HL Deb 31 July 1885, vol 300, cols 633-652. Contains Parliamentary information licensed under the Open Parliament Licence v3.0. https://api.parliament.uk/historic-hansard/lords/1885/jul/31/recent-legislation-thesocialistic

Hansard. HL Deb 21 June 1897, vol 50, cc 420-421. Contains Parliamentary information licensed under the Open Parliament Licence v3.0. https://api.parliament.uk/historic-hansard/lords/1897/jun/21/address-to-her-majesty

Hansard. HC Deb 21 June 1897 vol 50 cc440-441. Contains Parliamentary information licensed under the Open Parliament Licence v3.0. https://api.parliament.uk/historic-hansard/commons/1897/jun/21/address-ofcongratulation-to-her-majesty

Hansard. HC Deb 27 April 1908, vol 187 cc1033-40. Contains Parliamentary information licensed under the Open Parliament Licence v3.0.

Her Majesty Queen Victoria's Journals. Journal Entry: Tuesday 20th June 1837, Saturday 8th July 1837, Thursday 23rd November 1837, Saturday 2nd February 1839, Tuesday 2nd July 1850, Thursday 1st May 1851, Saturday 21st February 1852, Monday 23rd February 1852, Thursday 16th September 1852, Tuesday 10th March 1863, Friday 8th January 1864, Friday 1st April 1870, Thursday 29th February 1872, Wednesday 13th December 1871, Friday 28th March 1884, Thursday, 23rd December 1886, Wednesday, 13th January 1892, Thursday 14th January 1892, Monday 15th August 1892. The author would like to thank His Majesty King Charles III and the Royal Archives for granting permission to quote extracts from Queen Victoria's journals. (Her Majesty Queen Victoria's Journals. Journal Entry: 10 June 1840, 20 January 1896, 31 July 1900)

Hansard. HC Deb 17 March 1937, vol 321, c 2107. Contains Parliamentary information licensed under the Open Parliament Licence v3.0. https://api.parliament.uk/historic-hansard/commons/1937/mar/17/the-late-sir-austenchamberlain

Hansard. HC Deb 07 July 1960 vol 626 cc708-709. Contains Parliamentary information licensed under the Open Parliament Licence v3.0. https://api.parliament.uk/historic-hansard/commons/1960/jul/07/mr-aneurin-bevan-tributes

Hansard. HL Deb 18 October 1984 vol 455 cc1076-1077. Contains Parliamentary information licensed under the Open Parliament Licence v3.0.

Herbert, Christopher & Thomas, Hugh, *Edward VII, The Last Victorian*, 2nd Edition (London: St Martin's Press, 2022)

Hereford Times, 6 November 1841

Highland News, 2 June 1884

Huddersfield Chronicle, 22 May 1873

Illustrated Times, 23 July 1870

Jenkins, Roy, *Churchill* (London: Macmillan, 2002)

Jenkins, Roy, *Gladstone* (London: Macmillan, 1995)

Keeble, Sally & Dale, Iain, *The Honourable Ladies: Volume I, Profiles of Women MPs 1918-1996* (London: Biteback Publishing, 2019)
Kentish Gazette, 6 January 1858
Le Conte, Marie, *Honourable Misfits, A Brief History of Britain's Weirdest, Unluckiest and Most Outrageous MPs* (London: John Murray Press, 2021)
Leeds Times, 6 November 1841
Leonard, Dick, *Nineteenth-Century British Premiers: Pitt to Rosebery* (Basingstoke, Palgrave Macmillan, 2008)
Liverpool Daily Post, 26 January 1858
Logue, Mark, & Conrad, Peter, *The King's Speech* (London: Quercus, 2010)
Marr, Andrew, *The Making of Modern Britain, From Queen Victoria to VE Day* (London: Macmillan, 2009)
Morning Chronicle, 14 July 1837.
Morning Post, 1 July 1879, 3 February 1896, 25 December 1863
Newcastle Daily Chronicle, 8 November 1897
Norwich Mercury, 5 February 1896
Patel, Dinyar, *Naoroj, Pioneer of Indian Nationalism* (New York: Harvard University Press, 2020)
Ridley, Jane, *George V: Never a Dull Moment* (London: Chatto & Windus, 2021)
Roberts, Andrew, *Salisbury, Victorian Titan* (London: Weidenfeld and Nicolson, 1999)
Salisbury and Winchester Journal, 11 December 1858
Searing, Donald, *Westminster's World, Understanding Political Roles* (New York: Harvard University Press, 1994)
Sheffield Weekly Telegraph, 10 March 1900
South Wales Daily News, 25 January 1899
St James's Gazette, 30 March 1897, 21 June 1897
Steele, David, *Lord Salisbury, A Political Biography* (London: Routledge, 1999)
Suffolk and Essex Free Press, 18 May 1898
Sussex Advertiser, 29 May 1878
The Times, 26 October 1848, 20 October 1856, 3 December 1877, 20 May 1898, 4 December 1961,
Ward, Roger, *The Chamberlains: Joseph, Austen and Neville 1836-1940* (London: Fonthill Media, 2015)
Wood, Anthony, *Nineteenth Century Britain 1815-1914* (London: Longman, 1984)

Index

Aberdeen, Earl, 19, 51, 181
Albert Memorial, 101
Albert, Prince Consort, 24, 25, 34, 65, 84, 129, 146, 147, 152, 180, 185
Albert, Victor Prince, 5, 8, 42, 85, 95, 105, 175
Aldridge, Amanda, 42
Alexander II, Tsar, 14, 75,
Alexandra, Princess, 5, 8, 29, 40, 41, 55, 69, 128, 174, 176
Alfred, Prince, 14, 40, 43, 46, 101, 117, 128, 135
Alice, Princess, 65, 101, 181
Arthur, Prince, 3, 12, 56, 94, 160
Arts and Craft Movement, 63, 154

Baldwin, Stanley, 95, 119
Balfour, Arthur, 94, 99, 175
Balmoral, 16, 20, 51, 91, 147, 150, 160, 185
Barry, Charles, 21, 58, 83, 94, 113, 114, 135, 139, 185
Beatrice, Princess, 12, 26, 60, 114, 117
Beecham, Thomas, 66
Birmingham, 46, 47, 48, 56, 88, 122, 134, 137, 141, 163, 174
Bondfield, Margaret, 45
Bradlaugh, Charles, 7, 18
Brighton, 78, 112, 148
Bronte, Branwell, 143
Bronte, Charlotte, 53, 152
Bronte, Emily, 183
Brown, John, 26, 36, 45, 46, 50
Browning, Robert, 138, 180
Brunel, Isambard Kingdom, 19, 50, 57, 112, 139, 177

Brunel, Marc, 179
Buckingham Palace, 13, 19, 25, 30, 34, 36, 37, 40, 41, 46, 52, 56, 57, 60, 63, 65, 68, 72, 74, 88, 92, 100, 102, 105, 108, 123, 168
Burdett-Coutts, Angela, 28, 66

Cadbury, George, 141
Cambridge, Duke of, 5, 106, 135, 160
Campbell Bannerman, Henry, 93
Carlton Club, 24, 117, 183
Chartism, 10, 45, 58, 64, 72, 111, 137, 145, 161
Chamberlain, Joseph, 48, 57, 91, 150
Chaplin, Charlie, 61
Churchill, Randolph, 15, 27, 61, 184
Churchill, Winston, 15, 44, 61, 103, 105, 133, 173, 178
Conservative Party, 14, 32, 66, 72, 117, 127
Corn Laws, 14
Crimean War, 13, 17, 18, 33, 51, 52, 75, 77, 105, 155, 162
Cruikshank, George, 188

Darwin, Charles, 18, 62, 99, 170
Derby, Lord, 19, 32, 92, 151, 156
Dickens, Charles, 16, 40-41, 59, 68, 87-88, 91, 97, 118, 121, 123, 165, 183, 189
Disraeli, Benjamin, 1, 10, 19, 30, 34, 40, 47, 50, 53, 62, 65, 69, 127, 177

Elgar, Edward, 72, 79, 84, 92
Eliot, George, 163, 185
Edinburgh, 9, 28, 79, 150, 167, 170

Fenian Dynamite Campaign, 2, 34, 82, 180
Fisher, John, 69, 75
Fleming, Alexander, 121
France, 126, 130, 149
Frederick III, Kaiser, 90

Garfield, James, 141
Garibaldi, General, 59
Gladstone, William, 6, 16, 20, 22, 38, 57, 64, 76, 77, 81, 87, 90, 96, 103, 112, 122, 131, 136, 150, 170, 171, 177, 183, 187
Glasgow, 30, 37, 54
Great Exhibition, 68, 88, 107
Grey, Charles, 52

Haig, Douglas, 24
Harcourt, William, 61, 77
Hardie, Keir, 9, 35, 86, 115
Hardy, Thomas, 3, 84
Helena, Princess, 8, 55, 117, 176
Highland Clearances, 63
Hyde Park Riots, 114

India, 1, 4, 70, 95
Irving, Henry, 23, 111, 170, 172, 189

Jellicoe, John, 176

Kent, John, 125
Kipling, R, 111, 157, 189
Kitchener, Lord, 95

Labour Party, 31, 35, 41
Lang, Cosmo, 159
Langtry, Lillie 80, 151
Leo XIII, Pope, 39, 175, 183
Leopold, Prince, 35-36, 51, 56
Lister, Joseph, 45, 58, 123
Liverpool, 39, 85, 149
Livingstone, David, 68, 164
Lloyd George, David, 11, 19, 90
Louise, Princess, 43, 46, 47

Manchester, 60, 70, 109, 129, 138
Manning, Henry, 9, 76, 140
Marx, Karl, 31, 44, 185
Melbourne, Lord, 30, 71, 88, 93, 104
Metropolitan Police, 32, 82
Monet, Claude, 133
Morris, William, 63, 147, 154

Napoleon III, Emperor, 5, 126
National Liberal Club, 93
Nicholas II, Tsar, 51, 102
Nightingale, Florence, 155
Northcote, Stafford, 7

Olympic Games, 75, 107, 181
Osborne House, 8, 13, 81, 101, 118, 129, 147

Palmerston, Lord, 23, 31, 49, 64, 89, 101, 134, 153, 158, 180
Parnell, Charles, 148
Parry, Hubert, 34, 76, 79
Peabody Trust, 141
Peel, Robert, 12, 14, 26, 57, 71, 101, 123, 131
Pugin, Augustus, 21, 139

Reform Club, 120, 184
River Thames, 46, 72, 84
Rosebery, Lord, 39, 47, 61, 94, 128, 131
Royal Albert Hall, 51, 101, 122
Royal Navy, 10, 21, 47, 59, 85

Salisbury, Lord, 17, 48, 60, 70, 72, 114-115, 122, 165
Sandringham House, 8, 168, 181
Scott, George Gilbert, 101, 144
Seacole, Mary, 17, 75
Second Boer War, 3, 54, 150
Shaftesbury, Lord, 59, 99, 118, 149
St James's Palace, 13, 25, 108
Sullivan, Arthur, 3, 44, 74, 80, 117

Index

Teck, Mary, Princess of, 65, 80-81, 105, 175
Tennyson, Alfred Lord, 43, 56, 85, 92, 157, 168
Thackeray, William Makepeace, 56, 186
The Times, 134, 179, 188
Trollope, Anthony, 3, 23, 56, 170, 176-177

United States of America, 13, 85, 141
University of Cambridge, 34, 181
University of Oxford, 27, 99, 150

Victoria, Crown Princess, 16, 17, 168
Victoria, Queen, 1, 3, 5, 8, 9, 11-12, 13, 14, 15, 16, 17, 18, 19, 22, 23, 25, 26, 30, 31, 32, 35, 36, 38, 40, 41, 44, 45, 48, 51, 52, 55, 56, 57, 60, 63, 64, 71, 74, 76, 77, 79, 81, 88, 89, 91, 92, 93, 95, 97, 98, 101, 102, 103, 114, 116, 118, 126, 128, 130, 141, 142, 147, 149, 152, 154, 157, 162, 165, 168, 169, 178, 180, 181, 183, 185, 187
Villiers, Charles, 10

Wales, Prince of, 2, 5, 8, 11, 14, 31, 32, 37, 39, 41-42, 51, 55, 58, 61, 71, 73, 80, 81, 85, 94, 106, 107, 121, 128, 141, 143, 146, 151, 163, 168, 178, 179
Waterhouse, Alfred, 62, 93, 138
Wellington, 1st Duke of, 22, 27, 33, 92, 125, 138, 149, 161, 167
Westminster Abbey, 33, 63, 68, 90, 95, 97, 149, 158, 185
Wilberforce, Samuel, 99, 111, 130
Wilde, Oscar, 3, 20, 28, 29, 49, 55, 56, 172, 184
Wilhelm II, Kaiser (Previously Prince Wilhelm), 42, 90
William IV, King, 47, 106, 162, 174, 179
Wimbledon Tennis Championship, 42, 107, 108-109, 112
Windsor Castle, 33, 45, 106, 108, 152
Wood, Henry, 38, 122, 179
Wordsworth, William, 56, 168
Workhouses, 10, 61, 109